CHAPTER III

The Use of Alcohol in Three Salish

Indian Tribes

by

Edwin M. Lemert

The three Salish tribes whose drinking behavior
is described here live in villages near the Bute
Inlet, Squirrel Cove and Powell River on the coast
of British Columbia. The Homalthko, located at the
opening of the Bute Inlet, number nearly 200; the
Sliammon, near Powell River, count something over
100; while the Tlahoose, at Squirrel Cove, are the
least numerous, with a population around 80. These
Indians, when employed, work as independent
fishermen, logging camp laborers, or hand loggers.
For the most part their economic status is poor, the
tribes having few resources and the individual
natives little capital or equipment. Their fishing
boats are old gillnetters, having been obtained
originally during the war from Japanese fishermen
who were interned. These have been poorly maintained.
Fishing is carried on mainly in the summer, at which
time the natives travel up the coast to various inlets
where salmon runs are reported. Entire families may
make the trip, but usually women and children and old
people remain behind in the village. During the
winter the fishermen turn to logging or live on relief.
The loggers usually live at logging camps during the
week and return to their home villages on weekends.
While these Indians still exploit some natural food
resources, for the most part they are directly
dependent upon the money economy for their needs.

Reprinted from an article of the same title in
Quarterly Journal of Studies on Alcohol, Vol. 19,
1958:90-107 by permission of the author and the
Quarterly Journal of Studies on Alcohol.

Historical Background of Drinking

Like other Northwest coast natives, the Salish
Indians under discussion possessed no intoxicants
prior to contact with whites. Liquor in various
diluted and adulterated forms was introduced to them
during the fur trade period. Undoubtedly intoxicants
as well as the impact of the fur trade itself had a
dynamic if not revolutionary effect on their culture
and social organization. The use of alcohol became
integrated into their cultures largely in terms of
the competitive ethos of the potlatch, the well-known
gift-giving feast of the Northwest coast in which the
drinking and giving away of liquor became the basis
for invidious distinctions between individuals,
kinship groups and villages.

The evidence indicates that the Homalthko,
Tlahoose, and Sliammon developed drinking rituals
very much like the whisky feast of the Tsimshian
(Garfield 1939) and the Kwakiutl of Kingcome Inlet
(Lemert 1954). Thus, according to one old Homalthko
informant, whisky feasts were held at the potlatch
grounds at Salmon River in Toba Inlet "before the
priest came".

"In early days men on boats came around with
barrels of whisky and traded them. Then a
whisky potlatch was held. The whisky was
served in a cup by one person, who went around
to each person. He had to drink what was given
him. Pretty soon everybody all drunk".

An old Sliammon woman could recall her grandmother's
description of a whisky feast held in premissionary
times at Sliammon "right in front of where the church
stands now."

"One fellow went to Nanaimo and came back with a
barrel of whisky which he bought for twenty
dollars. We all sat along boards laid on top
of logs and beat time and sang. Three men carried
the barrel along in front of us. There was one
dipper and you had to drink it all down. Then
it was passed to the next person. The song they
sang was like this:

50

"I want a drink
Give me a drink
I want to be drunk" (pass out).

The Indians of these three tribes first began to be
Catholicized in the 1860's and by 1885 they had all
been converted and made loyal communicants of the
Church. this was done under the dynamic leadership
of Bishop Durieu, who developed a special control
and discipline for the natives. Letters of early
preists who contacted these Salish peoples refer
to their winter ceremonials and their whisky feasts
as "scandals" and speak of their degeneration at the
hands of whisky trader. The preists, especially
the forceful Bishop Durieu, made the renunciation
of all primitive potlatching and, above all, of the
use of alcohol, conditions of their conversion.

Informants unanimously insist that all dancing
and presumably whisky feasts ended "after the priests
came". However, surreptitious drinking continued
in the form of the drinking party, through which
renewal with the abandoned traditions of the past
or "the good old days" was achieved by informal
drinking, the singing of drinking songs, and the
recitation of myths and stories. The drinking party
has persisted up to the present day, although other
forms of drinking have appeared.

In the early period the alcoholic drinks consumed
were whisky, rum and various adulternated mixtures of
these, which sometimes included tobacco and camphor.
Home-brew is a more recent beverage, first introduced
about 30 or 40 years ago. According to one account,
a Seschelt Indian taught the Homalthko how to make
home-brew from a patent medicine called Bee-wine,
which was put into sirup and allowed to ferment.
After that, home-brew from salal berries and huckleberries
was made and drunk from a large galvanized tub. According
to another account, from a white trapper, the Homalthko
learned to make home-brew from the cook of a logging
camp at the head of Bute Inlet sometime after 1912.
Home-brew today is made with malt and sugar and yeast
from a recipe similar to that brewed by white Canadians.
However, oranges and other fruits sometimes are added
to the original ingredients by the Indians.

Occasionally a brew is made by adding a cake of yeast to a can of tomatoes and letting it stand overnight.

Present-Day Drinking

Drinking among the present-day Homalthko, Tlahoose and Sliammon is exclusively social. No case of solitary drinking has yet come to attention. Drinking ordinarily is in the form of a party or of an informal gathering at the host's cabin. The participants are relatives or known friends, with cousins often being the nucleus of the drinking group. Divorced and married women sometimes join these groups. Unmarried girls are occasionally present as spectators but do not drink except in rare instances when the party has become an occasion for sexual license. Old men and women are invited to such parties because of their special status or because they can sing drinking songs and tell stories. The village chief may be invited to a drinking party but he must be circumspect about his drinking, so usually he declines or appears only for a short time. Most parties are held on weekends. At New Year's, drinking and dancing go on for three to six days.

Where home-brew is drunk it is dipped out of the keg or tub in which it was made and the cup is passed from one drinker to another. Each must drink his share down, and to fail to drink would be an offense to the person giving the party, although to my knowledge this contingency has never arisen. The drinking continues usually until all of the brew is gone. The same is true when bottled beer has been obtained from the beer parlor. Whisky is drunk by passing the bottle until it is all gone. Sometimes it, too, is poured into a cup and the cup passed from one person to another, being refilled on the way.

Drinking also takes place on fishing boats, where it is more clandestine in nature. Bottles also may be circulated outside the community hall when a dance is being held. This also tends to be a more furtive type of behavior, inasmuch as open drinking in the hall is not permitted. Some drinking is also done in beer parlors, where the law since 1951 has permitted Indians to consume beer but not to carry it off the premises. There is a distinct impression, however, that these Indians are not entirely comfortable drinking in the presence of white persons, that they feel restrained from following their customary forms of drinking. Also, they run the risk of arrest for drunkenness off the reserve by drinking in the beer parlors.

There is little doubt that the objective of drinking by the Homalthko, Tlahoose and Sliammon is to get drunk. This is apparent from their consuming home-brew before it is completely fermented, in their gulping down of drinks, drinking until the supply is exhausted, and in their preference for strong liquor whenever it can be obtained. It also comes out in occasional spontaneous comments about how they like to drink, i.e., to get drunk quickly.

Drunken Behavior

In many respects the drunken behavior of these Indians is almost the reverse of their sober behavior. This generalization, of course, is subject to exceptions and there is considerable variation in the reactions of the Indians to the liquor they drink, depending upon age, sex and degree of education and their contact with white persons. However, there is a great deal of staggering, swaying, rolling, laughing, shouting and boisterousness in their drunken reactions, all of which is contrary to their everyday behavior in which they are restrained, impassive, even shy and timid. There is also a certain bleariness, actual or feigned, in the eyes of these Indians during their drunken states. However, the most distinguishing feature, at least in relation to their normal behavior, is the outburst of aggressiveness, especially in the younger Indians, which frequently comes with their gross intoxication. This is well illustrated in the following:*

* From field notes.

After I walked to the end of the float, Eddie
Palon came down the hill. As he did, he
staggered and fell down. Then he got up, came
toward me in a threatening manner and said he
had something to say to me. I told him I had
come to see the chief. He muttered that I was
trespassing and then he grabbed me by the coat
and pulled me out toward the dock. He told me
to put the box down. Then Chief Palon came up
and stood quietly back of Eddie. As I walked
up the path Chief Palon told Eddie he shouldn't
do that; he should go into his house and stay
there. Eddie swore at the chief and demanded
the ten dollars he owed him. The chief shoved
him away but he came back again. The chief
shoved him again and kicked him solidly in
the backside, almost knocking him down.
Meantime the chief's wife came and angrily
began to berate Eddie. This seemed to embarrass
the chief, who several times told her to be
quiet, finally shouting at her. However, it
was some time before she quieted down.

The chief commented that Eddie had done this
before - to a forest ranger. Then he said he
should stay in the house if he wanted to drink.
He added that Eddie is very shy when he is
sober - "Not like that; he runs away from
everyone."

A second illustration conveys some notion of drunken
behavior in a group or party situation:

I ran the boat near shore where I could call for
Joe Pell, whom I wanted to see. Four of the
Johnson boys and the grandson of the old deposed
chief came out on the little porch of one of the
houses on the beach. They were waving and
shouting. Finally George Johnson came down and
insisted that I run the boat up on the beach.
"Get your machine (tape recorder) and bring it up
to the house," he shouted. When I said it was
back at my cabin he insisted we go get it. Then
he jumped on the bow of the boat as if to enforce
his demand, refusing to move. Meantime a half

breed who had obviously been drinking with the
group came down, picked up a beer bottle, broke
it in half and menaced me with the sharp end.
Then he half laughed and threw the bottle away.

Finally, having little choice, I ran the boat
back for the tape recorder, at which George
grew very happy, his old mild self coming out.
The party had moved to another house by the
time we returned. The half breed and the
Johnson boys were drinking beer from bottles
and eating dried clams. The former chief was
sitting across the room with an old woman,
almost too drunk to sit up, and there were a
number of young girls present, though not
drinking. The grandson of the old chief and
the Johnson boys began to sing, a sentimental
popular song, to the accompaniment of a guitar
played by one of the boys, which I dutifully,
although painfully, recorded. At my urging,
the ex-chief tried to sing a drinking song, but
he could not remember the words and lapsed into
silence after a few attempts. Presently the
chief's grandson took the microphone and began
to deliver an impassioned speech in Salish,
becoming more and more wrought up as he
proceeded. This proved to be a violent,
vituperative attack on white men in general
and upon me in partiuclar. However, the old
chief soon grew restive and told his grandson
to "speak like a chief." Whereupon the younger
man changed his tone and began to make
perfunctory remarks in English about the need
for friendliness and how he wanted everyone
to have a good time at the party. The party
ended on this note, and I was allowed to retire
with my recorder.

In one or two instances among the Homalthko, when
heavy drinking has taken place, most of the villagers
have been seen outside their houses quarreling and
shouting, with occasional blows being struck. A
number of deaths have occurred during times of heavy
drinking. Police and neighboring whites are
convinced that most of these, which the Indians call
accidents, actually are murders, but proof is lacking.

55

In all three tribes, drunken men in a number of
instances have violently assaulted their wives,
blackened their eyes and given them nasty bruises.
One young Tlahoose Indian was sent to prison for
breaking the jaw of his fiancee during a drunken
fracas.

Irregular sex behavior and sex crimes, to the
extent that they have occurred, also have been largely
functions of drunkenness among the Homalthko and
Sliammon. Cases of seduction of young girls, resulting
in illegitimate childbirth, and adulterous unions
involving married women, likewise seem to have
intoxication as their main concomitant. One or two
cases of drunken rape are on the record of the three
tribes.

Ordinarily the Homalthko are very reserved in
their attitudes toward white men, and on the whole
they do not become involved in difficulties with
them. Yet when intoxicated some of them have engaged
in breaking and entering, burglary and theft from
whites. This most commonly takes place after the
Indians have become drunk and exhausted their supply
of liquor. On such occasions, somewhat like addicted
alcoholics, they are strongly driven and are willing
to go to any lengths to obtain alcohol. When liquor
is known to be on the boats of white fishermen, they
will surreptitiously steal it and, in one or two cases,
Homalthko and Sliammon Indians have openly attacked
white fishermen (at night, when visibility is nil) and
taken liquor from them. Incidents of the sort describe
here have not been numerous but they nevertheless
illustrate the compulsive nature of the need for
alcohol once the Indians have become drunk.

Older Indians tell of differences between their
drinking and that of "these young bucks". They insist
that the older pattern was to drink, sing songs, pass
out, wake up, drink some more and again pass out. "Now
days young Indians will steal your bottle from you.
Also when we were young we never said dirty words to
our cousins (female) when we got drunk." There is
some support for this in historical accounts of the
Homalthko, Tlahoose and Sliammon, in whose villages
stealing was relatively unknown 30 or 40 years ago.

However, older white men insist that the fathers and grandfathers of the present younger Indians were pretty much like them. The truth perhaps lies somewhere in between; certainly drunken aggressiveness has existed a long time, although stealing seems relatively recent.

Indian Drinking and White Drinking

A difficult question to answer is whether the pattern of Indian drinking is unique or is simply a post-frontier pattern, largely assimilated from white loggers and fishermen. Evidence for the latter view is not absent. The drinking of white neighbors of the Indians has much in common with that of the Indians. This includes drinking to get drunk, drinking until the supply is exhausted, and restless excursions to find more liquor when this happens. It is also true that many of the Canadian folk who live near these Indians become aggressive and engage in brawling, particularly at dances where drinking is heavy. Sexual indulgence is likewise a part of the white pattern, taking the form of "shacking up" with a bottle and a woman, if the latter is available. However, theft of liquor does not enter into white drunken behavior, largely because it is unnecessary. Also the direction which aggression takes among drunken whites differs from that of the Indians.

There is little doubt that contact and interaction with whites have left a definite imprint on the form of Indian drinking, inasmuch as whites first introduced liquor to them. However, it would be wrong to say that this resulted from their drinking together, except in particular situations which, from the white point of view, involve deviant behavior or deviant individuals. Here reference is made to the "klootchman", who drinks and lives with Indian women, and also to the white man who makes home-brew and invites Indians, usually women, to drink with him. Both of these forms of behavior tend to be disapproved by the white persons in the vicinity of the Indian villages, especially by older persons. How common such liaisons are is not known, but gossip and the numerical predominance of males in

57

the white population suggest that a fair number of white men at one time or another, when they were younger, have participated in the behavior.

One difference in the Indian drinking behavior is to be noted: this is the exaggerated symptoms of drunkenness which are often displayed, including bleariness of the eyes, head rolling, and staggering. Often this seems to be a parody or stereotype of drunkenness rather than the real thing. Also noteworthy is a distinct "sobering effect" in their drunkenness. This refers to quick transitions from drunken to sober behavior and back again, depending upon the situation, particularly when a necessary task must be carried out, such as starting a motor or navigating a boat through dangerous waters. Neighboring whites share the belief that the local Indians can get drunk on very little alcohol, or even through suggestion alone. Stories are told of whites putting soft drink in a whisky bottle and giving it to Indians, who proceed to act in an intoxicated manner after drinking it.

Because the local beliefs on this score reflect the more general white stereotype of the "drunken Indian," an effort was made to test the idea experimentally. The Homalthko often drink their home-brew when it is only 13 or 17 hours old, and also a brew of tomatoes which has stood overnight. In all three cases drunken behavior results. By making home-brew and tomato brew following the Indian recipes and testing it at the specified intervals, a notion of the alcohol content of these beverages was obtained. The results of the test are incorporated in Table 1.

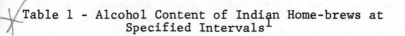

Table 1 - Alcohol Content of Indian Home-brews at
Specified Intervals[1]

Sample	Time (hours)	% Alcohol by Volume
A°	13	1.9
B†	13	1.4
A°	17	2.5
B†	17	2.0
A°	24	3.6
B†	24	2.8
C‡	24	2.1
D‡	24	2.5

These tests, conducted under optimum conditions,
suggest that the home-brews of the Homalthko are of
very low alcohol content, particularly when made
with a short fermentation time. Obviously a great
deal of such brew would have to be drunk very rapidly
in order to achieve intoxication. Yet the practice
of sharing the brew at parties makes it unlikely
that this is often true. This is not to say that
these Indians do not get intoxicated on strong
liquors, but it does give substance to the hypothesis
that they are capable of exhibiting drunkenness with

[1] The fermentations were carried out in glazed
earthern jars in a room at 81° to 83°F. I am
greatly indebted to Professor John G. B. Castor,
Department of Enology, University of California
at Davis, for carrying out these tests and
supplying me with the resultant data.

° The materials used in sample A were the equivalent
of 5 gallons of water with a can of malt sirup,
5 lbs. of sugar and 4 yeast cakes.

† The materials used in sample B were the equivalent
of 7 gallons of water, all the rest being the same
as in sample A.

‡ The materials in samples C and D consisted of a
can of tomatoes and a cake of yeast.

the ingestion of relatively small amounts of alcohol.
It is especially noticeable that younger Indians
give the impression of feigning intoxication, getting
drunk from "sniffing the cork," as it were.

The Function of Alcohol

The form of drinking among the Homalthko and
their related tribes is partly understandable in
terms of its function and meaning. First of all,
although many of the Indians express formal religious
disapproval of drinking, nevertheless to be able to
obtain and drink alcoholic beverages continues to
be a mark of status and prestige for the individual.
This derives from the culture pattern of the potlatch,
which in attenuated "feast" form is still observed
by these natives. The prestige function is most
apparent where the drinker or party giver is able
to secure distilled spirits. One Indian logger
epitomized this attitude by saying contemptuously,
"I don't drink home-brew, vanilla extract, hair
tonic, shaving lotion, perfume, or Listerine like
some guys do. I buy whisky and I have my ways of
getting it."

An interesting footnote to this is the practice
which some of the Homalthko have of putting home-
brew into whisky bottles on which labels are
carefully preserved and then somewhat proudly
offering it to be drunk. More sophisticated Indians
who encounter this subterfuge while visiting the
Homalthko village find it amusing or outright
laughable.

Being able to get "hard liquor" symbolizes the
economic success of him who can pay the bootlegger's
exorbitant price, the skill to manipulate white
friends, and also an ability to circumvent the white
man's law which forbids him to have the liquor. The
individual's manner of drinking, in which he swiftly
drinks down a large portion of wine or a water-glass
of whisky also carries an important prestige function
among the Homalthko.

60

From the standpoint of collective behavior the
drinking party can be viewed as one of the few ways,
in addition to religious ritual, through which the
Homalthko can feel a sense of social solidarity in
the presence of white man's society. It is also one
way - apart from feasts, which are rather costly and
now rarely given - through which continuity can be
established with the old culture. This is done
through the telling of myths and stories and the
singing of drinking songs.

In some ways the drinking party has stood in
direct competition with Catholic ritual. In recent
decades, perhaps since 1900, identity with
Catholicism has declined among the natives, and
there has been a corresponding growth in the
significance of the drinking party. At the present
time, however, as older Indians die off, there are
fewer who know enough of the old culture to make
the parties meaningful. This, combined with the
greater mobility of the younger Indians, makes the
drinking of the latter more random, capricious and
unpatterned. Yet withal, even this drinking remains
essentially an in-group activity.

Basic Personality and Drinking

Beyond the externally valued and collectively
expressed functions of drinking lie functions which
can be related to the basic personality structure
of the three Salish Indian tribes. By basic
personality structure is meant the average or model
psychic impact of a culture upon members of a
society. Presumably it is manifested in the creation
of psychic needs which are expressed in derivative
cultural forms, i.e., derived from what have been
called "basic" institutions of the culture. While
the concept has never been completely clarified, it
still has some usefulness here as an analytical
tool in comprehending certain aspects of Salish
drinking.

Salish personality might be described as formed around models of decorous and restrained behavior most clearly perceived in child-training practices. Parallel with this is a less apparent but real theme of aggressiveness related to the competitive ethos and war-making of the past. This is best observed in some of the night-time games and play of adolescent Indians. The integration of these contrary tendencies may be thought of as the key to the basic personality structure of the Salish peoples being discussed. In the past, aggression was channeled into the potlatch and warfare. When these latter came to an end in the middle of the last century, no cultural forms were left which gave sanctioned outlets for aggression. Consequently aggressiveness became a problem or anxiety-creating motive (Horton 1943).

It is pertinent to ask why aggressiveness should persist as a part of the Salish personality when its cultural relevance has disappeared. The answer is found in the multiple frustrations associated with contact and interaction with white persons and subjugation to bureaucratic governmental control. Aggressiveness also arises out of family interaction and the interaction of kinship groups. Due to exogamous marriage, husband-wife conflict has long been a part of Salish life, more recently aggravated by the greater independence of the women. Conflict between extended kinship groups also stays alive, to some extent in institutionalized form.

All of this speaks strongly of latent aggressiveness as a motive for intoxication among these Salish peoples. When they become intoxicated, it is in the above-mentioned three areas that aggressiveness breaks out, especially between kinship groups. Grudges are held for a long time, sometimes for years, and on occasions of drunkenness come to the surface, as indicated by the commentary of a native informant:

"Yeh, that last fight when Jimmy was drunk came out of another fight. About five years ago when Leo was drunk he beat up his wife, who is Jimmy's sister. Jimmy broke into the fight and hit Leo and put his eye out. Leo and some of the Pells have been waiting all this time,

62

remembering that and ready to get even. That's
a common kind of thing."

Other long-standing tensions between kinship
groups have been created over succession in
chieftanships, over conflicting claims to houses and
property, and losses rightly or wrongly attributed
to thievery. Deaths suspected of being murders also
fan the fires of kinship conflict. Factional splits
over compliance with religious observances center
around extended family groups -- a factionalism
which is especially pronounced among the Homalthko.

In contrast to this drink-facilitated
aggressiveness, transgressions by Indians against
white persons tend to be impersonal and more in the
nature of exploits. Thus when a dance was held in
a nearby white community a number of Homalthko who
had been drinking waited until the dance was in
full course and then raided the boats of the whites
for the liquor they knew would be there. Certain
Indians have acquired a notorious reputation for
similar exploits and among their own people enjoy
an enviable status, even though they may have been
sent to prison. These men also are the ones reputed
to have killed other Indians. The impression is
that their status is comparable in some ways to the
much feared "warrior" of precontact times.

Social Reactions to Drunkenness
and Aggression

White public opinion in the area of the three
Salish reserves generally is highly critical or
condemnatory of native drinking and draws a sharp
distinction between "drinking like a white man" and
"Indian drinking". This is based upon the known or
reputed cases in which, during drunken interludes,
Indians have beaten their wives, neglected their
children or destroyed property, or have been sent to
prison for crimes growing out of intoxication. In
white public opinion these events tend to be
generalized and are a part of the fixed local images
of Indian drinking.

63

Yet within the Indian communities themselves, while there is verbal disapproval of drinking, it is inconsistent and not substantiated by social rejection or penalties of any kind. The chief has no power to punish tribe members, and the council is equally impotent to invoke penalties for misbehavior. Any efforts of this nature could only stir up grudges and provoke more factional conflict than already exists. Furthermore, practically all adults have been involved in drunken escapades, at some time or another, so that disapproval or punitive action is likely to have a hollow ring. Once in a while some of the Indians have become frightened during drunken brawls and have called in the police or have asked white persons to do so. The next morning, however, they repent their action and later refuse to testify as witnesses. Significantly, drunkenness does not become a reason for a woman to leave or divorce her husband, even though he may have seriously mistreated her. This may be contrasted with the results of white drinking parties near the Homalthko village, which in some cases have led to changing of wives and desertions.

In native opinion the pleasures of intoxication appear to be insulated from other considerations; or if the undesirable consequences are thought of, they are discounted or outweighed. Indeed, the attitude is more that of a fatalistic acceptance, with little thought given to the matter. For example, the Sliammon soccer team was undefeated in its area, yet at the end of one season lost to an inferior team because a number of the players had hangovers. Despite the loss, no great blame was directed toward the players responsible. The damage or loss of property resulting from drunkenness also tends to be accepted with indifference, as when an Indian gets drunk on his boat and lets his fishing net drift away.

The Stereotype

Although white persons who come to know Indians well in any of the three villages differentiate them

64

as to drinking habits, those who have more casual contacts with them or for some reason are hostile towards them react categorically. They readily express the generalized stereotype of the Indian as innately or racially disposed to abnormal reactions to alcohol. Thus, white disapproval is one side of the coin; a belief that the Indian is helpless to control his drinking is the other side.

The latter belief is readily demonstrated in attitudes and actions of missionaries, who have blamed white men for the drinking problems of the Indians and have sought to solve the "problem" as they saw it, by castigating the liquor peddler and by eliminating the liquor traffic. Legislation prohibiting the sale to and use of liquor by Indians in the province has the same meaning, even more explicit. The administration of the law itself has also shown a tendency of police and magistrates to mitigate or dismiss the punishment of Indians who have committed crimes while intoxicated (Lemert 1954:356).

Symbolizing Drunken Behavior

While the perception by the Indian drinker of the frequently costly consequences of his drunkenness may engender in him a kind of ambivalent attitude, nevertheless in intimate interaction with his own people he is not confronted with any public opinion which would tend to create or reinforce a sense of guilt or self-censure. Indeed, as previously indicated, the values of intoxication seem preeminently in the other direction. These easily merge with the White stereotype and readily cancel out the external and formal opinion of the white community which is condemnatory of Indian drunkenness. While it cannot be proved directly, from inferential evidence it is very likely that many Homalthko and drinkers of the other two tribes tend to act out the White stereotype of the "drunken Indian" when they become intoxicated. The capacity to get drunk on beverages of low alcohol content, the dramatic symptoms of drunkenness, and the

sobering effect of emergencies all seem to point
to this conclusion. It is plausible to conclude
that the stereotype functions in the psychic process
to excuse otherwise socially unacceptable aggression
and depredations. Drunkenness frequently is invoked
as an excuse for socially deleterious acts in our
own society but with unpredictable results. These
Indians, however, are often saved by the stereotype
from unpleasant punishment in the courts of the white
man.

Alcoholism

As far as can be established, there are no
alcoholics in the accepted sense of that term among
the three Salish tribes. Several of the Homalthko
men have drunk heavily enough to suffer from delirium
tremens, according to the local physician's report.
However, thereafter they have tapered off their
drunkenness, usually within a relatively short period
of time. One woman living apart from the Homalthko
reserve went through such an experience after the
death of her baby, all taking place within the span
of a year.

The lack of chronic pathological drinking may
be simply a function of the nonurban, frontier type
of environment of these Indians, an explanation in
part supported by a low rate of alcoholism among
white people living in the hinterland or bush areas
in the province. In addition, it is to be noted that
the heavy drinker in the Indian community does not
become socially isolated as a consequence of his
drunkenness, nor does his behavior lead to a broken
marriage and loss of family support. Furthermore,
the values of his group actually uphold and sanction
his behavior. Another factor is that the local
situation more or less enforces sobriety, largely
because of the difficulty of keeping a continuous
supply of liquor on hand. The alternative for an
individual who feels strongly driven to stay drunk
is to travel to some city, namely Vancouver. However,
if he does this he seldom stays long -- ordinarily
until his money gives out. The reason for this is

66

that it is difficult or dangerous for an Indian to
live on Skid Row like other alcoholics. He is
likely to be more uneasy there than he is back home
without a ready source of liquor (Lemert 1954:363).

                The Position of the Chief

        The chief in the three Salish tribes must be
taken as an exception to comments made thus far. His
role and status is a source of no small conflict and
ambivalence where alcoholic indulgence is concerned.
This probably has been true since earlier times,
when liquor was first introduced to the Indians of
the Northwest coast. Some evidence of this emerges
from the following translation of a former Sliammon
chief's drinking song:

            Chief Johnson's Drinking Song

        Give me a drink, I am afraid to go,
        We keep on going. Come closer to me and drink.
        I'm drunk now. I'm drunk now, and we have a
        pretty good time.
        I don't like to drink but I have to drink the
        whisky.
        Here I am singing a love song, drinking, drinking,
        drinking.
        I didn't know whisky was no good and still I
        was drinking it.
        I found out that whisky is no good.
        Come closer to me, my slaves, and I'll give you
        a drink of whisky.
        Here we are drinking now.
        Have some more, some more of my whisky.
        Have a good time with it.
        Come closer to me, my slave.
        We are drinking now, we feel pretty good.
        Now you feel just like me.

        This song originally was the property of the
grandfather of a Sliammon man who presently is about
50 years of age. The song rather clearly speaks of
his awareness of the harm of liquor and at the same
time suggests his need for it as a means of decreasing
his sense of social isolation.

                        67

The former chief of the Tlahoose tribe lost his position by getting drunk and forcing the Indian agent to leave his reserve. He now drinks heavily, particularly when he comes down from the head of Toba Inlet where he lives alone on one of the old tribal village sites. The present Tlahoose chief tells others that he doesn't drink, but several from his village have reported that he does so privately in his own home with a few select cronies. He sometimes shows his displeasure with the drinking of others in his village by shutting off the generator in the light plant to bring their parties to a premature close. This may be connected with the historical fact that a chief was always invited to drinking parties even if he did not choose to attend. Failure to invite him was bound to arouse his resentment.

The former Homalthko chief took no public stand on drinking but preferred to shut himself in his house when drinking parties were in progress. He, too, drank with a few select companions. Now, since he is no longer a chief, he appears drunk in public without any apparent concern. The man who is currently the chief does very little drinking and openly criticizes those who do. However, there are reports that he drank heavily when he was younger and developed a stomach disorder which now makes drinking painful for him.

The chief's problem derives mainly from his status as a leader and a behavior model for his people, which means that drunkenness is inappropriate for him. At the same time he is supposed to show generosity, which would include giving drinking parties, and also, as a chief, to be the recipient of invitations to parties.

The chief's status as a leader of his people is highly attenuated by his subordination to the Indian agent, who is the real decision maker in matters affecting the welfare of the tribe. Frustration is inevitable and is magnified by the fact that many of the conflicts between the Indian and white culture arise out of this interaction. The Indian agent, of course, holds a higher expectation of responsible behavior for the chief, and there is the definite risk

68

that the latter will be deposed if he acquires a reputation for drunkenness. It can be well argued from a sociopsychological standpoint that the anomalous role of the chief contains the germs of true alcoholism, certainly more than that of the ordinary male member of the tribe.

Women and Alcohol

The heavily drinking woman among the Salish people also experiences conflicts, largely because her drinking is often associated with sexual promiscuity. In a goodly number of instances this involves white men, to whom she is attractive as an "easy" sexual partner. Continued contacts of this kind may lead to her detribalization. In contrast to the male drinker, the Indian woman can survive easily in the city. In Vancouver, there are Chinese men and some white men who are ready to support her, provide her with liquor, and probably treat her better than a man of her own tribe. Yet for the Salish woman to do this is to invite the hostility of her own people and also to violate the morality which Catholic indoctrination has given her. This means also that she will incur the displeasure of the priest, which most Indians fear very much. One Homalthko woman who lives with a white logger has a history of heavy drinking which ended in delirium tremens. Another woman from the Tlahoose tribe has lived with various men in Vancouver. From this she has acquired a reputation as a prostitute and drug addict as well as that of an alcoholic. The role of the woman is such that if she drinks heavily she is more likely than the man to develop some kind of drinking pathology.

Summary

The consumption of alcohol by Indians of the three Salish tribes discussed here originated with specialized contact and interaction with white

explorers and traders. The form of their drinking
still shows the impact of the early period. While
it is true that the form of present-day drinking
by the Indians is similar to that of the surrounding
white population, there are also differentiating
characteristics. The Indian drinking is also
differentiated from that of whites at the level of
function. An important relation between alcoholic
indulgence and the release of aggression appears
to exist. Alcohol addiction is absent, although
acute manifestations of alcoholism (delirium tremens)
have occurred in some cases. The role of the chief
and that of the women makes their drinking less
typical and possibly inclines them somewhat more
than others to pathological drinking.

REFERENCES

Garfield, V.
   1939   Tsimshian Clan and Society.   University
   of Washington Publications in Anthropology,
   Vol. 7:169-332.   Seattle: Univ. Washington.

Horton, D.
   1943   The functions of alcohol in primitive
   societies.   A cross-cultural study.   Quart.
   J. Stud. Alc. 4:199-320.

Lemert, E. M.
   1954   Alcohol and the Northwest Coast Indians.
   University of California Publications in
   Culture and Society, Vol. 2, No. 6:303-406.
   Berkeley: University of California Press.

CHAPTER IV

You Scratch My Back and I'll Scratch Yours:
Continuities in Inuit Social Relationships

by

John S. Matthiasson

Abstract

Prescribed social reciprocity and anticipated reciprocity, rooted in the traditional culture, is maintained among contemporary Tununermiut Inuit of northern Baffin Island, despite recent changes in economic adaptation and settlement patterns. A new vehicle for this reciprocity, alcohol, has emerged in networks between males, but traditional avoidance behavior in response to stress situations serves to curtail potentially violent alcohol-induced incidents.

A long-standing debate among Arctic ethnographers concerns the question of whether Inuit society is essentially communalistic or competitive (Hughes 1958).[1] Those who have employed the communalistic model have emphasized cooperation in hunting activities, distribution of game among kinsmen or fellow band members, shared responsibilities in child supervision and nurturance and other characteristics of traditional and contact-traditional

Reprinted from an article by the same name in Arctic Anthropology, Vol. XII, No. 1, 1975:31-36 by permission of the author and the editor of Arctic Anthropology.

[1] The emphasis in any particular ethnographic description is not always made explicit, but it is my contention that most Arctic ethnographers use one model or the other, and this personal choice has an influence on the overall image presented.

Inuit society and culture, as well as their expressions in modal personality traits, which support their model choice. Proponents of the competitive model tend to stress factors such as competition among hunters for scarce resources and among men for sexual partners, feuding and other examples supportive of their own model preference. Attributes of both models can probably be found, and an accurate representation of traditional and contact-traditional Inuit life should include both (Briggs 1974).

Despite this probable ambitendency, the image of the Inuit as a highly cooperative and communalistic people has become dominant, if not in the anthropological literature, at least in the public mind. In Canada in particular, where the Inuit constitute a large proportion of the indigenous population of the country, this image has led to a form of positive stereotyping which has had profound effects on, for example, government policies toward northern development and public corporations' attitudes toward differential hiring of native peoples (Matthiasson and Wing 1970). It may also have influenced Inuit self-conceptions. On a recent field trip to northern Baffin Island, I encountered the following note scribbled on the front of an old disc-list[2] by an Inuit clerk who is given to use of heavy sarcasm. "Eskimo people are very happy: Always smiling. Why not?" This was very likely a conscious expression of his resentment at being stereotyped, even if in a positive way.

Ethnographers who emphasize the cooperative, communalistic qualities of Inuit life often make

2 A disc-list is a compilation of the names of all Inuit living in and around a particular settlement. Usually compiled by the R.C.M.P., names on them are preceded by a "disc number", used to identify individuals in terms of ethnicity, area of residence and individual specificity. They are no longer kept in most settlements.

extensive reference to patterns of balanced reciprocity between kinsmen, hunting partners, spouses and other groupings, and to cultural mechanisms for the reduction of interpersonal hostilities and aggressions. I am probably adding further to the perpetuation of this communalistic model in this paper, in which I hope to demonstrate through two anecdotes the manner in which a cultural mechanism for the reduction and even avoidance of interpersonal hostility, and one which is based upon recognition of anticipated expressions of reciprocity, has been maintained in a post contact-traditional setting, although with a new basis for the pattern of reciprocity involved--alcohol.

The two anecdotes are based upon two sets of observations I made among the Tununermiut Inuit of northern Baffin Island in the Canadian Arctic in the winter of 1963-1964 and the summer of 1973. Both involve the same central figure, and both observations were made while I was living as a full-time participant with an Inuit family, a fact which diminishes the likelihood of artifice being present in either.

In 1963, approximately 90 percent of the Tununermiut were living as full-time hunters "on the land", in small, isolated hunting camps ranging from eight to 150 miles from the settlement of Pond Inlet. Monthly trips were made to the settlement to trade seal and fox skins for trade items such as flour, tea, sugar and cloth, but the general impact of the settlement and its contact agents on camp people was minimal (Matthiasson 1967). In the camp where I was living at the time there were five households, four of them connected by close kin connections. In one house an aged woman lived alone with her adopted teen-age daughter. This woman was the mother of J, the male head of another household. J's wife was the sister of Q, another head of household, and the daughter of A, who was head of a fourth household and also head-man in the camp. The husband and wife in the fifth unit had no relationship to the other four families, and in fact the wife had originally migrated after marriage from another settlement area. They had

75

occupied a camp house which had been abandoned the previous summer by a younger son of the head-man when he moved his family into the settlement. The three younger heads of households were all in their late 20's in age. During most of the winter I spent in their camp they regularly cooperated on joint hunting trips, although there were also occasions when individuals would venture off on other trips alone. J and Q rarely hunted without the assistance of one another, and in the area they were considered to be two of the most skilled hunters. Hunting trips, during which wives and children were left behind in the camp, would extend from two or three days to as long as three weeks.[3]

On any hunting trips which involved more than one day of absence from the camp, temporary transient snow houses would be constructed for sleeping purposes. They were generally abandoned after one night of occupancy. These "one-night-stand" snow houses would typically be small, with no sleeping platforms and little interior space for storage of carcasses and equipment. On occasion, however, extended periods of hunting would be carried out in fairly restricted geographical areas, and at these times larger, better constructed snow houses would be built, normally requiring several hours of work if designed for more than one person. These houses would typically have low sleeping platforms and comparatively spacious storage room.

In January of 1964, all three younger men in the camp went on a joint hunting trip, five or six days of which were to be spent in one particular area. A fairly large snow house had to be built to accomodate the three Inuit, the accompanying anthropologist and their equipment, and it had to be sturdy enough to survive without leakage for several days. We arrived at the site where the

3 On extended caribou hunting trips into the interior, wives and children accompanied the husband, but these usually took place in the spring.

house was to be constructed after traveling for approximately 15 hours in fairly stormy conditions. None of us had eaten any food other than bannock for several days because of a shortage of meat in the camp, a situation which necessitated the extended hunting trip in the first place.

After a brief discussion it was agreed that J would cut the snow blocks, which weighed on the average 40 pounds each, I would carry them to the construction site and Q would build the house. K was given responsibility for unharnessing the dogs and unloading the sleds. All went well for almost two hours and the house was near completion. We were all exhausted, hungry and anxious to see the job completed and be able to crawl into the house and rest. Q, however, was having trouble fitting a block of snow into the top of the house. Each time he placed it into position, it fell to the ground. This happened several times, and three blocks were tried before he lost his temper, kicked out with both legs and by exerting pressure with his arms broke down the entire structure. It crumbled about his feet. Q's work had been more exacting than that of the other men, but no more exhausting, and they all stopped their tasks to watch the spectacle. My personal reaction was one of anger and my strongest desire at the moment was to strike Q. I waited for one of the other men to give me vicarious satisfaction, but none did. Instead, they gathered together inside the fractured remains of the snow house, shuffled their feet, made exclamations about how irritating it is when a block of snow refuses to cooperate and then discussed alternative courses of action. It was soon agreed that Q should begin cutting blocks for a new house, K should carry the blocks and J should do the actual construction. A few blocks from the debris were salvaged and the entire operation began anew. No aggression or even hostility was displayed toward Q. He had made a personal, and apparently acceptable, response to a frustrating situation. With his new assignment, he would be able to work alone, away from the construction site, and it would not place new demands on his existing mood. Two hours later the house was completed, we removed our

77

parkas and climbed through the low opening into the house, ready for a good night's sleep. Nothing more was said about the incident.

I returned to the Tununermiut in the summer of 1973, and during that field trip I stayed with Q and his family, who now reside in the settlement of Pond Inlet. Shortly after my first trip, Q had been sent south for training as a heavy equipment operator. On his return, he and his family moved into the settlement, a move which anticipated a complete migration of all Tununermiut into Pond Inlet within the next few years. The camps no longer exist, although an abandoned one is used in the summer as a base for weekend fishing. Q now lives in a three-bedroom house, which he rents through the Settlement Housing Association, and is employed by the local Department of Public Works as an equipment operator. He has his own automobile, one of two in the community, and each year takes his family on a vacation trip to southern Canada. His life style has changed dramatically from that of a decade ago.

Despite his new affluence, there is one resource which is not readily available to Q: alcohol. There is no liquor outlet in the settlement and supplies must be ordered several weeks in advance from Frobisher Bay, the regional administrative center for the eastern Arctic. With uncertain and fairly infrequent mail service, one is never sure when a new supply will be available. Q is not a heavy drinker, although he does become inebriated on occasion. He has never had regular enough access to alcoholic beverages to develop a serious problem and it is questionable whether he would even with the opportunity. Nevertheless, an available supply of alcohol is important to Q, for alcohol serves a new need in the settlement: because of the rapid process of centralization of people in the area and consequent disruption of traditional relationships, alcohol now forms one base for the maintenance of links between adult males. That is, traditional patterns of relationships between males, which had been based on kinship, hunting partnerships, residential proximity and so on, are now formed and

often nurtured to a large degree through sharing
of alcohol.

Most adult Tununermiut males have found
employment in the settlement, as has Q, but 18 men
now work for one of the large oil companies carrying
out explorations in the high Arctic. These men work
on a rotating basis, spending 20 days on the site and
ten days in the settlement. Transportation to and
from the work site is by company aircraft. Although
no liquor is allowed on the site, it is readily
available to employees, who regularly spend time in
Resolute Bay while in transit to their home
settlement. There is no liquor outlet in Resolute
Bay, although there is a bar in the local hotel,
but Inuit living in the nearby settlement have much
better control over their liquor supplies than is
possible in Pond Inlet. With assured twice-weekly
flights from Frobisher Bay, they can be fairly certain
to have an adequate supply available for times when
it is wanted.

Several of the families living in the Resolute
Bay settlement were originally Tununermiut, having
been brought to Resolute in the 1950's to assist in
the construction and later maintenance of the Royal
Canadian Air Forces base; through the intervening
years contact has been maintained between the two
populations, although sporadically.[4] Oil rig workers
from Pond Inlet stay in the Inuit settlement when they
are forced to spend time in Resolute Bay in transit
to or from their work site. They have, therefore,
ready access to a regular source of alcohol and it is
rare that a man will return home from the site,
having passed through Resolute, without having a bottle
or two in his luggage. In the present employment
situation, there are at all times 12 Tununermiut at
the work site and six workers taking their regular
ten-day rest and recuperation time in the settlement.
Consequently, returning workers constitute a major

[4] On my departure from Pond Inlet, for example, I
was asked to deliver several letters to people
in Resolute Bay as I passed through it.

79

factor in determination of when drinking can take place in the settlement, and, for those persons who wish to take advantage of the liquor they make available, it is necessary to maintain a sound basis of reciprocal relations with them. A party, or male get-together, is usually held whenever men return from the site. Workers preparing to leave for the work site also provide a rationale for liquor consumption. Before departure, many of them, unhappy with the prospect of returning to work, will decide to "have a few drinks." Usually they will meet at the home of some individual who lives near the airstrip and spend several hours drinking and waiting for the aircraft to arrive, or for the pilot to have a meal after it has. Other men will drop in and have one or more drinks with the departing workers. At times, the nucleus of the drinking group will move from one house to another. Women rarely take part in these departure gatherings and are not normally present, although the wife of the host will likely be in her own home for at least part of the time.

One evening, while I was staying in Q's home, a gathering of this type was held there. A young man from the settlement was waiting for an aircraft to leave for the work site. Waiting with him was a young man from Arctic Bay, a nearby settlement, who had just returned from the site and was hoping to get to Resolute Bay to make connections with a flight south. The young Tununermiut became increasingly maudlin as the evening progressed and his rate of alcoholic intake increased. After the available liquor supply had been exhausted, he made several telephone calls to friends who might be willing to loan him a bottle, but the settlement was dry. By this time in the evening, most of the other participants had left, and Q's wife had gone off to visit a friend. Q, the two oil workers and I remained. Highly inebriated and increasingly losing control of his faculties, the young Tununermiut finally tore the telephone from the wall. Q was seated in such a way that he saw what had happened, but for several minutes he did nothing. Then he stood up, walked across the room to the phone and in a quiet voice stated that it was his phone, after all, and the young man really had no right to break it. He examined the damages and returned to his chair. Although he had by this time consumed a considerable amount of alcohol himself, Q was not noticeably inebriated. When, shortly after, the announcement was made over the local radio station that the aircraft was ready for departure, the four of us walked to the airstrip to bid the workers farewell and then Q and I returned to his home. By that time his wife was home, furious at the state of the telephone. Q spoke to her consolingly and then made the necessary repairs to the wiring. Nothing further was said about the incident. When the young oil worker's brother returned from the work site the following week, having had a stop-over in Resolute Bay, he brought with him a bottle of whiskey for Q, and several men in the settlement dropped in to Q's home that evening to have a drink or two from it.

The two anecdotes recounted happened a decade apart, under two quite different sets of conditions. Nevertheless, they share certain common characteristics and, I believe, offer evidence of continuity in interpersonal relationships in Inuit society, and the perpetuation of traditional mechanisms for avoidance of aggression and continuing hostility. In recounting them, I am, of course, supporting the cooperative model of Inuit social structure. In each anecdote an individual is driven to resort to violent action as a means of expressing frustration. In the first case it is the inability to make a block of snow stay in place during construction of a snow house which provokes the frustration, and in the second, an inability to locate more alcohol. Neither frustrating circumstance is produced by the previolence interactive setting or other actors in the situation. But, in both cases the violent reaction has deleterious effects on a second person. In the first, the snow house had to be rebuilt at a time when the other men in the hunting party were weary, hungry and cold, and in the second, Q's telephone had to be repaired. In neither case did the violent

81

action trigger a violent response on the part of
the other actors present, including those who had
been injured by it. I interpret the reason for this
to be the dependency of the injured parties on long-
term interaction with the individual, in either case,
who caused the injury, and the fact that certain
resources, which may not be the same over time, are
considered to be both scarce and valuable. In the
first case, Q's sister was married to one of the
other hunters present and his father was head-man
in the camp where they all lived. Q was also a
highly regarded hunter in a context where hunting
skills constituted a major source of personal prestige
and were critical for survival. K, the third
hunter present, was dependent upon Q's father for
continued residence in the camp. Q and J, his
brother-in-law, were hunting partners. In the
second case Q wanted access to the liquor brought
into the settlement by returning oil workers.
Possession of alcohol assisted him in maintaining
a set of relationships with other males in the
community. Some were kinsmen while others were not,
but all were important to Q in his efforts to
maintain his status, which had been established when
he was a full-time hunter and was now increasingly
difficult to validate in traditional terms. His
response, then, was an appropriate one, which resolved
a difficult and unexpected situation through recourse
to a traditional Inuit pattern of interpersonal
hostility resolution.

Discussion

     Alcohol has been present in the eastern Canadian
Arctic since the first explorers and whalers entered
its waters centuries ago, but it has only recently
become easily accessible to most Inuit. Availability
of alcoholic beverages to Eskimos and Indians has a
longer history in the western regions, but even there
it is relatively recent. Because of this, some analyst
of sociocultural change in the Canadian Arctic have
looked carefully at the manner in which Inuit have
adopted and adapted to the use of alcohol (Honigmann

82

and Honigmann 1965, 1970; Graburn 1969). More casual
observers are often quick to make generalizing
statements about Inuit drinking patterns. In both
sets of instances, I submit, depictions of Inuit
drinking patterns, and social and psychological
consequences of them, are to some extent results of
attitudes towards rapid change, personal thoughts
about the morality of drinking and selections of one
or the other model of traditional Inuit culture, or,
in some instances, intermingling of the two I
proposed earlier. Graburn, for example, sees the
introduction of home-brewing techniques to Sugluk
as the harbinger of social and psychological
breakdown, resulting in increased acts of violence,
promiscuity and in general, interpersonal hostilities
unchecked by traditional mechanisms for conflict
resolution. It seems that for him, the cooperative
basis of Inuit social relationships is threatened
by this abusive use of alcohol (Graburn 1969:186).

Non-Inuit residents and visitors to Inuit
settlements usually view the introduction of
alcohol as disastrous and blame it for most problems
that contemporary Inuit experience.[5] On several
occasions in 1973, while I was living in Q's home,
I was asked by Euro-Canadians how I was able to
accept the drunkenness by which they assumed I was
surrounded. The resident Anglican missionary, whose
wife happened to be dispatcher for the airline which
had regular flights back and forth between Pond Inlet
and Resolute Bay, met each aircraft and noted any
cartons of liquor and the persons to whom they were

5   In 1967 I taught the first anthropology course
    offered in Rankin Inlet, N.W.T., as part of the
    Arctic Research and Training Centre of the
    University of Saskatchewan. I required students
    to call on all Inuit families in the settlement
    and ask a series of predetermined questions.
    These students reacted with a startled response,
    and withdrew whenever they encountered drinking
    in Inuit homes. An open bottle of beer on a
    kitchen table was often enough provocation to
    elicit such a response. It seemed that a
    drinking Inuit was a drunken Inuit.

addressed. Like others, he attributed spurious and
genuine problems to alcohol. Among such observers the
cooperative model seems to have gained popular
acceptance.

In the second example I have used here, a
violent action directed against property in his home
was met with calm equanimity by Q, even though he
had been drinking heavily himself. John and Irma
Honigmann have claimed that similar expressions of
violence against furniture and household furnishings
were not unusual during drinking episodes in Inuvik
in the late 1960's. They also suggest that "native
drinking in Inuvik is in practise comparatively
normless, and sanctions designed to limit it are
only rarely imposed", and that"drunken violence
tends to be mostly inflicted within the same circle
of friends and relatives in which one is prone to
drink" (Honigmann and Honigmann 1970:100). Also,
"savage attacks are launched against mothers, fathers,
siblings, spouses and drinking companions".
(Honigmann and Honigmann 1970:100) (Emphasis mine).
Rather than drawing on either the cooperative or
competitive models of traditional Inuit society to
explain the violence provoked by excessive social
drinking in Inuvik, the Honigmanns introduce the
concept of "frontier culture" and identify these
drinking patterns as one of its characteristics.
Their evidence suggests most persuasively that a
frontier culture does exist in Inuvik, and probably
in other large, well-established settlements in the
western Canadian Arctic as well, where Inuit contact
with Euro-Canadians and, often, Indians, has been
long and intense, but I doubt that it is a reality
in Sugluk and am convinced that it does not exist
in Pond Inlet, although many of its postulated
features are characteristic of Inuit behavior in
Pond Inlet, such as emotional attachment to the land
and hunting prowess.

As I mentioned earlier, the centralization of
the Tununermiut into the settlement of Pond Inlet has
occurred mainly within the past decade. The
availability of alcohol to them, even though limited,
has been recent, and is only one of many sudden and
often traumatic changes which they have experienced

84

since centralization. The Euro-Canadian and Inuit
populations in Pond Inlet today are effectively
separate social entities, with little--and that
highly structured--interaction between them (this is
in part the result of voluntary social segregation
by the Inuit). As I plan to illustrate in a separate
article on political change among the Inuit of the
eastern Canadian Arctic, the networks which bound
together isolated camps before centralization have
been preserved in the transformed settlement. There
has not been adequate time, because of the swiftness
of the centralization process and the circumscribed
arenas for interaction between Euro-Canadians and
Tununermiut for a form of frontier culture to develop.
Given the rate of overall change within the
settlement, it is doubtful whether a frontier culture
will ever emerge in Pond Inlet. For example, the
Honigmanns have referred to the individualism of
participants in frontier culture (Honigmann and
Honigmann 1970:14), but in Pond Inlet cooperative
efforts are evident in a variety of enterprises, such
as the locally-controlled Inuit language radio
station.

     In the anecdote which I provided from camp
life, an individual struck out in anger in response
to frustration. Frustration-provoking situations
were common in traditional and contact-traditional
Inuit life. He did not inflict bodily harm on any
of the other participants in the setting. If he
had, the response of his companions might have been
different. In the second anecdote there is also
violence directed at an inanimate object. The
centralized settlement of Pond Inlet is also filled
with frustration-provoking conditions and situations
for the people living in it, for they have
experienced a rate of sociocultural change which
must be almost unique in human history. The use and
abuse of alcoholic beverages has become
characteristic of the lifeways of some Tununermiut,
although not all. The anecdote about its use which
I have recounted is extreme. Nevertheless, while I
did observe drunken behavior on several occasions,
I never saw it erupt into displays of interpersonal
aggression and when situations did develop in which
violence directed toward another person was

85

potential, other individuals, also present in the setting, were quick to ward it off. In fact, apparent drunken behavior was often more a posturing than the consequence of high intake of alcohol. A relaxing of constraints was often an accompaniment of male drinking parties, such as times of departure or return from work on the oil rigs, but the amount of alcohol consumed by individuals was usually so small, due to limited resources, that it is doubtful whether control of the situations was in fact lost. Certainly "normlessness" would not be an appropriate term to characterize such settlings.

In conclusion, I would suggest that drinking behavior among the Tununermiut, in the absence of a frontier culture, is not as socially and psychologically disruptive and damaging as casual observers of the settlement of Pond Inlet, and others like it in the eastern Arctic, have concluded. There have been casualties as a consequence of the introduction of alcohol, but the victims have typically been individuals who have spent extended periods of time "outside" the settlement, in Ottawa and/or Frobisher Bay (an unusually high proportion of Tununermiut were "brought out" during the early 1960's to work on Department of Northern Affairs and Natural Resources projects such as the development of a Roman orthography for the Inuit language). Being a scarce resource, alcohol has taken a place as a means of maintenance of networks between males. Traditional patterns of avoidance of socially damaging expressions of interpersonal hostility are employed to prevent the eruption of alcohol-induced violence. In at least one respect, then, alcohol has provided a means for the expression of traditional Tununermiut relationships based on patterns of reciprocity in a society which is more characterized by a tenacious tendency toward cooperation than competition.

REFERENCES

Briggs, Jean
    1974   Eskimo Women: Makers of Men.   In Many
    Sisters: Women in Cross-Cultural Perspective.
    Edited by Carolyn J. Matthiasson.   New York.

Graburn, Nelson H. H.
    1969   Eskimos Without Igloos: Social and
    Economic Development in Sugluk.   Boston.

Honigmann, John J. and Irma Honigmann
    1965   Eskimo Townsmen.   Ottawa.
    1970   Arctic Townsmen.   Ottawa.

Hughes, Charles C.
    1958   Anomie, the Ammassalik, and the
    Standardization of Error.   Southwestern
    Journal of Anthropology, Vol. 14-4:352-77.

Matthiasson, John S.
    1967   Eskimo Legal Acculturation: The
    Adjustment of Baffin Island Eskimo to
    Canadian Law.   Ph.D. Dissertation, Cornell
    University.

Matthiasson, John S. and Wing Sam Chow
    1970   Relocated Eskimo Miners.   Occasional Papers
    No. 1, Center for Settlement Studies,
    University of Manitoba.   Winnipeg.

CHAPTER V

Alcoholics Anonymous: Cultural Reform Among

The Saulteaux[1]

by

Jack Steinbring

The area of those bands now identified as
Northern Ojibwa (Dunning 1959:8), remains as E. S.
Rogers pointed out in 1962, Terra Incognita (1962:3).
Only Hallowell (1954), Dunning (1959), and Rogers
(1962) have completed and reported on extended
residential field research in the region. Landes
(1938) and Hilger (1951) have reported on prolonged
field studies for immediately related groups.

The term „Lake Winnipeg Ojibwa" applies only
to the Northern Ojibwa bands which now occupy the
east shoreline of Lake Winnipeg. These bands live
at the mouths of west-flowing rivers which have
their source in the Canadian Shield. This
designation has utility in the fact that Ojibwa bands
on the west side of this great inland sea occupy a
very different habitat and have adpated to it in
becoming at least variants of what is usually
referred to as the Plains Ojibwa (Howard 1965).
Other than this, however, the „Lake Winnipeg"

Reprinted from "Acculturational Phenomena Among the
Lake Winnipeg Ojibwa of Canada" in Verhandlungen
des XXXVIII Internationalen amerikanestenkongress,
Stuttgart 1968, Band III:179-188 by permission of the
author and the Director of the Linden-Museum,
Stuttgart.

[1] I am very grateful to a number of institutions
for helping me in the work which led to this
report. Among them were the University of Winnipeg,
the Canada Council, and the University of Manitoba.
To the Canada Council and the University of
Winnipeg, I am additionally grateful for travel
funds which made my attendance at the congress
possible.

89

designation would still prove to be weak in
attempting any refined distinctions between the
eastern lake-shore bands and those upriver. Hallowell
(1954:123) called attention to a gradient in this
upriver distribution. It applies to acculturational
characteristics, and it is clear that the visible
attributes of Western Acculturation increase as
one moves downriver to the loci of transport,
economic, and Christian religious establishments.
Recent field work (Steinbring 1965, 67; Elias 1967)
suggests the vague possibility of a "maritime-
interior" division based on residence related to
settled fishing and a semi-mobile, hunting-trapping
pattern in the interior. Reconstruction will be
difficult in this and probably it is an historically
connected matter, not a classical dichotomy of the
Chukchi type (Potapov 1964:799).

Originally there were ten Northern Ojibwa
communities occupying river mouths along the east
shore of Lake Winnipeg. Two of these bands (Loon
Straits and Rice River), were officially relocated
and placed on a larger reserve with the Hole River
(Wanipigow) Band. Today there are 8 officially
established reserves, and of these four have become
connected to the northern expansion of Manitoba
provincial highways. The Brokenhead and Fort
Alexander Reserves have been connected to the road
system for several decades, while the Hole River
and Little Black River Bands have received all
weather roads only within the past few years. The
Canadian Shield on the east side of Lake Winnipeg
has greatly limited road extension. The more
accessible physiography on the west side has made
it possible for most bands there to share in this
potentially unlimited urban contact for a much
longer period of time.

When anthropological field work by the University
of Winnipeg commenced in October 1963, the Little
Black River Band had experienced road connection
for less than a year. The Hole River Band, to the
north, had been connected about two years earlier.
It, however, had been long associated with a
regional mining road, shipping activities, a Metis
community with stores, intensive timber and pulp

90

exploitation, and commercial fishing. In addition,
two "competing" missions had been operating for many
years. It was clear to begin with that the most
favorable anthropological opportunities for the
examination of road attachment would rest with the
Little Black River Band, with excellent controls being
provided by the more exposed bands. The population
of Little Black River was then less than 140, with
insufficient manpower to produce a work-force or for
commercial fishing. It had no mineral or timber
resources, and, up to the time of the road, it had
only one Christian church. Contact with the outside
world had been by dog team and boat, and through
occasional trips to hospital by plane. Only two of
the 23 families appear to have expressed any interest
in expanding this contact through the future
possibility of a road. Some were undecided, and
many were openly apprehensive. Today this
uncertainty is brought out as informants cite the
disadvantages to their new location, two miles
upriver from the lakeshore. Relocation had been
demanded by the prohibitive cost of building at least
two bridges so that both the north half and south
halves of the band could be served. Today, very few
admit to any agreement about this relocation, which
was accomplished in two days by tractor along the
frozen river. They cite the swarms of summer insects,
the lack of fish, the mud, or the fact that every
single one of them has a close relative who has been
killed or badly injured in an automobile accident.

It has always been customary to view the abrupt
exposure of nonliterate peoples to the Western world
as having essentially negative force. Guns, whiskey,
tuberculosis, venereal disease, money, Christianity,
and now automobiles may be cited to elaborate this
view. To the Little Black River Band of Manitoba,
the extension of the road system also brought an
answer to growing cultural stress. When the road
finally arrived, most of the adults of the band
became members of Alcoholics Anonymous[2] and were
proud to say so.

[2] Alcoholics Anonymous is an institution founded in
    1935 for the purpose of arresting alcoholism
    through mutual support. It has a membership of

Because of its semi-isolation, the Little Black River Band represents the clearest part of a larger movement. This phenomenon appears to have first emerged at Powerview, Manitoba, with the establishment of the Sunrise Chapter in 1956. Diffusion of AA from the urban center occurred through a work force associated with the construction of a hydro-electric dam at Powerview. The membership of this chapter was largely from the north bank area of the Fort Alexander Band, and got both inspiration and practical assistance from "Roy", a long established regional figure in AA from the nearby pulp mill town of Pine Falls. From Powerview, AA spread west to the administrative center of the Fort Alexander Reserve, where the Sunset Chapter was formed, just west of Pine Falls. It was now developing strength and the bands to the north were beginning to learn about it, the more remote ones indirectly through water traffic along the east shore of Lake Winnipeg. This communication was limited, but highly meaningful because of the family and totemic relationship between bands. AA became a favoured thing, and the judgment of a relative or totem mate was to be respected.

When the road system was extended from Powerview to Manigotagan in 1959, AA spread with it. In that year the Daybreak Chapter was established at Manigotagan by "Frankie", a Metis gentleman of outstanding personal qualities. Most of the membership was Saulteaux speaking ("low" Ojibwa) and even the local Whites spoke this language. From Manigotagan, it spread to Bissett where the Golden Group was formed, again largely of off-reservation persons, as well as some Whites and Metis from this mining town. Subsequently a timber operation at Manigotagan moved to a location near Bissett,

over 300,000 distributed throughout 85 countries. A complete description of the movement can be found in its official publication, Alcoholics Anonymous, Works Publishing Company, 1946. A discussion of its religious dimension is conveyed by Arthur H. Cain in: "Alcoholics Anonymous: Cult or Cure", Harper's Magazine, Volume 226, No. 1353, February 1963, pp. 48-53.

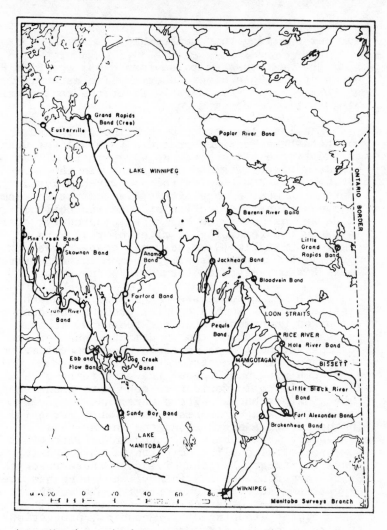

Fig. 1 Map showing distribution of Native Bands in the Lake Winnipeg region of Manitoba, Canada.

93

further swelling that membership.

The next chapter to be formed was the Side Hill Group at the Hole River Reserve. The establishment of this chapter came shortly after the construction of a 7 mile connecting road.

The last chapter to be originally formed in the southern Lake Winnipeg area was the Twilight Chapter at the Little Black River Reserve, just halfway between Powerview and Manigotagan. In the 1959 northerly road extension the highway had passed just four miles east of the Little Black River settlement. Two years later, a section of road was built in 2½ miles approximately to the reserve boundary. Late in 1962, the remaining 1½ miles of road were completed, and in 1963 the local chapter was formally begun. It is still common to hear current local history cited in terms of "when we got AA".

In order to understand the absorption and modification of such a complex group phenomenon as AA, by an unmarkedly acculturated band, it is necessary to examine the functions. Whether one regards alcoholism as an acute, psychosocially defined disorder, a strictly medical problem, or as a combination of these, the occurrence of a chronic alcoholic would have been rare among the Lake Winnipeg bands. There were, and are, very severe "drinking problems", to be sure, especially in the larger bands such as the one at Fort Alexander. But, there appeared to be little, if any, actual alcoholic addiction of the chronic phase for treaty Indians living on these reserves. Of the numerous persons interviewed, none had ever experienced surreptitious drinking, "blackouts", a rationalization of drinking behaviour, persistent remorse, the dropping of friendships, protection of alcohol supply, tremors, psychomotor inhibition, or obsessive drinking. These are among the 39 attributes established by the Alcoholism Subcommittee of the World Health Organization. At Little Black River, there were many members who had never experienced any kind of serious drinking problem, and there were some (mainly ladies) who

94

had never been drinkers. "Old Jane" was a case in point. At an AA meeting, the local Metis school teacher (an abstainer himself) asked this 75 year old woman about her "drinking problems". She replied that she always used to drink too much when, her husband was alive. It developed that her husband had been dead for over 20 years!

In the established functions of AA as they developed within urban Western culture do not appear emphasized in the process of cultural integration, the social scientist is obliged to examine the new characteristics of function, and also the manner in which this phenomenon was absorbed in the first place. If these matters can be sufficiently explained, the results may offer predictive value.

There is a collective feeling among Native North American peoples that their culture is disappearing, that they are experiencing a fundamental kind of loss. This has been felt across the entire breadth of the continent and has been met by a bewildering variety of reformative movements (Voget 1960). The introduction of Alcoholics Anonymous exhibits a number of reformative characteristics[3]).

Hallowell (1954:277) has demonstrated an important relationship between Ojibwa personality and magico-religious belief. All human difficulties, even death, were explicable in terms of malevolent supernatural forces. This system, through tremendous historical depth, had, among its components, the facility of rationalizing one's behaviour. Christianity sought to break down such beliefs. At Little Black River, Christian teaching commenced in the 1870's, at about "treaty time", but until the present decade was carried on by lay ministers of

[3] I was once vigorously criticized by a local missionary for using the term Nativistic in connection with AA. He advised me that a drunk from the most acculturated regional band now refused to listen when he "encouraged" the drunk to attend AA meetings. The drunk's reply: "I'm not going to join any damned Nativistic revival".

Native background. In reviewing the stories about
these people it is clear that they themselves carried
a combination of Native and Christian ideas. One,
for example, is reported to have observed the Windigo,
a cannabalistic monster of the other world. This same
man, a Metis, was married to an Ojibwa woman and
raised seven children throughout his 55 years of
service to the Little Black River Band. He used and
administered Native medicinal preparations, was
faultless in his use of the Native language, and was
the source of all formal education for half a century.
The result of this man's work and the less balanced
combinations of his predecessors was a graduality
in the assumption of Christian religious beliefs.
When the last lay minister left in the 1950's and
a new aggressive echelon of trained, totally
Christian clergy stepped in, a stronger need for a
new form of rationalizing negative behaviour became
felt. Despite its minimal and intermittent use,
alcohol supplied the answer. To the people of
Little Black River, much of Man's misfortune is
attributed directly to alcohol. And alcohol is
associated in the minds of Little Black River people
with the deteriorating impact of urban-industrial
expansion. Alcohol provided a symbol of unity, a
consolidation of purpose, and Alcoholics Anonymous
provided, for a time, the ready-made organizational
matrix.

        This sequence of events and less tangible forces
was far from enough, however, to provide a practical
basis for the incorporation of a fairly complex set
of social ideas and activities. To properly
understand the integration of AA, we must turn to
an examination of the specific structural and
functional attributes of AA which provided for
alignment with pre-existent Ojibwa culture traits.

        Alcoholics Anonymous, generally speaking, is
a male dominated and male oriented group. This
fact aligned well with indigenous conditions.
Northern Ojibwa culture is male oriented,
inheritance is patrilineal, primary economic roles
are filled by men, and leadership is entirely male.
It is most interesting that, while the Band

96

Auxiliary has always been an enthusiastic and instrumental group, efforts to establish an AA auxiliary have repeatedly failed, one such failure occurring only months before this presentation. It is of further interest to note that the AA auxiliary or Alanon[4] has succeeded in at least one of the other more acculturated bands. In Ojibwa culture, the verbal arts are highly developed. Story telling is a favoured form of pastime, and oratory has traditionally been an activity of men, in, or moving toward, roles of leadership. Ojibwa oratory is dramatic, charged with subtle innuendos, and carried on best by the traditional persons of authority, the elders. The testimonial of AA seems to have been predestined for this, and it arrived at a time when the authority of the elders was beginning to be questioned by the younger men. For several years practically all of the men, even teenagers, belonged to AA, and it was clear from the start that it would be a long time before the young men could rise to the oratorical heights of their fathers and grandfathers. There was a renewed respect for the older men, and AA may be seen to have provided a means toward the reconsolidation of traditional authority which continues today in varied form.

The confessional aspects of the AA testimonial might also have aligned with indigenous procedure. Confessions among the Ojibwa are reported from several sources in connection with the services of a conjuring shaman. The most recent instance of this in the literature is reported by Dunning (1959:180), and the practise is confirmed by Little Black River data acquired during the 1967 field season.

Whereas boasting (like any other human excesses) was reprehensible conduct among the Northern Ojibwa, there was at least one way in which a person could legitimately call attention to his deeds and achievements. This was again through a public recitation. In this way a man might describe a dream which gave him power, or describe, in great detail,

[4] Al Anon is the group formed universally for the spouses of AA members.

an encounter with a bear while out hunting. These
stories are always the same, told over and over
again, but to a never tiring audience.

The AA testimonial is a regular feature of
meetings. The same story is told over and over again
by each member. These stories detail the conditions
of a man's life, before and after joining AA. They
are legitimate stories of achievement.

Whereas some of these testimonials contain a
richness of sordid former happenings, some are
peculiarly thin. In a sense, the latter speakers
suffer a kind of subordination since there is effort
to present an abundance of negative material. These
are the persons who have had only limited experience
with alcohol. This does not apply to the younger
men, who make up in detail for their shortcomings
in oratorical skill.

Whereas, boasting outside the somewhat formalized
public recitation, is traditionally unacceptable, one
possible instance in AA does come to mind. A certain
member of one of the chapters, in not too apologetic
terms to his formerly polygynous people, cites the
fact that: "Before I joined up with AA, I had ten
wives."

The organizational aspects of AA also played an
important part in its acceptance. Decentralization
and localization align well with the autonomous
character of Northern Ojibwa bands. These features
of AA permit the development of close, band-centered
chapters, capable of fully local function, and,
significantly, the full use of Native language. In
a sense, AA also reinforces, in its administrative
characteristics, basic band and totemic organization.
Band and totemic exogamy are still widely practised.
No person is permitted to marry another person from
his or her band, or from the same totemic group such
as a caribou, lynx or sturgeon. One way in which
this system is reinforced comes through the highly
popular AA dances. Several times, throughout the
year, AA chapters sponsor dances to which many come
from all of the bands. These dances provide
wholesome opportunity for young people of different

98

bands and totems to meet, and through which
appropriate marriages may develop[5]. None of the band
halls is large enough to hold the people who flock to
these dances. Music and dancing are of immense
importance in the modern life of Northern Ojibwa
people. Guitar and fiddle playing are widely favored
means toward individual achievement and recognition.
All in all, the association between AA and the
institution of music and dance provides considerable
reinforcement for both.

The people have always been aware, however, of
the dangers in exaggerating the entertainment aspect.
This was rather dramatically brought out when one
large AA chapter repeatedly sponsored dances for
profit. The situation, reportedly, became quite
tense, as no effective effort was made to exclude
drunks from these dances. This may have been
partial cause for the formation of a new chapter,
growing mainly from the disenchanted ranks of the
larger one.

In AA, local pride has been remarkably evident.
There has been marked competition between bands to
develop the "best" AA chapter. Other bands have
been accused by the Little Black River people of
being "jealous" of them. Sometimes, in fact, evil
deeds like breaking and entering an isolated cabin
or disturbing a trap have been explained by the
jealousy of other bands, "because of our AA". The
same views have been expressed by other bands,
towards Little Black River. It has been apparent
throughout that there is nothing very anonymous
about AA in these Ojibwa bands. Pride attaches to
individual membership, and few resist telling that
they are members. In many cases they have
unhesitatingly identified all or most of the other
members. At Little Black River, this was simply a
run down of all but one or two of the responsible
adult males, and quite a few of the ladies. The
non-members whose identity did change in a limited

5   In this sense it is quite the same as the annual
    gathering of wild rice, except that it is not
    limited to a season of the year.

way, were as a rule, from the highly acculturated
families, and one has now moved permanently from
the reserve.

The Christian religious dimension of AA seems
to have had appeal. Possibly it may have fallen in
line with a diminishing concern for the orthodox,
large denominational local church. As is the case
elsewhere, fundamentalist groups are appearing more
frequently in response to local demands at Little
Black River, another result of road extension. For
some reason too, AA meetings have always been held
on Sunday.

To the anthropologist attempting to investigate
the conditions under which another person or group
can use help, one fact about the integration of AA
stands out more dramatically than any other. This
is one of the fundamental concepts of AA. Simply
stated it is: "AA will not come to the man. The man
must come to AA." This exemplifies one secure
theoretical finding of modern, professional Social
Work, namely self-determination. This is the essence
of free choice, unaffected by external, and in this
case culturally, threatening pressures. The people
of Little Black River have demonstrated this choice
each time they have referred to recent events in
terms of "when we got AA". Because of this free
choice, the feeling of having something of one's
own is greatly enhanced, a condition implied each
time they have expressed the opinion that another
band is "jealous of our AA".

From a sentimental stance, it seems tragic in
1968, that AA, as a formal institution of the Little
Black River Band, has collapsed. While it continues
in varying strength at all of the more acculturated
communities, at Little Black River it emerged quickly,
shone brightly, and then died. But, there is a good
chance that the anatomy of its death may equal in
value the analysis of its integration.

To those who know Algonkian leadership patterns,
the failure of a formal AA is not difficult to
understand. While most of the initial membership had

100

prior knowledge of AA and was quite ready to accept
it, practical leadership was begun by a highly
acculturated man who had owned a car out on the
unconnected highway, and who had joined AA in a town
to the south. For a full year, he was the only
member, and when the last section of reserve road
went in, he presided at the gatherings in his home.
In this formative period, meetings were always on
the home reserve, and they were conducted in the
Native language. Because of the immediate successes,
the "leader" became regionally prominent. He
became a delegate to conferences, and frequently
attended meetings in other bands and in White towns.
The less acculturated membership started expressing
dissension, privately, in what one might call the
"typical Ojibwa way". The elaborate Ojibwa gossip
system was soon heard to say things like "that White
man". And, along these lines, the gossip system had
plenty of ammunition. The "head man of AA" had been
born in a different band. He was quite literate in
English. He had the only full time, regular money
income on the reserve, as caretaker of the government
day school. When the road was finished, he started
a taxi service and quickly got more government income
for handling materials previously transported by
water and air to the school. Before long, he put
a picture window in his house and shortly later he
installed a billiard table. Along with the price
of each game, his wife would collect money for coffee,
hamburgers, and canned soda pop. Some time before
the road was completed, this man's standard Canadian
family allowance was increased by the government
placement of an English speaking foster child.
Following completion of the road, another English
speaking foster child was placed in the home, and a
few months after this the "head man of AA" commenced
the exclusive use of the English language, except when
acting as interpreter for government officials. He
also built a garage and developed a small docking
service for Whites occupying off reservation property
on the lakeshore. Commonly he would provide meals
and facilities for government contracted carpenters
doing work on the reserve.

All of this, and a good deal more, was fed into
the gossip system. AA meetings became very rare.

101

And, in the spring of 1967, an election was coming
up. In what might well have been an effort to
achieve power, the "head man of AA" became nominated
for chief. His identification with outside government
and urban ways prompted the gossip system to label
him "the Agent's man". It is important to recognize
that this man's primary claim to authority and respect
within the band was through his AA activity.
Practically all of his other experience identified
him with the aggression and goal striving behaviour
of non-Ojibwa life. It would seem reasonable to
suppose that his overwhelming defeat came very close
to a true reaction toward his brand of AA, and,
moreover, toward his materialistic philosophy now
far removed from the spirit of the group.

Even more instructive was the election of his
opponents, each of them a devoted adherent to AA.
The chief is a young man, literate, an excellent
hunter, loyal to his people and to the two elder
councillors who carefully guide his actions. These
men abstain from alcohol. When they meet together
or with members of their families, they discuss the
benefits of doing so. They, and many other adults
of the band, support each other without formality.
A few have returned to drinking but mainly in
moderation. When the interviewer asks a person if
he or she belongs to AA, the answer is: "no".
However, if the interviewer asks the question, "are
you AA?" the answer is very often "yes". The
response obtained in the first inquiries about this
contradiction nicely defined the new AA, and
reflected, not insignificantly, on the role of a
rather rare type of anthropological participant-
observer:

"I'm just like you, Jack. I got my AA right
here (pointing), in my head."

The multiplicity of human forces, and the absence
of control combine to grossly limit confidence in the
predictive processes of social science. Our
observations on the adoption of AA by the southern
Lake Winnipeg bands, however, reveal a number of
rather clear alignments, most of which are posed by

102

generalized indigenous conditions. In 1965, after
viewing an absolute correlation between highway
extension and adoption of AA over a period of 6 years,
it seemed very reasonable to predict the further
adoption of AA by the Northern Ojibwa as the road
moved north to connect more of the Lake Winnipeg
bands. While no new bands have since been connected,
this is probably still a safe prediction. With its
decentralization, unity of expression, close group
experience, provision of independent choice, male
orientation, the testimonial, not to mention others,
this phenomenon tends to fulfill some basic
prerequisites to a reformative movement. And, to
those bands living north on an extending road system,
it will have been introduced by other Native people
of the same cultural and linguistic affiliation.
However, it is now clear that the formality of such
adoption may be greatly conditioned by the exact
factors of introduction. In those bands like Berens
River, which have become urban industrial satelites,
formality will probably characterize the adoption.
In other cases, like the Little Grand Rapids Band
(an interior community) and possibly the Bloodvein
Band, the adoption will probably be less formal.
In the Kenora, Ontario area AA is largely formal
and can be identified with "Pan-Indian" activity.
An AA conference mainly for Native members has taken
place there, and such a conference has been held at
the Fort Alexander Reserve near Pine Falls, Manitoba.
This latter Ojibwa community shows promise of
becoming an important center for "Pan-Indian"
developments.

As population increases, both for urban society,
and for Native peoples the stresses of culture
contact accrue. As Man finds his cultural integrity
threatened, and thus his own sense of well-being, he
strives to defend against changes which cannot be
smoothly accomodated. Even without the unique
alignment of culturally important attributes,
Alcoholics Anonymous serves reform. Presently there
is no assurance of whether or not it will ever be
identified as a formal Nativistic phenomenon[6]. All

6   Some feel that AA forms a substitute for the Grand
    Medicine Society of the Ojibwa which passed away

over North America there have been hundreds of
reformative movements, some large, most of them small.
All of them have been geared to a reconsolidation of
values, a new direction, a reconstitution of group
identity, a new hope.

An informant summed it up quite neatly when I
asked what the name of the Side Hill Chapter meant.
He replied, "We are climbing".

regionally in the 1920's (Hallowell 1936). Such
speculation will require a type of evidence which
this phenomenon will not yield without a rather
unique set of investigative procedures. However,
on one of the reserves a tin can containing the
AA "bible" was buried in the backyard of the
meeting hall. It was annually re-excavated and
read at the "Birthday" meeting. This, they said
was "the way the Old People did it". Such a
practise was, in fact, common to the Grand
Medicine Society.

REFERENCES

Dunning, R. W.
    1959 Social and Economic Change Among the
    Northern Ojibwa. University of Toronto Press.
    Toronto.

Elias, Peter Douglas
    1967 "Relationships Between Formal and Informal
    Groups, and the Distribution of Power in an
    Indian Community", Unpublished Manuscript,
    Laboratory of Anthropology, University of
    Winnipeg.

Hallowell, A. Irving
    1942 The Role of Conjuring in Saulteaux Society.
    Publications of the Philadelphia Anthropological
    Society, Volume 2.
    1955 Culture and Experience. University of
    Pennsylvania Press. Philadelphia.

Hilger, Sister M. Inez
    1951 Chippewa Child Life and Its Cultural
    Background. Bureau of American Ethnology,
    Bulletin 146. Washington.

Howard, James H.
    1965 The Plains-Ojibwa or Bungi. South Dakota
    Museum, University of South Dakota,
    Anthropological Papers, No. 1.

Landes, Ruth
    1937a Ojibwa Sociology, Columbia University
    Press. New York.
    1937b "The Ojibwa of Canada", in Margaret Mead
    (ed.), Cooperation and Competition Among
    Primitive Peoples. New York.
    1938 The Ojibwa Woman. Columbia University Press.
    New York.
    1968 Potawatomi Culture 1936-1958. Unpublished
    Manuscript, Laboratory of Anthropology,
    University of Winnipeg.

Rogers, Edward S.
    1962 The Round Lake Ojibwa. Occasional Paper
    5, Art and Archaeology Division, Royal Ontario

Museum, University of Toronto.

Steinbring, Jack
1965 "Culture Change Among the Northern Ojibwa", Transactions of the Historical and Scientific Society of Manitoba, Series III, Number 21: 13-25.
1967 "Ojibwa Culture: The Modern Situation and Problems", in: Kenora 1967, Resolving Conflicts -- A Cross- Cultural Approach, University of Manitoba Press. 46-71.

Voget, Fred
1960 "American Indian Reformations and Acculturation", National Museum of Canada Bulletin No. 190, Contributions to Anthropology, Part II.

World Health Organization
1952 Second Report, Alcoholism Subcommittee, Expert Committee on Mental Health, Geneva. 26-30.

CHAPTER VI

Acculturation Stress and the Functions of

Alcohol among the Forest Potawatomi

by

John H. Hamer

    The purpose of this study of the Forest
Potawatomi is to consider some of the motivations
for drinking and the social functions of alcohol
in a society where the pressures of acculturation
have been severe.[1] The community, located in the
Upper Peninsula of Michigan, was in 1961 a small
village of 162 persons in 29 families.[2] Because of
the personal nature of the material to be discussed,
this village will be given the pseudonym Whitehorse.
It is suggested, on the basis of the observations,
that drinking in this community (a) gives the
individual a means for coping with an unpredictable
universe, as well as an escape from anxiety about
the expression of overt aggression; (b) permits

[1] The field work on which this report is based
was conducted during the summer and fall of 1961
under a grant from the Michigan State Board of
Alcoholism.

[2] Hamer, J. Social problems in Whitehorse: An
Indian community in the Upper Peninsula of
Michigan. In: Pearman, J. R. An Exploratory
Study of Welfare Programs and Needs in the Upper
Peninsula of Michigan. Mimeographed; 1961.

persons temporarily to assume desirable status
positions when there has been interference with,
and inadequate substitutes for, the traditional
social structure; (c) serves as a means for catego-
rizing groups in an acculturative situation by
rendering the behavior of one predictable by the
other; and (d) provides a kind of solvent of tension
which helps, periodically, to bring the white and
Indian communities together on a basis of
friendship.

Background

The Potawatomi are a tribe once significant
in numbers and influence in the Great Lakes region.
Their social organization was based on the patrilineal
hunting and gathering band, with the women cultivating
some crops such as maize, squash, beans and tobacco.
Though the political system was rudimentary, with
chiefs granted temporary authority only on hunting
and war parties, the Potawatomi were not only adept
as warriors but were noted for their role as
peacemakers (an activity largely implemented through
intermarriage) in disputes between other tribes (De
La Potherie 1753:301-303; Caton 1876:3-30; Morse
1822:131-135; Skinner 1924). For purposes of this
paper the most important aspect of their religion
was the well-known guardian-spirit quest by which
the individual acquired a supernatural protector for
life. Complete protection was impossible, however,
for there was always the danger of sorcery should
one antagonize a person whose guardian spirit was
more powerful.

The experiences of these Indians with fur traders,
missionaries, white settlers and the government have
been almost wholly unfavorable, with the possible
exception of the early years of contact. By the
middle of the last century those who had not been
forcibly removed to reservations in the southwest
wandered aimlessly in northern Wisconsin and the
Upper Peninsula of Michigan until the second decade
of this century (Foreman 1946:105-122; Lawson 1920).

In 1914 the wanderings finally came to an end when the government purchased 3,359 acres for the Whitehorse Band in the Upper Michigan area.

There are several historical references to drunkenness among the Potawatomi as being attributable to the introduction of intoxicants by the early fur traders, provision of rum by the British and French to obtain their support in military ventures and, in the nineteenth century, widespread use of whisky in exchange transactions between white storekeepers and Indians (Lawson 1920; Keating 1824:88-134; Pokagon 1899:82-107, 249). Experience with the white man was not itself the only reason for the development of heavy drinking patterns; the pre-existing tensions between spouses, lack of social controls, beliefs about the curative properties of alcohol, personality attributes of dependency, and strict control on interpersonal aggressiveness, made drinking an acceptable innovation in Potawatomi culture.

There is much evidence that husbands traditionally held higher status than wives. For example, there are references to the generally brutal treatment of wives by husbands as well as the existence of a dual standard for infidelity by which the woman was subject to punishment but not her lover (Morse 1822; Keating 1824). This dominant status of the man appears to have declined, under the pressures of acculturation, to the point where women held an increasingly negative stereotype of men by the end of the nineteenth century (Pokagon 1899). The decline in male prestige is especially relevant in the light of the alcoholic fantasies concerning male status that will be discussed later.

Recent studies have suggested that community condemnation and social controls are significantly related to amount of drinking (McCord 1960:38-43). In the case of the Potawatomi, with the exception of maple syrup expeditions in the spring, war parties, and games of lacrosse, there were few organized activities which would provide for the subordination of the individual to the group. Considering their

109

individualistically oriented hunting and gathering
culture, measures of supernatural and individual
self-control, such as Hallowell (1955:363) has
demonstrated worked so well in the Chippewa, were
probably sufficient. By the middle of the nineteenth
century, when alcohol was being used extensively and
the deculturation process had set in, the limited
potential for formal community sanctions led to the
development of a situation in which incest, murder,
theft, and disrespect for parents, though considered
"most atrocious", often went unpunished (Keating
1824:88-134; Copley 1908:261). Intoxication was
invariably the rationalization for these crimes
and the perpetrator went free.

Further, there seem to have developed beliefs
in the therapeutic properties of alcohol, since
even as early as the middle of the eighteenth
century Ottawa shamans are reported to have used
brandy to excess, thinking it would cure disease
(Kinietz 1940:307). This belief continued through
the nineteenth century (Pokagon 1899:82-107, 249)
and one old informant indicated that some members
of the Whitehorse community still believe alcohol
provides a remedy for blood poisoning.

Though historical records can provide only
crude indications of personality traits, in those
documents alluding to contact between Potawatomi
and the white man it is possible to discern certain
tendencies toward obsequiousness, avoidance of self-
blame through projection, and periodic outbursts of
aggression. There are the reports of early
missionaries and explorers that the Potawatomi were
exceptional among the Indians of the Great Lakes
region in their docility, generosity, and general
desire for approval from the white man (De La Potherie
1753; Thwaites 1899). In the historical records of
the nineteenth century there are numerous examples of
obsequious apologies by various leaders for not
being able to meet the demands of the white settler
for more land. These indications of dependency often
occur simultaneously with accusations and blame of
the whites as solely responsible for the increase
in drunkeness among the Indians (Copley 1908;

Beckworth 1884:179-180). Hence there is demonstrated
a willingness to project the responsibility for
undesirable individual characteristics onto others,
a trait usually associated with alcoholism in
industrial societies.

Much evidence is available to show that the
emphasis placed on control of interpersonal aggression
led to periodic outbursts of hostility. In a most
extreme form these aggressive acts were expressed in
cannibalistic episodes, which the data indicate
were common occurrences not only in times of famine
but frequently as an excuse for gaining the power
attributed to an enemy (Keating 1824:88-134). This
extreme physiological expression of anger was not
confined to men, for upon return from a war party
scalps and severed heads were thrown on the ground
for the women to beat and insult; later they
performed dances with the heads held aloft on poles
(Skinner 1924). Even in the course of everyday life
the accounts of travelers indicate a strange contrast
between the impulsive obscenity of Potawatomi
conversation and their very guarded actions (Keating
1824:88-134). The stranger was well advised to be
cautious despite initial demonstrations of
friendliness, since the least sign of hostility or
error in etiquette could be used as an excuse to
make him an enemy. Thus, while self-control was
stressed in social interaction between members of the
community it seems to have been a fragile thing. It
is not surprising, therefore, that intoxication became
a rationalization for assaulting, even murdering,
kinsmen or band members.

Contemporary Culture and Drinking

Only a few of the oldest inhabitants can remember
childhood experiences involving fasting and the vision
quest; the younger generation have little knowledge
of the old Indian way of life. It is evident that
there has been nothing to replace the old forms of
religion, warfare and technology so abruptly

111

dislocated by the white man, but the atomistic
social structure and subsistence type of economy
have changed only slightly. Because there is
practically no social organization at the community
level, social interaction continues to be concentrated
in the family. Part-time work in the woods and
government relief checks provide a bare subsistence,
which is not dissimilar to subsistence patterns of the
last century. It is in this relatively deculturated
setting supported by the traditional lack of community
sanctions, psychological tendencies toward dependency
and severe aggression anxiety, along with a decline
in the formerly high status of the male, that
drinking has become a way of life. To understand
the functions of drinking in the present cultural
context it is necessary to consider the desire for
alcoholic beverages, their use, drinking norms,
and behavior while intoxicated.

Desire for Alcohol

        The principal beverages used in Whitehorse, as
in most low income areas, are beer and wine, though
whisky and vodka are drunk occasionally when
government checks are received or when it is provided
by visiting white men. Actually there is no
preferred beverage, except in the sense that, according
to most informants, the higher the alcohol content
the more desirable the drink. Only one man, a Chippewa
who had married into the community, was observed to
make "home brew" (dandelion wine). The normal
procedure is to purchase one or two "jumbos" (quarts
of beer) or a quart of wine (20% alcohol content
preferred) whenever one makes a trip to the store,
which in the summer, considering that refrigeration
is nonexistent, can be as often as every other day.
Of most of the adults it can be said that whenever
they have money they also have beer and wine. The
ethnographer's experience in bringing candy to
children shows, at least indirectly, the great desire
for liquor. Inevitably this candy would be received
by adults, without any expression of gratitude, and

112

distributed perfunctorily to the children. On the
other hand, a gift of wine or beer for adults was
always received most graciously.

There is a desperation about the desire for
alcohol which sometimes pushes the characteristic
mode of indirect expression to the extreme. For
example, informants, who were reluctant to ask for
favors pertaining to the ordinary problems of
health and subsistence, felt no qualms about using
a ritualized request for money to purchase beer and
wine. Illustrative of this approach were the
frequent petitions addressed to white men, a more
likely source of money than other Indians, to borrow
a dollar or two to purchase gasoline, to look for
a job, or to buy food "to feed the children". A
short time later the supplicant would be found with
a "jumbo" of beer or a quart of wine. The Potawatomi
uses this method not only because of an unwillingness
to ask directly for favors but because he knows that
it is the stereotype for evoking pity in the white
man's culture and that, if he is successful in
obtaining the money, the donor will not be surprised
or angered to find that it has been used to purchase
alcohol, since this fits in with the latter's
stereotyped expectations of Indian behavior.

The importance of drinking in the lives of the
Potawatomi is shown in a comparison of their income
and expenditures. The average monthly income of each
of 12 families in Whitehorse, in the course of a year
(1960-1961), was $170.14; in 6 of these families 50%
of this income was spent for food, 30% for liquor and
tobacco, 8% for clothing, 5% for transportation, 2%
for organized entertainment and 5% for miscellaneous
purposes. It should be emphasized that these
proportions are only estimated; it was impossible,
except in one or two families, to obtain reasonably
accurate records.

Use of Alcoholic Beverages

Practically all drinking in Whitehorse is
social. Only one woman, by her own admission,
preferred to drink alone. While much of the drinking
in homes or cars involves the custom of passing the
bottle from one person to another, tavern practices
are similar to those of the white man. It is
customary to imbibe as long as the supply lasts, with
time periods varying from a few hours of drinking to
a 2 or 3 day binge. One informant said that it was
not unusual for an individual to drink five or six
12-ounce bottles of beer in an hour or to consume
a gallon of wine in the course of an all-night
drinking session. This is undoubtedly a questionable
claim, particularly in regard to the wine, but the
extent to which this is an exaggeration is indicative
of the pride these people take in their drinking
prowess. One woman bragged that she sometimes
consumes 2 pints of whisky, with little noticeable
effect, during the course of a work day in the woods.
On several occasions the ethnographer observed both
men and women each to consume between 5 and 6 quarts
of beer within a period of 6 hours. As to the
aftereffects of drinking, the usual procedure is to
taper off with an "eye opener" and, if possible,
a sizable meal. One informant suggested that most
people have found that a thin soup of water tomatoes
and noodles is a means of curing a hangover. It is
generally agreed that hangovers are unpleasant, but
not unbearable, and certainly not a sufficient reason
to avoid drinking.

Most parties are small-group affairs occurring
spontaneously, but weddings and birthdays are
usually planned and may provide the occasion for
community-wide celebrations. At wedding parties the
usual custom is for the bridegroom to obtain the back
room of one of the local taverns after agreeing to
purchase a designated amount of beer. The hosts
generally start with the idea of inviting a limited
number of people, but in the end most of the inhabitant
of Whitehorse, invited or uninvited, are present.
People drink and dance to jukebox records or, when
any of the more talented Indians are present, the

guitar and piano. On such occasions it is not
unusual to see people of all ages, including children,
thoroughly intoxicated. These parties usually
continue until the tavern closes, or the conviviality
is broken by one of the inevitable fights. Often
the closing of the tavern is the signal for the party
to break up into smaller groups, with people
continuing to drink in their cars or homes until all
financial resources are exhausted.

    Most of the small-group parties are highly
mobile affairs, moving from home to local taverns
and even out into the woods. A considerable amount
of drinking occurs while driving between home and
tavern, the only concern being to avoid the main
highways for fear of being stopped by the police.
But this vague anxiety about being arrested has not
been sufficient to deter drinking while driving;
three adults died in automobile accidents, attributed
to drunken driving, in the interval between November
1960 and the end of October 1961.

Drinking Norms

    Of the 74 adults (18 years and over) in
Whitehorse, only 7 could be considered as moderate
drinkers or nondrinkers. Although there seem to be
no formalized requirements as to the age at which
individuals may begin to drink, several informants
were of the opinion that young people in their early
teens did their first "heavy" drinking at weddings
or birthday parties. Children learn very early,
however, not only the importance of drinking in the
life patterns of adults, but also some of the
relatively subtle concepts, such as the distinction
between a drinking and a nondrinking day for their
mothers and fathers. When it is the former, and while
the adult drinkers are still in a pleasant mood, they
will often join in the joking and receive occasional
drinks, but the development of quarreling and physical
aggression among their elders is the signal to flee
to the woods until the drinking bout has ended. Most
informants indicated that they had begun to drink
consistently, sometimes as often as once a week,

115

and occasionally to the point of intoxication, between their fourteenth and sixteenth birthdays. This new pattern of behavior was usually accepted passively by adults, and fits in with the permissive patterns of child rearing associated with the individualistic orientation of the culture.

It was possible, after establishing rapport with the people of Whitehorse, to get beyond the usual platitudes about the values of drinking moderately and to discover how highly esteemed was the practice of becoming intoxicated. Typical responses to the question of whether Indians ever felt guilty about drinking were the following:

> Most people don't feel guilty about drinking; say they are going to quit when they have a hangover, but never do.

> Hardly anyone who doesn't drink here. I don't think people consider it a problem. People don't feel that it is wrong to drink; like to have a good time.

These statements were supported by observation and long hours of listening to casual conversations. With the exception of discussions with nondrinkers, the topic would invariably be switched to the subject of who had been drunk the previous evening, injuries to someone who had been in an automobile accident while drinking, or various schemes, involving a minimum of work, for obtaining "beer money."

All informants agreed that to drink means to "get shined up" (intoxicated) and, if possible, to continue imbibing until one passes out. This goal is well illustrated by the following excerpt from a conversation with a Potawatomi woman in which the differences between the drinking habits of the white man and the Indian were being discussed:

> Indians here, if they have beer, will drink it all, while white people will take a bottle of beer and drink it and go to bed.

116

As has been reported of the Chippewa (Friedl 1956), Potawatomi individuals often appeared highly intoxicated after only a few bottles of beer.

In discussing the meaning of drinking with the people of Whitehorse, it soon became evident that they considered it a form of recreation, a way of overcoming shyness, and a means of gaining courage. Most informants agreed that there was no alternative recreation as enjoyable as the drinking party. There was also a widespread belief that through the use of alcohol people could overcome the shyness which made it difficult to converse with others. As one woman suggested, it was only when people had liquor available that they could feel "happy" or "get together with others." Another woman, the wife of a former tribal chairman, indicated that her husband could never attend a meeting to discuss tribal business without his "drink of courage."

Behavior

The reactions of the Whitehorse Potawatomi to alcohol can be viewed as progressing through three stages; an initial period of euphoria, followed by one of aggressive activity, and ending in a state of complete passivity. After the first few drinks individuals are able to converse freely and are noticeably more friendly and generous. An example is that of the man for whom it was not uncommon to spend $25 on liquor, not only for himself or a few companions, but for all of those whom he happened to meet in the course of an evening. Amiability is generally followed by acts of physical aggression, usually of short duration, ranging from minor fist fights between men to attempted rape and assault with a knife. There was a concensus among informants that Indians fight among themselves only when drunk and seldom remember these altercations when sober. A high frequency of such altercations was observed between husbands and wives, following which, both spouses appeared as if physically drained, and either continued to drink themselves into a stupor

117

or returned quietly to their homes to sleep. The latter action is typical of all persons in the third stage of intoxication. Considering that there are seldom recriminations for such behavior, it is not surprising that everything which goes wrong, from physical disabilities to lack of cooperation between families, is attributed to intoxication.

Promiscuity and jealousy between spouses are noticeable accompaniments of the aggressiveness which occurs with drinking. Women were often observed to make amorous advances, particularly toward white men, after imbibing a small amount of liquor. Since women are very reserved, even shy, when sober, one had the impression that the relatively small amount of alcohol consumed was an excuse, rather than a cause, for the reduction of sexual inhibitions. When the period of supposed intoxication has passed they are as reserved as usual and profess to remember nothing of what had transpired during the drinking situation. As a consequence of such behavior, there is a rich folklore among local white men, confirmed by Indian men, concerning the way in which a few drinks will aid in obtaining sexual favors from Whitehorse women. Over the years there have been occasional complaints to the local authorities about white men bringing liquor to the reservation and using it to gain sexual access to the women. While these requests for the white authorities to intervene imply that the white man is completely responsible for the resulting promiscuity, there is evidence that the wives use drinking as an excuse for taking revenge on their husbands.

Most informants agreed that jealousy between spouses was a major problem in the community. The causes of this conflict can be traced to the breakdown in the traditional kinship system and the disparaging attitude of wives toward their husbands. The latter is illustrated by the following quotations from Potawatomi women.

> Women have more to say about the community,
> but the only time men will speak out is when
> they are drunk. The men here never fight with
> other Indians or white men; they only beat up
> their wives.

> Women around here don't respect their husbands
> because they don't deserve it. One time my
> old man was too busy drinking to chop wood or
> buy food, so I went to the police. But he
> helps now, because he knows he will be sent
> to prison if he doesn't.

Even in playing games, such as the various coin-operated games to be found in most taverns, women, if they have had a few drinks, take great pride in outdoing men.

Though formally stated rules and sanctions governing behavior while drinking are lacking, there is a noticeable attempt by the majority to avoid certain individuals who are considered to be "always getting into fights". While it is expected that fighting will occur during the course of drinking, such altercations should not result in severe injury to the participants. For example, it has become an established practice to avoid George M. who becomes so violent when drinking that he may seriously injure others, as he did when he broke his wife's jaw. On the other hand, despite a number of fatal automobile accidents attributable to intoxication, there has been no attempt to develop rules for controlling the use of cars while drinking. Possibly this would require more community organization and cooperation than presently exists in Whitehorse, or it may be due to a belief that the white man should be responsible for solving that problem.

Since heavy drinking is the norm in the community, it would be difficult to classify the Potawatomi of Whitehorse as alcoholics. There are only two individuals who might be classed as compulsive drinkers; the vast majority seem capable

119

of getting along without liquor. It is through the use of alcohol that the people are able to escape from the prosaic pattern of subsistence living. There no longer are dances, curing ceremonies, war parties, and elaborate hunting expeditions, and this loss has not been compensated for by acquiring the white man's social activities or material conveniences. Considering that these people work in order to eat and drink, show little interest in activities which do not involve drinking, and spend most of their time talking about subjects which are either directly or indirectly related to intoxication, it would seem that alcohol has taken the place of these traditional aspects of culture that have been lost.

Social Functions of Drinking

Intoxication has become a means of fantasy for regaining the high status which Potawatomi men held prior to the coming of the white man. The lack of a community structure for imposing sanctions, which was conducive to the early development of intemperate drinking, prevents the development of an organized approach for coping with the problems of acculturation. In the contemporary culture the atomistic social structure makes it difficult for men to find substitutes for their traditionally prestigious roles as hunters, religious practitioners and warriors. Also, given the high rate of unemployment in the vicinity of Whitehorse, in conjunction with lack of skills and work ethos among Indians, it has not been possible for men to improve their status through participation in the economy of the white man. At the same time women have not only been able to retain their traditional positions as mothers, housekeepers and lovers, but have also succeeded in enhancing their status, since the numerous children they bear provide added income for the family as a result of government relief programs. In addition, their willingness to dispense sexual favors makes them favorites with

120

some white men who, in turn, have become more
favorably disposed toward all the Indians at
Whitehorse. In these circumstances women quite
openly express a contempt for Indian men, with
claims that they do more work and contribute more
to the maintenance of the family than the latter.
As a consequence men seek to regain status through
a make-believe world, induced by intoxication, in
which they make demands on their wives and argue
with others. Women, however, have developed
complementary roles vis-a-vis men in the drinking
situation; for the assumption of a role of aggressive
dominance by the men has enabled the women to play
a revenge-taking role, arousing jealousy in the
former by sexual advances toward others within or
outside the community. These complementary positions
are functional in the sense that the intoxicated
participants are able to assume roles which would
be socially disruptive if carried out when sober.
Thus, drinking provides a temporary solution which
is acceptable to the people of Whitehorse, but does
not resolve the problem of declining male status
and increasing female resentment.

The stereotyping of the Indian as a drunkard
by the white man, and the Indian's response thereto,
provides for a reciprocal understanding and
predictability of their different roles. The whites
associate the poverty of the Indians with the excessive
use of alcohol, and therefore assume that Indians
are inherently irresponsible. As a consequence, the
inhabitants of Whitehorse are believed to be
incapable of more than a minimum of conformity to
the norms of the dominant white community. There
is, for example, a kind of patronizing tolerance by
law-enforcement officers, which often takes the form
of penalizing Indians less heavily than white men
for infractions of the law occurring while inebriated.

The Potawatomi conform to this self-fulfilling
prophecy by accepting the status of inferiority
associated with their frequent intoxication.
Except for a few who express resentment over the
inability to obtain full-time employment, most
Indians approach prospective white employers with

the idea of obtaining a few days' work in order to "make a little beer money." This approach is perfectly understandable to the employer who usually predicts with some degree of accuracy that his new employee will perform creditably for 2 or 3 days, until he receives his pay, then will disappear on a drinking spree. Since there are no kinship or communal institutions for effectively sanctioning this behavior, the stereotype of the drunken Indian receives support. In this way, for both groups, a predictable dominance-submission role pattern has developed out of the drinking process.

Considering the latent tension between the white and Indian communities, resulting from the generally negative view of the latter by the former, there exists a potential for open incidents of conflict. A break does not occur, however, partly because of the long tradition of dominance by one group over the other, but especially because of the inconsistent image of the Indian held by the white man. Thus, while the poverty, idleness and alleged immorality of the Indian are overtly deprecated, there are many in the white community who secretly confess an admiration for what they mistakenly believe to be an idyllic life of drinking and leisure led by the inhabitants of Whitehorse. Some white men act on this assumption and become frequent participants in mixed drinking parties. As a consequence, the minimum of friendly contact, arising out of the mutual pleasures of imbibing alcohol, has the function of reducing tension between the two communities by reinforcing the positive image of the Potawatomi as a kind of bacchanalian ne'er-do-well.

There is some evidence in Whitehorse that intoxication entails social costs, in terms of the number of victims of automobile accidents, a high frequency of severe respiratory diseases traceable to exposure while on the way home from drinking parties and the contradiction of wanting education for children but not providing examples of self-control which would aid in the attainment of this goal. The

122

inhabitants of Whitehorse are not only aware of
these hazards but also realize that their drinking
patterns create a kind of cultural stagnation which
makes change difficult. For example, of 12 persons
questioned directly on this subject, 1 spoke
positively of future plans and development, 2
expressed indifference, and 9 were of the opinion
that the community would remain about the same or
gradually disappear. Nevertheless the vast majority
of Potawatomi find the existing drinking practices
worth the costs.

It is difficult, however, to conceive of
drinking as dysfunctional for the community of
Whitehorse, because the deculturation process of
the last 150 years has left relatively few
institutionalized norms with which the practice may
interfere. It is possible that the frequent
intoxication is inconsistent with the often expressed
goal of full-time employment and would be a hindrance
to successful occupational role playing if work
were available. Nevertheless in the area where
Whitehorse is located the available jobs are
limited to short-term work in agriculture and in
the woods. When these minimum conditions of
employment are combined with government distribution
of surplus food and subsidized medical care the
group is able to survive. Therefore, and without
any inconsistency in regard to the unachievable goal
of full-time employment, the Potawatomi have accommodated
to their severe acculturation experience and the
present subsistence standard of living through the
pattern of widespread and frequent drinking of
intoxicants.

Psychological Functions of Drinking[3]

[3] This section on the psychological functions of
drinking is taken from "Guardian Spirits, Alcohol,
and Cultural Defense Mechanisms", Anthropologica,
N.S. vol XI, no. 2. (1969): 215-241. Reprinted
by permission of Anthropologica and by John H. Hamer.

Dependency

Many theories also include a conceptualization
of aggression as a response to sought after but
unrewarded dependency. In a recent publication
Gavalas and Briggs (1966:97-121) have summarized
the major theories of dependency as falling under
the heading of those stressing the causal importance
of anxiety, fear of independent behavior, conflict,
and concurrent reinforcement of dependency and
competency. In this paper we shall follow the
conflict theory as it seems appropriate to the
individualistic, highly controlled personality found
among the Forest Potawatomi.

Mowrer (1960) has developed a theory of conflict
in which the opposing emotions of hope and fear are
aroused as a consequence of the individual
experiencing both reward and frustration of his
responses over a period of time. This tends to
result in anger which leads either to intensification
or inhibition of the response. The application to
dependency may be formally stated as follows:

> Dependency occurs when nurturance is sought
> from others with only intermittent success;
> as a consequence the individual learns to
> experience mixed emotions of hope and fear
> when approaching others. The conflict serves
> to heighten the threshold of response, which
> when frustrated results in anger.

On the basis of this definition it is possible
to construct a paradigm of how the proposed cultural
defense mechanism relates to dependency.

(a) When the cultural norms call for guardedness
in social interaction the individual will experience
ambivalent emotions of hope and fear in attempting
to associate with others. The long period of
nurturance required in the socialization of the
human primate is such that to some degree
individuals in all societies are going to experience
dependency, simply because it is humanly impossible,
and even dangerous, to avoid frustrating the desires

124

of the small child to attract attention and to be near a nurturant adult. At the same time many tribal societies, including the Potawatomi, tend to maximize contact between mother and child until the weaning period. After weaning, however, the rules may call for quite the opposite form of behavior not only in terms of a stress on independent, self-reliant action, but more especially a redefinition of the role of adults and gradually even of peers from positive nurturant others to negative, powerful, competitive others. It is this drastic negative, reinterpretation required of the small child which leads to mixed expectations about receiving support from people.

(b) Approaching others involves the contrasting emotions of hope and fear, but withdrawal reduces the fear. On the other hand the desire to be near and receive attention from others remains, so that once fear has been reduced the approach will be made again. The individual is caught in a dilemma. As Mowrer (1960:424) suggests there would seem to be three options in such a situation: (1) the finding of another source of nurturance; (2) elimination of punishment for seeking nurturance; (3) individuals lose interest in the quest. Choice of alternative (2) is unlikely considering that Potawatomi socio-economic norms stress independence and (3) is improbable given the degree to which nurturance expectations have been highly rewarded in the early socialization process. Therefore (1) becomes the most probable alternative. Nevertheless, given the anticipated uncertainty about the response, a premium will be placed on circumspection in initiating social interaction. Since, however, behavior is never completely consistent with the rules and because others are also seeking attention and reassurance, there will be intermittent success.

(c) It might be expected that intermittency of reinforcement would lead to a balancing out of fear and hope in the long run, but Sears et al (1965: 48) have suggested that the process actually serves to heighten dependency.

Dependency occurs when nurturance is sought
from others with only intermittent success;
as a consequence the individual learns to
experience mixed emotions of hope and fear when
approaching others. The conflict serves to
heighten the threshold of response, which when
frustrated results in anger.

In their study of American nursery school
children they found some evidence for a relationship
between intermittent reinforcement in early childhood
and a high level of positive attention seeking at
age four (Sears et al 1965:48-75).

(d) Nonetheless, a built-in paradox exists
regarding the conflict induced between hope and
fear (Gavalas and Briggs 1966:108-109). There is
some empirical data to show that the direction of
the conflict is difficult to predict since it may
inhibit as well as energize responsiveness.
Mowrer (1960:425) sites one study which shows the
time factor to be important; the initial response
to frustration tends to activate, but if
reinforcement is not forthcoming over a period of
time depression sets in and the response tendancy
is ultimately extinguished. It is possible,
however, that the cultural defenses against overt
expressions of dependency discussed in this paper
are so spaced that there is insufficient time lag
for extinction to occur.

On the basis of the above reasoning it is
possible to advance the following hypotheses
concerning the relation between dependency and
culturally constituted defense mechanisms in the
historic and reservation experiences of the Forest
Potawatomi.

(1) Traditional child rearing practices in
the past and in the present tend to
encourage the fear-hope conflict in
interpersonal relations which is the
basis of dependency.

126

(2) Emphasis on the avoidance of open nurturant,
helping, or caretaking behavior is
compensated by the prevalence of this
behavior within the institutionalized
framework of the traditional guardian
spirit relationship which has been replaced
in recent times by social drinking.

As indicators of dependent behavior we shall use
three developed by Sears et al. (1965:27, 33). One
is "negative attention seeking" which refers to the
attempt to gain attention through aggressive
behavior; a second is "reassurance seeking" involving
the quest for help and emotional support; while a
third, "positive attention seeking" is the attempt to
win the admiration and cooperation of others. In
their study of nursery school children they found
some evidence that negative attention seeking was
associated in both sexes with low demands and
restrictions by the parents. For reassurance
seeking both parents showed high demands for
achievement along with coldness and encouragement
of independent behavior. Positive attention seeking
was clearly associated with parental restrictions
on aggressiveness and in the case of boys, rejection
by the father. There are other attributes that
researchers found associated with these measures of
dependency, but these appear to be the principal
ones, and those for which we have information from
the Potawatomi.

From the small amount of ethnographic data and
the memories of some of the oldest informants, there
are indications that traditional Potawatomi
culture was very similar to that of the Ojibwa and
and Ottawa (Quimby 1960:122-132). Therefore, in
the discussion to follow extensive use will be made
of the more abundant Ojibwa material.

Child Training

Densmore (1929:48-51) in his account of Ojibwa
infancy indicates that even during the second decade
of this century the contact between mother and child
impressed him as being of greater intensity and
warmth than that found in European societies. The
permissive period may also have been of greater
length, for Keating (1824:132) suggests that before
the middle of the last century Potawatomi mothers
nursed their children for prolonged periods of three,
four years, or longer. The criterion for change
seems to have been the arrival of a new sibling,
at which time the mother would induce a relatively
abrupt separation by sending the child away to a
kinsman, covering the breasts with unpleasant
tasting substances, and/or frightening the child
when he tried to suck (Hilger 1951:28-29).

After weaning, stress seems to have been placed
on independence with the consequence that the
formerly nurturant adults took on the opposite
attributes of distance and aloofness. The cultural
basis for independence training has been well
summarized in Barry, Bacon, and Child's (1959:53-59)
study on the difference between the accumulative,
cooperative, agricultural, and pastoral societies as
compared with those with hunting and fishing economies.
The results of their statistical comparisons show
that the accumulative groups emphasize obedience,
responsibility, and nurturance in youngsters
while the hunting and fishing types socialize
achievement, self-reliance and independent behavior.
Though the Ojibwa are one of the societies considered
as ranking high in the importance placed on independenc
it is the consequence of this training in terms of
reversal of the earlier nurturant adult-child
relationships which is important in this study.

Densmore (1929:58-59) states that the Ojibwa
parent attempted to instill self-control in the
child through games and various fear techniques.
He notes by contrast with white children the far
greater demands "to keep still when surprised or
frightened". Keating (1824:96-97) reports that the
principal technique of discipline utilized by the

Potawatomi in the early 19th century was fear; children were continually being told that to disobey their parents would bring down the wrath of the Great Spirit upon them, and in the case of boys, would deprive them of all success as hunters or warriors. Another form of punishment, apparently used somewhat sparingly, was to require the child to blacken his face and go without food for varying periods (Keating 1824:123). In 1929 Jenness (1935: 95) found among the Parry Island Ojibwa that withdrawal of food was an "ordinary punishment" for young children six to eleven years old. They were given a bowl of soup once a day for several days and told to fast the rest of the time, remaining in a corner of the wigwam and attempting to dream in order that the punishment would not be wasted.

Landes' (1938a:2-4) discussion of early Ojibwa childhood fits in well with the dependency model proposed in this paper. She found that even though warmth and affection was stressed during infancy, there was concern that too much nurturance would detract from making the new arrival into an efficient, contributing, member to the subsistence activities of the household. Boys especially, as they grew older, were urged to acquire power by going without food. She says the four or five year old child: "...often objects to the fast, stamps and cries, or runs around to snatch some food for himself". There was no escaping the parent, however, who would rub charcoal on his face and send him out to play with the other children. If he managed to maintain the fast for the rest of the day he would be rewarded with an "especially good meal" in the evening. A child of eight who on the day he was supposed to fast demanded bread rather than charcoal when confronted with the choice, would be severely punished by his father. Like Keating, she also found that withdrawal of food was used as a punishment for disobedient children.

There is in the situation described by Landes, which is reminiscent of that described by our older Potawatomi informants much that fits into the conflict

sequence. A child approaches the adult in hope of
a nurturant reward of food only to be rebuffed.
The immediate response is anger and a short
interval of rejection, which is followed by a
lavish reward of food reinforcing the hope for
future nurturance. Hence in the early attempts
at coping with adult demands for independence
and power, the child is likely to have developed
mixed expectations of hope and fear which were
alternately reinforced by the adult. Through the
process of fasting for a vision his dependency
threshold was increased by intermittent reinforcement,
but the learning experience of the vision quest led
to a transfer of expectations of nurturance from
people to super-natural beings.

The process of transference is frought with
conflict which would seem to have potential for
increasing the threshold of the dependency response
vis-a-vis the individual and his sought-after
vision. Landes (1938a:4) notes that some dreams
were considered acceptable and others "evil". Guide
lines for "correct" dreaming were laid down by
parents, but it is evident that boys met with
intermittent success, thus reinforcing the hope-
fear conflict. Whatever the outcome the boy was
admonished to: "... identify himself with it so
thoroughly that he 'can pretty nearly talk to his
manido'" (Landes 1938a:5). Parker (1960:605) has
indicated the significance of this change from early
childhood to adult status when he says that it was
based on a developing awareness of the precarious
subsistence of the small isolated group of kinsmen.
There was the absence of the adult males on long
hunting trips, the boy's own inability to contribute
significantly to the group, the continual reminders
of his spiritual vulnerability, and the proddings
to grow up as rapidly as possible. All were
mediated through parental withdrawal of "over-
effectionate behavior".

Though the pre-adolescent male apparently
experienced increasing frustration in his attempts
to gain the nurturant attention of adults, there

130

was no immediate repression of expressions of childhood anger. In fact there is considerable evidence from early explorers and missionaries that Indian children were overtly aggressive and relatively uncontrolled in their behavior (Hallowell 1955:135-136). Nevertheless, as an individual became aware that others possessed supernatural powers in differing and usually unknown amounts, he became wary of overt expressions of hostility. Hallowell (1955:148) suggests that expression of open anger toward another became the equivalent of a challenge to a duel by sorcery. Green (1948:227) is even more emphatic in proposing that Ojibwa boys were subjected to a severe conflict when they were urged to be successful hunters. While this would indicate great power and entitle them to the respect of others, such power was feared as well as admired and could result in others becoming sufficiently jealous to direct their power against one who was reckoned a success. In such a situation the only alternative was a surface friendliness and agreement which could antagonize no one. This would seem to fit in with the statements of 17th century French missionaries that the Potawatomi were the most "docile" and eager to please of any of the Indian groups that they had encountered, and the evidence from historical accounts of the 18th century t'at they could easily be persuaded to switch alliances between the Americans, British and French (Lawson 1920:44-45, 60-61, 76-77, 82-83). Moreover, extreme friendship seems to have been a sign of the practicing sorcerer. Thus the individual learned that he existed in a society which was individualistic and highly competitive not only in regard to subsistence, but also in terms of the supernatural power which made a man a success or failure. He gradually came to fear people and, as Hallowell (1955:305) suggests, sought help from supernatural others who "became parent surrogates from puberty onward".

> ... Formerly the boy has been dependent upon older human beings, who in addition to teaching him necessary skills, had trained him to rely upon himself to the extent of his ca⸗ ⸗ .ty.

Henceforth he was to rely primarily upon
superhuman beings, that is upon inner
promptings, derived from further dreams or the
memories of his fasting experience.

Both Hallowell (1955:228, 305) and Landes (1938a:
3-5) indicate that sexual differentiation was
important in the socialization of reliance on
supernatural power. Girls could dream and acquire
power, but there was no great emphasis, given their
primarily domestic role, on self-reliance and the
climactic puberty ritual of acquiring one or more
supernatural protectors was not a required part of
their experience. Densmore (1929:61) mentions that
the relationship between mother and daughter was
very close and Hilger (1951:6) suggests that mothers
liked to have a number of daughters because they,
unlike sons, tended to be willing to care for their
parents in old age. Further data is provided by
Landes (1966:121, 123) who says that the early
training of a girl was directed toward developing
an attitude of subordination and cooperation
while at the same time greater ambiguity in
expectations about the adult female role made for
greater variation in acceptable behavior than was
found among males. Perhaps Parker (1960:617) has
best summarized the situation in his comprehensive
survey of the literature:

> During both the early childhood phase and in
> adult life, females are able to satisfy normal
> dependency needs to a far greater extent than
> males.

The limited evidence is more than suggestive in
light of the aforementioned study by Sears et al
(1965:70-75), in which they found a positive
association among their daughters in the nursery
school setting, but a negative association between
the two variables in regard to boys. On the other
hand dependency in boys occurred with the withholding
of love and affection by both the mother and father.
They felt, however, that the withholding of
nurturance could not be absolute and was likely to
be of the kind that would encourage intermittent

132

reinforcement of the dependency response.

Guardian Spirits and Dependency

There should be indications of the hope-fear
conflict, intermittent reinforcement, and anger
arising out of frustrated attempts to receive
nurturance from others if the guardian spirit
complex is an institutionalized means of
sublimating dependency in adult life. In this
section the consequences for males of acquiring at
puberty a life-long guardian spirit will be examined,
according to the suggested indicators of dependency:
reassurance and positive and negative attention-
seeking.

Reassurance

For purposes of this paper reassurance means
the restoration of confidence in another by
providing sympathy, protection, and help. It seems
that one of the principal goals in seeking a
supernatural helper was to obtain a substitute for
the reassurance formerly provided by the parent.
As previously noted these supernatural beings
became "parental surrogates" and once an adolescent
male Ojibwa had established such a relationship,
help from human beings, in time of crisis, was
considered both unnecessary and dangerous (Hallowell
1955:305; Landes 1937:55). Furthermore, the ritual
by which this substitution was made involved a
symbolic regression to a nearly complete state of
helplessness, reminiscent of infancy. The process
was one of weakening the body through fasting
to the point where one could hardly walk, with most
of the time being spent curled up in a nest of leaves
in a semi-comatose state (Hilger 1951:42-43). The
spirit is said to have taken "pity" on a supplicant
in this condition; the meaning of the word for pity
in Ojibwa carries the connotation of adopting and

133

caring for another as a parent or grandparent would care for a child (Landes 1938a:6). Landes (1966: 98) describes the typical response of the helper as follows:

> My grandchild (or brother or sweetheart or any other relationship term which has emotional significance), I have taken pity upon you (this is a very respectful phrase, not a patronizing one). I have seen you in your sufferings, and I have taken pity upon you, I will give you something to amuse yourself with.

After an individual had established such a relationship he continued to approach his spiritual benefactor at times of crisis in a state of helplessness. He would always carry a special medicine bundle as a token of the power and help promised by his guardian and, as one of Hilger's informants reported, even the thought of this helper in times of trouble was sufficient to make things "brighten up" (Barry et al 1959:61). Keating (1824:119-120) has also mentioned this helping quality in discussing the link between a Potawatomi and his spirit as it existed during the early nineteenth century: "...he consults it in all his difficulties and not infrequently conceives that he has derived relief from it". For the Potawatomi friendship with the animal spirit was considered personal and under no circumstances to be shared with others.

In regard to confidence building, it is significant that the only way in which an individual could develop a reputation for unusual accomplishment was through the attainment of special powers from his guardian spirit. By this means some attained the most prestigious position in the society, that of shaman, but a few acquired sufficient confidence from their vision quest to aspire to such heights. Nevertheless, one could feel confident of successfully negotiating various life crises through the aid of super natural support

134

and adherence to the traditional norm proscribing warm interpersonal relations. The latter form of behavior provided a means of avoiding tests of strength with others, who might possess more powerful supernatural protection, which could not only destroy self confidence, but in some cases life itself (Hallowell 1955:362).

Positive Attention Seeking

This phrase refers to individual utilization of a culturally recognized and acceptable competency as an attention getting device. Among Algonkian speaking peoples probably the most notable means for males to gain the admiration and cooperation of others was through the demonstration of prowess in hunting, curing, games and/or warfare. The only source of power to do these things was the guardian spirit. In the case of the Ojibwa Hallowell (1955: 361) observes:

> Every special aptitude, all his successes and failures, hinged upon the blessings of his supernatural helpers, rather than upon his own native or acquired endowments, or even the help of his fellow human beings.

An individual suspected of having great power was respected by others, but because of a conceptualized rank order of power there was always someone who had more and was consequently more successful in attracting the attention of others through concrete examples of his competency. One could not, however, be certain about the amount of power possessed by the next person, nor was it possible to control fluctuations in power which were in reality, the result of the element of chance in hunting, curing, games and warfare. Also, while the individual might excell in performance and impress others, he was simultaneously arousing their envy and fear which would ultimately be directed against himself (Parker 1960:616; Green 1948:227).

135

Thus a conflict situation develops, involving hope that people will be impressed with a display of prowess combined with fear that the jealousy aroused will constitute a danger to the self. One can then only turn for support to the supernatural helper, but due to the element of chance there is no real escape from the conflict. The spirit's reaction is of necessity ambiguous, sometimes resulting in support and frequently in rejection, according to the rationalization of the supplicant because of anger or disappointment with the latter. Therefore, it is a fair assumption that intermittent reinforcement of nurturance occurs, heightening dependency on the spirit protector.

Negative Attention Seeking

A third more desperate means of rousing nuturant support was through overt or covert displays of hostility. Despite frequent mention in the literature of the reverence and awe in which a guardian spirit was held, Parker (1960:611) has suggested that an element of ambivalent hostility existed in the relationship. Landes (1938b:19) has made specific mention of this ambivalence, pointing out that the form of the protective spirit was often that of an animal which the supplicant desired to kill. Also available is some evidence from early accounts that intoxicated Indians would rage against their supernatural partners, even seeking to destroy them with their guns (Landes 1938b).

Another aspect of negative attention seeking involved what could be considered repressed hostility toward spirits being projected on to human subjects, in the sense that persons claiming extreme power, such as shamans, could challenge others overtly by trying to hurt or frighten them. A well known shaman relying on the power of his supernatural helper might confront a rival with the claim that he was superior and threaten to destroy the latter within a designated period. (Hallowell 1955: 289; Landes 1938a 188-20, 205-208). To embark upon such a venture involved grave risks because the medicine used was so powerful it might ultimately result in the destruction of the self and the immediate members of one's family. Nevertheless, there is evidence of shamen even challenging whole communities by making exhorbitant demands for curing or protecting people from illness (Landes 1938a: 201-204).

In short the available data show that the Potawatomi might acquire help and sympathy from an anthropomorphic being. The acquisition of competency as a means of gaining the attention of others was unpredictable, resulting in the element of hope-fear vis-a-vis approach to the spirit helper. Even if the individual's confidence was increased because of help from his spirit, the contrasting element of fear was never far behind due to the fact that a show of greater competency led to jealousy and the danger of challenge from mortals with more power. Nevertheless, it would seem that fortuitous support and assistance from super-human helpers was sufficient to provide intermittent reinforcement of dependency. There is also limited evidence of occasional overt anger against spirits and hostile challenges of other humans and their guardian mentors, which is suggestive of frustration in obtaining nurture by supernatural means.

Dependency as a potentially disruptive motive in a society where survival was contingent on isolated, economic, self-sufficiency was thus gratified in a socially acceptable manner. Nurture could be sought indirectly from a nonhuman source, the approach being based on secrecy and privacy. These elements provided support for the underpinnings of circumspection and highly controlled emotional affect validating social atomism.

Reservation Setting

Both Parker (1960:621-622) and James (1961) have suggested that the reservation way of life has

encouraged dependency among the Ojibwa. In a
recently published article Cohen and VanStone (1963:
46-49) in comparing traditional folk tales with
essays written by Chipewyan school children for
evidence of self-reliance and dependency found that
there was a tendency toward a balance in the
occurrence of these attributes in the tales, but
an increase of dependency over self-reliance in
the contemporary essays. They attribute this
change to the acculturation experience. There is
evidence, as the following data show, that the
conditions of reservation life for the Potawatomi
of Whitehorse have also been conducive to increasing
dependency, but social drinking has replaced the
guardian spirit complex, as a culturally constituted
means of coping with it.

In general the younger generation at Whitehorse
has little knowledge of the old Indian way of life
and only a few of the oldest inhabitants can
remember childhood experiences involving fasting
and the vision quest. Nevertheless, the psychological
norm in this small Potawatomi community with its
stress on suppressed hostility and highly
introverted inner controls is very similar to what
Hallowell (1955:345-366) has deduced as typical of
traditional Ojibwa personality. To understand the
reasons for this seeming psychic continuity it is
necessary to give consideration to the culture that
supports it.

The time factor is of no small consequence.
The Forest Potawatomi gave up their semi-nomadic
existence for a sedentary way of life as recently
as the first decade of this century. In addition
to adapting to a new pattern of subsistence they
are spatially and socially isolated from the
dominant white community. This means that the
number of potential relationships with persons
outside the community is minimal. Indeed, as noted
previously, interaction with the white man is
largely confined to occupational and convivial
drinking situations. Hence the avoidance of
conflict in order to maintain the limited potential

for interaction within the community is essential.
Therefore stress on rigid emotional control and
social reticence is one way of furthering this end.
But in addition to historical support and the
social functions of the traditional oriented
personality type there is a third variable,
indifference, which has developed out of the
frustrating and ambivalent experiences of trying
to cope with a hostile social environment. The
seeming emotional coldness and unresponsiveness
of the individual in a social setting also
constitutes a kind of "I don't care" attitude,
which provides a defense against further rebuffs
from within and outside the community .

Child Training

     There is no attempt to maximize the early
independence of the small boy by urging him to
obtain the power and protection of a supernatural
being. Nevertheless, it does not take the observer
long to realize that in their dealings with others
adults show considerable reserve and convert
hostility. In dealing with their children they are
inconsistent in the imposition of sanctions, hold
an anomalous position as cultural models, and lack
support from other potential sources of nurture.
All of these things limit the opportunities for the
child to obtain satisfaction of dependency needs.
As in the last century the child, during the first
two years of his life or until the arrival of a
new sibling, receives consistently favorable
responses to his demands for warmth and acceptance.
Following infancy, however, the socialization
process becomes relatively inconsistent, with the
parent sometimes lavishing food and attention on
the child and at other times being too preoccupied
to make more than an indifferent or mechanical
response.

     Covert hostility in Whitehorse is as evident
as that inferred from sources concerning traditional

Algonkian speaking peoples. For the ethnographer
it was most noticeable in the form of jealousy,
invariably related to the fear that someone else
was receiving more attention than the informant.
So intense was this feeling that it was sometimes
difficult to interview the members of one household
without being accused by others, quite overtly if
they were intoxicated, of not only favoring, but
having ulterior motives in regard to women informants.
This fear of not receiving enough attention on
the interfamilial level applied as well to
intrafamilial relations. Though overt aggression,
except when intoxicated, runs counter to the
social norms there was continual gossip and rumor.
For example, there was frequent talk of marital
infidelity, parental neglect of children, and
failure of siblings to assist each other in time
of need. Furthermore, this thinly concealed
hostile rivalry seems to have become a part of
parent-child relations in the reservation
situation. As one old grandfather explained it,
many parents are "jealous" of the accomplishments
of their sons and daughters, fearing that the
latter will get more benefits from the school,
government agencies, or the occasional friendly
white man.

It is difficult for even the most sympathetic
adult to decide what values and beliefs should be
transmitted to the younger generation. Parents
lack knowledge about the subtleties of Euro-American
culture and are uncertain of the appropriateness
of many aspects of traditional Indian culture.
Perhaps as a consequence of this dilemma parents
tend to have contradictory performance expectations
for their children. This begins in early childhood
with promises to help the child in a given task or
to provide an opportunity for participation in some
desirable activity, only to fail in following through.
In latency parents occasionally expect and demand
a high standard of competence in the carrying out
of household chores and subsistence activities,
while at other times they are permissive almost
to the point of negligence. Examples of the latter

140

include allowing small children to simply disappear
for the day without knowing their whereabouts,
and permitting them to wander unsupervised in the
woods or swamps in areas where men are cutting
fence posts or gathering cedar brush. Nevertheless,
inconsistence in its most dramatic form appears
in the periodic drinking parties which are so much
a part of everyday life. In this situation the
child is initially favored with candy and affection
only to be later ignored for hours or occasionally
even days, while adults are engrossed in their
own pleasures and disputes.

Potential sources of nurturance other than
parents are older siblings, grandparents, and
persons outside the community. Grandparents often
show more affection and responsibility than
parents in socializing children. Their prestige,
however, as models of deportment and their role as
protectors is undermined by the disparagement and
contradiction of their efforts by parents. Older
siblings provide only limited nurture, for their
lives are made difficult not only by the short
interval between births and the heavy demands of
parents, but by the fact that the latter overtly
show favoritism to one child.[4] It is unlikely that
children find much support in the school system,
considering the high rate of truancy and the fact
that most children drop out before finishing. The
only other external contacts are with contract
physicians, administrators from the Bureau of
Indian Affairs, and welfare case workers although
because of the formality and infrequency of these
contacts there is little opportunity to form
personal relationships.

[4] The number of persons per family increased from
3.8 in 1937 to 5.6 in 1961. Also, the percentage
of population under 5 years of age in 1961 was
17 as compared with 11.1 in the surrounding white
community (Hamer 1962:A1A3). These figures
proved some indication of the relatively large
number of small children in most families as
well as an implied close spacing of pregnancies
in recent years.

141

Thus the inconsistency of parents in socializing goals and standards of performance in both boys and girls indicates the existence of a social milieu conducive to the development of the hope-fear conflict. Covert hostility and jealousy between generations make it difficult for grandparents to alleviate this conflict Furthermore, potential outside sources of nurture are by nature of their respective bureaucratic roles too emotionally uninvolved to provide support. Under the circumstances, a child seeking help or emotional sustenance from adults is likely to meet with only intermittent success, the conditions which the hypothesis defines as leading to dependency.

Drinking as Positive Attention Seeking

Individual Potawatomi no longer seek power from a spirit helper that will enable them to acquire more prestige than another. Instead they use their position of relative poverty to gain the cooperation of others prior to and within the drinking situation. Unlike the covert method for acquiring admiration in the past, however, in the quest for alcohol one may make overt demands on others. Nevertheless, the abovementioned plea for money to purchase beer and wine, usually directed toward neighboring white men as the most likely sources of cash, is couched in such indirect, ritualized terms as: "I don't know where I will find the money to get bread for the children's breakfast" or; "I need money for gasoline so I can look for work". The real meaning behind this devious petition is seldom missed. White men are better potential source of money than Indians. They are also likely to be more sympathetic both out of a sense of guilt concerning the conditions of poverty at Whitehorse and a vicarious pleasure stemming from the previously mentioned stereotype of convivial beer parties and casual sex relations on the reservation.

Though acts of friendliness were traditionally associated with a form of witchcraft which is no longer the norm, the amicable approach continues to be used in the drinking situation, as a means of

142

manipulating others. This indirect form of attempting
to attract admiration is used by intoxicated women to
lure men, both white and Indian, into promiscuous
relations. The purpose is either that of obligating
them to render future personal favors or as a means
for gaining revenge against an erring husband. Men
may also use the convivial drinking relationship
to extract promises of a monetary loan, the use of
tools, or other material rewards.

Reassurance Seeking

     An examination of themes of conversations
occuring during the early stages of intoxication,
but seldom found in sober exchange, indicate
numerous attempts to arouse pity. In this phase of
the drinking process it is the listener who is
expected to and usually does express an interest
and sympathy seldom shown in the isolation of ordinary,
sober, existence. For example, one informant would
talk openly of a longing for her deceased mother whom
she felt was the only one to show real feeling and
understanding for her. Another combined lamentation
about his long deceased wife with ritual repetition of
the phrase "Jesus will come again". For several
people there was a noticeable increase in concern
about health and the possibility of death, leading
to long detailed stories of the development and
difficulties of curing an ailment, and invariably
ending on a note of self-pity.

     Given the limited encouragement for problem
solving and the resolution of social conflicts, the
individual has little opportunity for developing
confidence through interpersonal associations. As
a result there is a tendency to resort to fantasy.
In the traditional culture he could bolster his
confidence by relying on supernatural power, but
now he turns for similar results to the make-believe
power, but now he turns for similar results to the
make-believe world of a small circle of drinking
companions. The process involves seeking direct

143

assurance from others and creating temporary make-believe status positions of prestige. The former situation is illustrated by the man who after two or three beers invariably insists on reminding others that he is not a "bad guy", and expects his drinking companions to reciprocate with declarations of their esteem. Simultaneously, or as an alternative, he may attempt to assume such fantasy positions as a person of authority, superior parent, paragon of generosity, or status equal to the white man. In the event that a fictive status is assumed, it is generally conceded that the Potawatomi display an optimism and emotional affect seldom shown on other occasions. In fact this exuberance may reach the point, as one informant suggested, where "a man thinks he knows too much". A case in point involved two men who, as long as a beer or wine were available, would expound for hours on their rights to the tribal chieftaincy and what they were going to do to the man who had usurped this position. It is of interest to note that one of these men who had actually been chairman of the tribal council for a short period, indicated that it was very difficult for him to attend and direct the infrequent council meeting without consuming a "drink of courage". On the other hand, pretending the role of the superior parent is a somewhat more indirect method of seeking reassurance. It involves in the beginning a great deal of bragging about the exceptional performance of one's children, and ends with the announcement that the latter are going to go to college, and acquire a place in the white man's world. This declaration is frequently made despite the fact that the listeners know the son or daughter referred to, has dropped out of high school several years prior to the discussion. The same form of exaggeration occurs in the case of penurious individuals who seek to create the illusion of unusual generosity by offering drinks to all comers and even going to the point of pawning expensive chain saws and rifles in order to keep a drinking party going.

Relaxed social interaction with the white man is at best difficult, but with the aid of alcohol it does occur in the recreational setting. The problem of how to attain status equality is easily resolved by buying the white man a drink, and then behaving with a show of animated joviality as an equal. Sufficient confidence results from encouragement provided by the white drinker to enter into open competition in tavern games, even dancing, without fear of retribution or overwhelming shyness.

Though self-assurance from visions induced by alcohol is only temporary, it is reinforced by the frequency and pleasure of intoxication. Nevertheless, just as in the guardian spirit quest few individuals acquire enough confidence in their supernatural power to challenge others overtly. For the contemporary Potawatomi, status fantasies of intoxication are seldom, if ever, acted upon when the individual becomes sober. No one, white man or Indian, questions or belittles this type of status claim within the context of the drinking situation, but attempts at implementation in the world of reality lead only to social rebuff, if not outright ostracism.

Negative Attention Seeking

In the second phase of the drinking sequence spasmodic outbursts occur in which the individual aggressively asserts his rights, attempts to manipulate others, or is physically aggressive. All of these actions provide a temporary means of mastering the social situation by forcefully attracting the attention of others.

Drinking occasions were the only times that Potawatomi were observed to vehemently assert their rights to respect from others. At a drinking party it was not uncommon for an informant to remind the ethnographer that many of his questions were unwarranted infringements of the latter's privacy and that henceforth questions would not be answered. After he thought sufficient time had elapsed for the ethnographer to have been suitably impressed by the outburst, the same

informant would issue an invitation to be sure and
pay him a visit when interviewing other families.
Another example is that of a heavily intoxicated
man who would become insistent about his
exclusive rights to water from a pump which was not
only far removed from his premises, but customarily
used by other members of the community. Even the
contract doctor, grocer, and other dispensing
services in the white community observed that Indians
tended to demand their rights only when intoxicated.

Contempt is another method often used when
drinking, though as a means of commanding the
attention of others, it is especially disruptive
of kinship bonds. For example, in the case of a
husband and wife it was not uncommon for the latter
to make a slurring remark about some attribute
of her spouse, provoking an immediate denial to be
followed by prolonged argument or direct physical
aggression. In either case the wife succeeds with
dramatic effect in obtaining immediate recognition
from her husband, while simultaneously justifying
her feelings and expressions of hostility at his
negative reaction. Another type of situation
involves the mother-in-law who seeks to regain
control over her son by using drinking as an excuse
to express contempt for her daughter-in-law. Though
this creates conflict between husband and wife it
often brings the son, if only temporarily, back to
the mother's home to provide affection and care.
It was not even unusual for intoxicated individuals
to bait the ethnographer with thinly veiled
expressions of contempt for his work, in an effort
to persuade him to spend more time with them, so
that he might obtain the "true story about the Indian"

The most extreme of these attempts to control
others end in overt aggression, as a kind of last
desperate effort to regain the real or alleged loss
of attention to another. Nevertheless, stealing,
physical assault, and the smashing of others' property
occur only in the drinking setting and are either not
remembered or else minimized when the period of
intoxication has passed.

146

Drinking patterns at Whitehorse provide encouragement of the hope-fear conflict in two ways. First of all the individual knows that nurturant responsiveness is linked only to the modus operandi of social drinking. On the other hand sobriety is associated with the introverted, withdrawn personality of adult life which has its cultural foundations in a subsistence economy and the tensions of living in a small, socially isolated community. Thus the hope-fear ambivalence is supported by persons being giving and warm in one situation but generally cold and circumspect in another. Also, there does not seem to be a sufficient time lapse between drinking episodes to lead to the extinction of the conflict response. On the contrary, the frequency of drinking seems to provide the kind of intermittent reward which according to the paradigm is likely to lead to the reinforcement of dependency.

Secondly, and as a consequence of this intermittent reinforcement, there is a noticeable amount of frustration and overt anger. The expression of hostile feelings invariably follows the reassurance of the initial drinking phase. This is not to say that all the aggression necessarily relates to frustration in the ongoing social situation, for it may represent a cumulation of rejection by others or be totally unrelated to dependency. Nevertheless, the inevitable sequence of nurturance followed by hostility seems to be more than a coincidence. The switch from helpfulness or friendly verbal exchange is often so abrupt that it is as if there were a sudden recall of some past slight or rejection which justifies the aggressive outburst. Aggression is excused in sober afterthought because it is attributed to alcohol, but the event is not forgotten and provides sufficient reason for an ambivalent attitude toward future interaction.

It is clear that only within the confines of the drinking situation can one overtly manipulate others, express hostility, and seek emotional support. Thus, the individual is protected from mental breakdown in the sense that most violations of the cultural norms

147

other than serious physical assault, are excusable
when associated with the imbibing of alcohol.
Supporting this rationalization of deviation is a
complete lack of guilt feelings about drinking to
intoxication. As a consequence, the social system
is protected by the channeling of dependency
expressions into the fantasy world of intoxication.

Summary

     In traditional Potawatomi culture it seems
probable that the child experienced high, initial
indulgence of his attachment to adults. The
permissive period was followed, however, by a
reversal of the process of encouraging   dependency
in favor of the socialization of self-reliance.
On the reservation a high degree of dependency is
still rewarded in the infancy and toddler stages
of development, but there is no emphasis on
training the child for the kind of socio-economic
self-sufficiency which was so important in the
past. In fact the uncertainty and apathy of adults
as to how they should train their children leads
to discontinuity of nurture. Thus in the past the
desire on the part of parents to avoid indulgence
of their children with warmth and affection in
order to instill independence, while intermittently
rewarding them with an abundance of affection for
a job well done, would seem to be consistent with
the conditions necessary for the development of the
hope-fear conflict. The unintentional discontinuity
of nurture in Whitehorse leads to analogous results.
As a consequence of the socialization process and
adult roles, both past and present, which place a
premium on circuumspection and fear of warm personal
ties in social interaction, it is difficult for
dependency to be overtly expressed.

     The guardian spirit quest and social drinking
provide institutionalized outlets for sublimating
dependency. Both institutions furnish individuals
with an opportunity to give and receive nurture,
and provide a situationally acceptable means for

releasing aggression which may be related to the
frustrations of rejection. Also, the ease and
frequency of consulting a spirit or joining a
drinking party makes dependent behavior emotionally
rewarding. It is not, however necessary to view the
relation between dependency and these two
institutions as teleological. Rather it is sufficient
simply to indicate the obvious, that while guardian
spirits and social drinking have several other manifest
and latent functions, they also furnish individuals
with an indirect way of expressing dependency needs.
Historically the Potawatomi social system provided
a maximum of opportunity for individual action.
The most important status differences were structured
along sexual lines, but the disappearance of the
hunt and military expedition as a basis for validating
the superiority of men over women has led to a decline
in the prestige of the male. As a consequence men
seek to create through drinking a fantasy status of
authority which enables them for a short time to
reassert an aggressive dominance over women. Social
conflict is avoided by attributing this unrealistic
form of status dominance to intoxication. Beyond
the help it provides in maintaining a modicum of
intracommunity harmony, alcohol also serves as a
symbolic means for predicting behavioral differences
between the whites and Indians in the area and helps
to limit the development of tension between the two
groups.

    Among contemporary North American Indian societies,
the Potawatomi of Whitehorse may be considered as
representing the extreme and chiefly negative
consequences of drinking as a way of life. Nevertheless
the adaptive aspects of heavy and frequent consumption
of alcohol are recognized by these people as
outweighing the social costs.

REFERENCES

Barry, H., M. Bacon and I. Child
1959 "Relation of child training to subsistence economy", American Anthropologist, 61:51-63.

Beckworth, H.
1884 Some accounts of the Indian Tribes formerly inhabiting Indiana and Illinois. Chicago: Fergus Historical Society of Indiana Series, No. 27.

Caton, K. D.
1876 The Last of the Illinois and a Sketch of the Pottawatomies. Chicago: Fergus Historical Society of Indiana, Series no. 3.

Cohen, R. and J. W. VanStone
1963 "Dependency and self-sufficiency in Chipewyan stories", National Museum of Canada, Bulletin No. 194:29-55.

Cooper, J. M.
1933 "The Northern Algonquian Supreme Being". Primitive Man 6:41-111.

Copley, A. B.
1908 The Pottawattomies. Historical Collections of the Michigan Pioneer and Historical Society, No. 14. Lansing: Michigan Historical Commission

De La Potherie, C.
1753 Histoire de l' Amerique Septentrionale, Tome II. Paris.

Densmore, F.
1929 Chippewa Customs. Washington, D. C.: Bureau of American Ethnology Bulletin No. 86.

Foreman, C.
1946 The Last Trek of the Indians. Chicago: University of Chicago Press.

Friedl, E.
1956 "Persistence in Chippewa culture and personality", Amer. Anthrop. 58:814-825.

150

Gavalas, R. J. and P. F. Briggs
    1966 "Concurrent schedules of reinforcement:
    a new concept of dependency", Merrill-Palmer
    Quarterly, 12:97-121.

Green
    1948 "Culture, normality and personality
    conflict", American Anthropologist, 50:225-237.

Hallowell, I. A.
    1955 Culture and experience. Philadelphia:
    University of Pennsylvania Press.

Hilger, I. M.
    1951 Chippewa child life and its cultural
    background. Washington, D. C.: Bureau of
    American Ethnology Bulletin 146.

James, B. J.
    1961 "Social-psychological dimensions of
    Ojibwa acculturation", American Anthropologist,
    63:721-746.

Jenness, D.
    1935 The Ojibwa Indians of Parry Island.
    National Museum of Canada, Bulletin No. 78.

Keating, W. H.
    1824 Narrative of an Expedition to the
    Source of St. Peter's River, Lake Winnepeek,
    Lake of the Woods, etc., Vol. 1.
    Philadelphia.

Kinietz, W. V.
    1940 The Indians of the Western Great Lakes,
    1615-1760, Occasional Contributions from
    the Museum of Anthropology of the
    University of Michigan, No. 10. Ann Arbor:
    University of Michigan Press.

Landes, R.
    1937 Ojibwa sociology. New York: Columbia
    University Press.

    1938a The Ojibwa woman. New York: Columbia
    University Press.
    1938b "The abnormal among the Ojibwa Indians",
    Journal of Abnormal and Social Psychology,
    33:14-33.
    1966 "The Ojibwa of Canada", In Cooperation and
    competition among primitive peoples. M. Mead,
    ed. Boston: Beacon Press.

Lawson, P. V.
    1920 The Potawatomi. Wis. Archeologist 19:76-
    105.

McCord, W. and J. McCord
    1960 Origins of Alcoholism. Stanford: Stanford
    University Press.

Morse, J. A.
    1822 Report on Indian Affairs. New Haven.

Mowrer, O. H.
    1960 Learning theory and behavior. New York:
    Wiley.

Parker, S.
    1960 "The Wiitiko psychosis in the context of
    Ojibwa personality and culture", American
    Anthropologist, 62:603-623.

Pokagon, S.
    1899 O-gi-maw-kwe mit-i-gwa-ki: Queen of the
    Woods. Hartford.

Quimby, G. I.
    1960 Indian life in the Upper Great Lakes.
    Chicago: University of Chicago Press.

Sears, R., L. Pau, and R. Alpert
    1965 Identification and child rearing.
    Stanford: Stanford University Press.

Skinner, A.
    1924 The Mascoutens or Prairie Potawatomi

Indians, Bull. publ. Mus. Milwaukee 6:38-41.

Thwaites, R. S., ed.
    1899 The Jesuit Relations and Allied Documents,
        vol. 51, Ottawa, Lower Canada, Iroquois:
        1610-1791. Cleveland.

154

CHAPTER VII

Alcohol and the Identity Struggle:

Some Effects of Economic Change on

Interpersonal Relations

by

Richard Loward Robbins

Introduction

Kenelm Burridge (1969) has recently drawn
attention to the role of economic change in
promoting various types of millenarian activities.
He proposes that the introduction of a money economy
into a society will bring about a questioning of
the nature and distribution of power, and that this
questioning will effect an effort to change the
means by which persons may secure prestige, this
effort manifesting itself in millenarian activities.
However, there are other activities of a less
spectacular sort that appear to result from the
same circumstances. Codere (1950), for example,
notes that following the introduction of wage labor
among the Kwakiutl there was an increase in potlatch
activity. Salisbury (1962) observes an increase in
ceremonial exchanges among the Siane following the
introduction of indentured labor, and Middleton (1960)
remarks that following the introduction of migrant
labor among the Lugbara there was an increase in
witchcraft accusations. In each of these instances
the introduction of a wage-money economy produced
not an increase in millenarian activities, as
Burridge proposes, but an increase in those

Reprinted from Alcohol and the Identity Struggle:
Some Effects of Economic Change on Interpersonal
Relations, American Anthropologist, Vol. 75, No. 1
1973:99-122 by permission of the author and the
editors of the American Anthropologist.

institutionalized and ritualized activities that
serve to express and resolve interpersonal conflict.
The aim of this paper is to explore this phenomenon
focusing initially on the drinking behavior
characteristic of Naskapi Indian males in
Schefferville, Quebec.[1] More specifically, this
paper will investigate the following hypothesis:
<u>When economic change alters persons' means of access</u>
<u>to status-conferring goods or activities, or increases</u>
<u>the availability of such goods or activities, there</u>
<u>will be an increase in frequency of interpersonal</u>
<u>conflict, and an increase in occurrence of those</u>
<u>cultural processes which serve to resolve this</u>
<u>conflict</u>. A secondary hypothesis holds that
Naskapi drinking interactions serve as a locus of
interpersonal conflict which stems from recent
changes in their economic life, and that these
interactions further provide the opportunity for
the resolution of this conflict.

Theoretical Framework

   The study of interpersonal relations requires
the delineation of the conceptions held by actors
in a given interaction of their social position
vis-a-vis others (see Miller 1963). Such conceptions
include a person's self-identity - his notion of
his place in an interaction; his social identity -

[1] The author's research in Schefferville was
   conducted from February through August 1966,
   supported by a grant from the National Science
   Foundation (Grant #GS 939) administered by John
   J. Honigmann, and from June through August 1968
   while the author was serving as Field Work
   Director, supported by a training grant from the
   National Institute of Mental Health (Grant #5 -
   Ti - MH - 8166). A grant from the SUNY Research
   Foundation made possible revision of an earlier
   draft of this paper. My thanks also to John J.
   Honigmann, Kary Jablonka, and Alice Hicks, all
   of whom provided valuable comments on the paper.

the place in the interaction he conceives others attribute to him; and his public-identity - the way others actually view his social standing (see Goodenough 1963; Miller 1963).[2] This identity-interaction framework implies certain assumptions about the nature of man and the meaning of human behavior, the most basic being that a person's image of himself and of others affects his behavior and beliefs (Hallowell 1955). Secondly, it implies that a person's identity serves as a guide to him and others in orienting their pattern of interaction (Goffman 1956; Goodenough 1963). Further, a person's identity is formed and maintained in the course of his interaction with others (Mead 1934; Schwartz and Merten 1968), and persons need to acquire information which confirms the image they entertain of themselves (Laing 1962). Finally, persons are constantly striving to bring within their orbit persons, possessions, or behaviors which confirm to them that they are indeed the persons that they believe themselves to be (Wallace 1967).

In striving to become what he believes to be a desirable person, the individual attempts to develop or acquire those attributes which serve in his society to define that identity. These attributes or features may include a certain physical appearance, the fulfillment of kinship obligations, the attainment of membership in certain groups, or the kind and quantity of personal possessions (see Wallace 1967; Miller 1963). Thus, in a given society the personal attribute of generosity may be one aspect of a favorable identity, as may the possession of such things as yams, pigs, horses, or automobiles. Given this framework the major problem posed in this paper entails examining the social consequences of changing patterns of access to those attributes that serve to define a desirable identity, and examining the behavioral strategies adopted by persons to maintain their identities in the face of this change.

[2] The various constituents of identity (self, social, personal, etc.) have been referred to by a number of terms (see Robbins 1972), although the three used here cover most.

This paper will also focus on identity-resolving forums. Such forums are social gatherings which exhibit the following characteristics. First, they are times in the flow of community activities which are set aside for the permitting of behaviors that are otherwise disallowed (see McAndrew and Edgerton 1969; Leach 1965). Second, they have inherent in them statements or actions which demarcate ambiguities, inconsistencies, or conflicts in interpersonal relations, in this sense resembling what Turner (1957) refers to as a "social drama." Third, during such gatherings persons are permitted and encouraged to adopt poses intended to demonstrate that they do indeed possess the attributes of the identity they claim (Barth 1969). Finally, the forums serve as a time during which participants in the gathering have the opportunity to seek information to allow for the aligning of the identity they believe they possess with the identity they believe others attribute to them. In sum, such gatherings or interactions involve the enactment of behavioral strategies to permit persons to maintain, attain or protect desired identities or social positions. Some examples of social gatherings which exhibit these characteristics are initiation ceremonies (Burton and Whiting 1965; Cohen 1964), trance ceremonies (Bourguignon 1965; Hamer 1966), ceremonial exchanges (Wallace and Fogelson 1965), and, as I propose to demonstrate, Naskapi drinking interactions.

The Social and Economic Background of the Naskapi

Located on the Quebec-Labrador border, the frontier mining town of Schefferville might appear at first glance to be indistinguishable from the suburbs of any large, North American city. Completed in 1957, the town was built by the Iron Ore Company of Canada, supporting a Euro-Canadian population of some 4000 persons, and a native population of some 700 persons. The town, accessible only by rail and air, contains a department store, two supermarkets, a movie theater, two bars, three

158

restaurants, and virtually all the other conveniences one associates with modern urban life. Located some three miles from this main residential area is what the townspeople refer to as the "Indian Village," a settlement that, in fact, contains two socially distinct Indian groups; a community of some 400 Montagnais Indians who migrated to Schefferville from the Southern settlement of Sept-Iles, and some 300 Naskapi Indians who migrated to Schefferville from the Northern Ungava settlement of Fort Chimo.

The Schefferville Naskapi comprise the remnants of that group which Speck (1931) referred to as the Ungava Band, whose occupation of the area around Fort Chimo can be traced back to the mid-19th Century (Turner 1889-90). Aboriginally this group subsisted primarily on fish and caribou. Their social organization lacked any large-scale, permanent social groupings or formal political controls (Honigmann 1964), with leadership and prestige being contingent upon a person's skills as orator or hunter (Leacock 1958; Rogers 1965). The only gradiation in status was reflected in the number of wives a man possessed, and the number of hunting trophies he acquired, some portion of slain animals being kept and displayed (Turner 1889-90). In 1957 the Naskapi left a life still based on hunting, but supplemented by government relief, and migrated to Schefferville, living at present in a permanent settlement of 37 government-built houses, depending for subsistence on wage labor and relief. Most importantly, wages earned at the Iron Ore Company have made available to them such Western goods as television, phonographs, refrigerators, washing machines, and electric stoves, goods whose availability has had a profound effect on the character of their interpersonal relations.

Attributes utilized in a society to define a person of social worth determine not only the nature of interpersonal relations, but also the means to power, that is, the ability to influence the behavior of others, especially towards oneself. For a Naskapi to maintain or attain such power, to be, as they put it, a "good man," he must exhibit certain personal characteristics, honor his kin obligations,

159

be a good provider for his family, and possess certain goods which are used for either display or exchange.

When asked to define the attributes of a good man a Naskapi will usually first reply that it is someone who shares what he has with others and who minds his own business. This latter attribute of reticence (see Preston Ms) makes requisite the avoiding of placing oneself or others in potentially conflict laden situations, and avoiding the appearance of, as the Naskapi put it, placing oneself "above others." On one occasion, for example, a woman was struck on the hand with an iron pipe by a youth she was berating for his excessive drinking. The resulting injury was serious enough to require 20 stitches, but when asked for information on the matter the woman's husband merely replied, "It's none of my business." Reticence is also reflected in the evasiveness of individuals when they are asked their opinion on some matter, and in the reluctance of persons to appear in any way to be claiming that they are better than others or boasting of their exploits. In fact, the only situation in which reticence is lacking is during drinking interactions.

Generosity, the second important personal attribute of a good man, is to some extent related to the Naskapi's aboriginal subsistence pattern. Most societies in which food is scarce tend to place an emphasis on sharing because of the vicissitudes of obtaining it (see Evans-Pritchard 1940; Thomas 1959), those successful in the food quest sharing with others if only to insure a like return when they experience a food shortage. However, of more relevance in the Naskapi's present setting is the fact that sharing enables a person to obtain prestige reflected in the deference paid to the giver by the receiver of gifts. Giving or sharing is, in effect, a silent boast of success, with the acceptance of the offering affirming that success (see Ridington 1968). Not to share, on the other hand, marks an admission of failure, while the refusal of an offering indicates a negation of the giver's boast of success. Before the Naskapi moved to Schefferville, items marked for sharing or exchange

160

were products of the hunt. However, with game now scarce and of lesser utility in the Naskapi scheme of things, items to be shared consist mostly of store-bought goods such as radios, watches, and, most importantly, alcoholic beverages.

In addition to exhibiting the requisite attributes of reticence and generosity, a Naskapi must also honor obligations defined by kinship if he is to maintain his desired identity. That all persons in the Naskapi community are kin is understood by all; however, it is also recognized that all people do not honor obligations wrought by a kin tie. Thus, the fact that a person may stand in a relationship as father to son is one thing; that he fulfills his obligations as a father is something else. Kin relationships in the Naskapi community can be divided into two general types. There are those that tie together persons of equal or near equal status, or using Foster's (1967) terms a "colleague contract," and those in which there is some status differential between persons, or a "patron-client" relationship (Foster 1967). Colleague contracts among the Naskapi include a man's relationship to nistash (older male sibling, male parallel-cousin), to nishim (younger sibling, younger parallel-cousin),[3] and nistaw (male cross-cousin or wife's brother). One illustration of this type of relationship is the tie between Joseph and Willie. They are nistaw to each other and both acknowledge the closeness of their tie. Their relationship is maintained by the frequent exchange of alcoholic beverages, rarely a week passing when they did not together visit one of the two local bars or exchange beer which one or the other had purchased. They frequently go hunting together, and exchange household visits virtually every day. Furthermore, they have agreed that Joseph's 12-year-old son will marry Willie's

3   The term nishim denotes both male and female younger siblings and male and female younger parallel-cousins, although colleague contracts refer only to male relationships.

10-year-old daughter when both come of age.
However, while the equality of their relationship
is understood by both, the balance of the
relationship is contingent upon the equal fortune of
the two participants in the interaction since the
colleague relationship assumes that each gives to
the other in like manner, kind, and quantity. In
other words, if one participant in the relationship
should have greater access than the other to those
goods which are marked for exchange, the balance
of the relationship would be disrupted and the tie
between them would approach that of patron to client.
There are, in fact, persons in the community who
have no jobs, but who reside with nistaw who are
employed. These relationships tend toward that
of patron to client with the wage-earner providing
food and shelter, and the unemployed person
chopping wood, carrying water, or doing other such
chores. Thus, for those who are unsuccessful in
wage earning it has become difficult, if not
impossible, to maintain the proper balance in their
colleague contracts.

There are also relationships in the Naskapi
community characterized by some status difference
which have been disrupted by the lack of access of
persons to those attributes needed to maintain a
favorable identity. Marriage, for example,
generally marks the transition of a Naskapi male
from boy (nabash) to man (nabow), although such a
status is not recognized until the birth of the
first child. At such a time a man should be able
to establish a household, and assume the position of
household head, one of the few roles in which a
Naskapi may overtly exert authority. However, for
such a status to be viewed as an attribute of a
favorable identity, the husband must demonstrate
that he can provide well for his family, and
fulfill his marital and parental obligations. But
there are some males in the community who because
they do not have access to steady wages are unable
to provide for their family at the level recognized
by their spouse or others to be desirable. These
men tend to be frequently derided by their marital
partners as well as by their children. Their
authority in the household is further undermined by

the government practice of making relief checks out
to the woman of the household, a practice initiated
to prevent men from spending relief money on
alcoholic beverages.

The final attribute to be treated here that is
necessary for successful identity maintenance is a
man's personal possessions. Thorsten Veblen in The
Theory of the Leisure Class was one of the first
social scientists to treat the importance of various
forms of economic goods in the establishment and
maintenance of status differences within a society,
an importance that has long since been recognized by
anthropologists (see Mauss 1961; Sahlins 1965;
Foster 1967, among others). A particularly lucid
report on the part that economic goods play in
determining social position in a hunting society is
Robin Ridington's paper dealing with the Beaver
Indians (1968). To the Beaver, success is measured
by the amount of supernatural power (ma yine) a
person possesses. A person's ma yine, however, can
only be validated by his success as a hunter, for
it is in the sharing of game that others convey
recognition of the power of the giver, with game then
serving as a trophy which confirms a person's claim
to a desired identity. As was noted, hunting and
the trophies it produces has ceased to be important
in determining a Naskapi's social worth, since game
itself is scarce, and, for the most part, they no
longer accept products of the hunt as status symbols.
Instead, the Naskapi now aspire to possess such items
as television, radio, record players, and automobiles,
goods whose display now confirms a person's claim to
a desired identity.

In sum, for a Naskapi to attain or maintain a
desirable identity (i.e. "good man"), he no longer
needs to demonstrate success at exploiting the
physical environment. Instead, his social worth is
now determined by his ability to exploit the social
and economic institutions of Schefferville. His
avenue to a desired identity has ceased to be through
success at hunting, and now is through his success as
a wage earner, since it is the goods purchased with
such wages that are shared to maintain the attribute

163

of generosity, and it is these goods that are given to kinsmen to fulfill kin obligations. Further, it is the goods purchased with these wages whose display and possession mark a man as a good provider for his family.

As is the case with virtually all Schefferville residents, the Naskapi are largely dependent for wages on employment at the iron ore mines (see Table 1).* The Iron Ore Company began employing Naskapi workers in 1957, almost immediately after their arrival from Fort Chimo. However, as of August 1966, only 11 men were permanent employees, 10 being members of the local union, a branch of the United Steel Workers of America. Two other Naskapi were at one time permanent employees, but were dismissed for job infractions. Only one Naskapi ever held a job at the Company other than unskilled laborer, but his promotion lasted only one month because of his inadequate command of English. One reason for the relatively low number of permanent Naskapi employees is the hiring practice of the Company prior to 1967. Company and union regulations stipulated that a person must have worked 65 consecutive days before he could either become a union member or gain seniority, a rule which under ordinary circumstances would have benefitted the Naskapi, for, along with the Montagnais, they constitute the most permanent labor force in a community with considerable labor turnover. However, the Company had a practice of employing native workers for 60 days, laying them off a few days, and then rehiring them, in this way denying their claim to seniority. Ten of the permanent employees had already accumulated the necessary time when the union was formed in 1959, so they could not be dismissed, while the remaining person gained seniority when his foreman "forgot" to report that he worked 64 consecutive days. In effect, these hiring rules created a situation where only a few of the adult males in the Naskapi community have access to full-time employment and the income realized from it, while the remaining Naskapi must depend on

*Tables begin on Page 194.

less lucrative part-time employment. While it was partly chance that 10 Naskapi had worked the necessary consecutive period when the union was formed, additional factors enter into their success. They had constantly stayed on the job while others would take unannounced leaves from their jobs to go hunting or to take a vacation. They also had to limit job infractions such as appearing late to work, coming to work inebriated, or taking unexcused absences, thus quickly adapting to the norms of employment and the new temporal routine a job required.

Part-time employment available in the mines for the rest of the Naskapi population depends upon the yearly fluctuations of labor demand, and the seasonal nature of mining operations in the North. To illustrate, Table 2 indicates the number of men who worked and the number of man hours worked by Naskapi employed on a part-time basis from 1962 to June of 1966.

There are few alternatives to employment at the mines (see Table 1). The town occasionally employs Naskapi workers on a part-time basis, usually for snow removal, but this adds little income to the Indian community. For example, in 1964, when only 6 Naskapi found part-time work in the mines, 22 men worked for the town, but their combined income from this source was only $3200, far short of the potential income to be earned working for the Company. A number of persons have been able to find jobs as guides in the hunting and fishing camps scattered in the area, but not only is this work seasonal - from June to October - it comes at a time when employment in the mines is likely to be available. The only other source of significant income is government relief. However, as noted, these payments do little for allowing the identity maintenance of the male household heads, since relief checks are made out to the women. These payments also do little to rectify the difference in the range of household incomes (see Table 3). In 1966 there were 37 separate Naskapi households, and while the average income over an 18-month period was $4774, including relief payments, the incomes ranged from a high of $10,888, to a low of $300.

One key point of change affecting the Naskapi is that economic change has created greater status differences between persons than existed before the move to Schefferville: in effect, the differential between success and failure has increased. Further, there has been a scramble among persons to obtain these goods which are most relevant for identity maintenance. To demonstrate it is only necessary to examine the way the Naskapi have allocated their income from wage labor. Money itself lacks status-conferring qualities for the Naskapi. It is not displayed nor is it circulated outside a close circle of kin, so unless it is translated into goods which can be displayed or circulated it lacks any social value. The goods available to the Naskapi can be divided into five categories.[4] Category 1 consists of such items as food, clothing, and shelter, items which may be labeled subsistence goods. Category 2 includes such items as washing machines, freezers, refrigerators, and sewing machines, goods which have some household utility. Category 3 contains such items as guns, outboard motors, fishing equipment, and canoes, goods, which at least in the past had considerable survival benefit. Category 4 is made up of television, radio, record player, and camera, goods which are considered luxury items, while category 5 consists of such consumable luxuries as alcoholic beverages, tobacco, movie-going, and billiards.

In terms of social meaning, none of the goods in category 1 is attended by any sort of prestige.[5]

[4] I was unable to obtain a native classification of goods available in Schefferville (if one, indeed, exists), so the scheme used here is based primarily on my observations of how goods were used.

[5] This may be changing. The Naskapi now appear to be taking an interest in purchasing mail order clothing such as suits with the explicit aim of

166

There is virtually no difference in the appearance
of Naskapi homes, except, as we shall see, in the
furnishings. There is little difference among
individuals in dress, and little difference in types
of food purchased, with slight advantages being taken
of the wide variety of foodstuffs available at the
two local supermarkets. Goods in category 2 would
appear to function as household aids, but their
utility is more potential than actual. Freezers,
one of the most frequently purchased items in this
category, are supposedly used to store fish and
caribou, but the amount of game actually obtained
and left over after sharing and consumption hardly
requires a large upright freezer. Washing machines
tend to be difficult to operate because the Naskapi
homes lack running water. In winter water must be
carried from the adjacent lake, a trip of some 25
to 300 yards (depending upon the location of the
homes), and in summer must be carried from a half
mile distant stream, the water in the lake being
unfit for consumption because of a lack of
sanitation facilities in the village. Furthermore,
when using the washing machine, trips for water
must be made twice, once for the wash cycle, and
once for the rinse. While such goods are not, and
cannot, be used to their full potential they may
still have some utility for the women of the
households, but I suspect that their prime importance
lies in the status that the possession of such goods
bestows upon the head of the household. Items in
category 3, bush tools, were once basic items of
survival, but are now recreational implements. The
Naskapi still go into the bush, but rarely do such
trips last more than 3 or 4 days. Goods in category
4 function primarily for display purposes, serving
to demonstrate the success of the owner. Television,
a popular item in this category, is purchased,
although there are only 14 hours of English-language
programming each week, with few Naskapi being able to
understand even them. Combination radio and phonograph
consoles are purchased even though the record player
portion is never used. Of the items in category 5 -
tobacco, billiards, movie-going - alcoholic beverages

    "dressing up."

are most important. Aside from its value as an
intoxicant, alcohol serves as a source of prestige
to those who purchase and distribute it.

Using the Naskapi household I resided in as a
standard of measurement, along with observation of
the consumption patterns of other households, I
estimate that 15-20% of Naskapi income is allocated
to goods in category 1. Little is spent on housing
although it is possible to invest in new homes
(most being overcrowded), but such investments have
not been made. The frequency of purchase of items
in categories 2 through 4 is summarized in Table
4. What is of particular interest is the high
frequency of purchase of goods in categories 2 and
4, and the relatively low frequency of purchase of
items in category 3. Cost is not a factor in this
resource allocation pattern for prices of items in
the different categories are comparable, a three
horsepower outboard engine costing about the same
as a television or freezer at the local Hudson's
Bay Company store. The number of guns in the
community is deceiving, since most are 22 caliber
rifles dating back to Fort Chimo days, and few
persons own higher caliber rifles useful in hunting
caribou, while only 2 persons own shotguns for
hunting duck, geese, or ptarmigan.

The most frequently purchased item in Category 5
is beer. It is difficult to gauge precisely how
much is spent on such beverages since local merchants
keep no records of native purchases. However, one
individual stated that he spends approximately $40
a week on beer in addition to an unspecified amount
at the local bar. This represents some 30-40% of
his weekly income, and since he is not atypical in
his consumption patterns one may estimate that some
25-50% of Naskapi income is allocated to alcoholic
beverages.

Two things about the way Naskapi spend their money
are relevant here. First, there is a marked preference
for those goods which are most meaningful for
distinguishing status differences within the community.
Put another way, there appears to be a scramble for

168

those goods which are most important in maintaining
a person's identity or power. Second, the resource
allocation pattern has effected a translation of
differential income into a differential distribution
of those things or behaviors needed to maintain a
desired identity.

     In sum, the above account of Naskapi life in
Schefferville reveals at least three changes in
their economy which could be expected to produce
changes in their patterns of interpersonal relations.
First, there was a transition from a hunting economy
to one based on wage labor, a shift which changed
the way persons could obtain those goods needed to
attain status or to maintain one's identity. All
societies, of course, have some criteria for
defining persons as successful or unsuccessful,
whether the criteria be caribou tails or television,
as well as having some way of determining who has
access to these criteria. However, when there is
a precipitous change in the means by which persons
obtain access to status or power-conferring goods
or activities one can expect that those persons who
were successful under the old system of power
distribution would find their status threatened by
the introduction of a new system of power
distribution (see Sharp 1952). Among the Naskapi,
for example, there are persons who were (and are)
successful hunters, but who, for whatever reason,
are not successful wage earners. These persons have
seen their power and prestige decline relative to
those who, while perhaps not successful hunters, are
successful wage earners. Thus, in the past a leader
was selected primarily for his hunting ability, but
in Schefferville, all four individuals who have been
elected chief since the move from Fort Chimo are
persons who are permanent employees at the Company,
and are not particularly noted for their hunting
ability.

     Second, the move to Schefferville meant that
status symbols were more numerous and easier to
attain. The fact that such things were more numerous
meant there was an influx into the Naskapi social
system of what Salisbury (1962:190) terms "free-

floating power," goods which have status-conferring qualities but which lack fixed rules of distribution. These goods, aside from being more plentiful, also are easier to obtain than hunting trophies, for whereas a hunter's access to status-conferring goods is limited by the vicissitudes of consumating a kill, a wage earner's access to such status is limited only by his ability to translate wages into goods with status-conferring qualities. One can then expect that the change in availability and quantity of status-conferring goods will result in what may simply be called a free-for-all to obtain these goods, and a scramble to obtain access to the new means by which such goods are acquired.

Third, because of the hiring practices of the Iron Ore Company after 1959 the avenues of access to power were partially closed so only some persons, those employed full-time, were able to maintain their identities at the new level required by life in Schefferville. This resulted in greater status differences between persons than one would expect to exist in a society based on a hunting economy. One may then postulate that this increased differential between success and failure would make it more difficult for some persons to fulfill obligations wrought by their ties to others.

One can deduce from the propositions enumerated earlier that any circumstance that dramatically changes persons' identities will require a reordering of interpersonal relations,[6] and that such

6 Changes in persons' identities are, of course, an ever occurring circumstance as persons move through the life cycle and as their situation in life changes. However, these are largely small-scale, predictable changes in which the reordering of interpersonal relations is effected by various rites of passage. When such changes occur on a large scale, as will happen given economic change, it will become necessary for virtually all relationships to be reordered, and will result in a dramatic increase in the need for identity resolving forums (see

170

circumstances will promote an increase in those social interactions in which the identity claimed by a person is different from the identity attributed to him by others, relationships which Wallace terms identity struggles (1967; see also Wallace and Fogelson 1965). The change in the means of access to identity-maintaining and power-conferring goods will initiate struggles between those who formerly enjoyed favored access to such goods and those whose access improved under the new system of power distribution. Further, there will develop a struggle between persons vying for the increased power injected into the community in the form of Western goods, with those who are successful in obtaining such goods asserting, in some form, what they see to be their newly acquired status. Finally, the greater status differential between persons resulting from economic change will effect struggles between persons involved in relationships in which one partner can no longer fulfill his obligations to the other.

The question that now presents itself is if indeed one can expect the above consequences to economic change, in what form do the struggles postulated to exist present themselves?

Alcohol and the Naskapi

Social scientists have long noted a relationship between alcohol and anxiety, frustration or failure (see Horton 1967). Graves (1967), for example, demonstrates that persons who do not have access to desired goals tend to drink more heavily than those to whom such goals are attainable. Whittaker (1963) views Sioux drinking as a reliever of tensions caused by the basic insecurities of reservation life, and Simmons (1959) sees Peruvian Mestizo drinking serving as an opportunity to "reduce anxiety due to a distrust and fear of others." These and other studies have tended to focus only on alcohol

Peacock 1968).

consumption itself rather than the behavior
generated by alcohol use, assuming that it is the
physiological reaction alcohol is supposed to
have on the person that is of prime importance.
However, the utilization of this psychodynamic
framework does little to explain the dynamics of
Naskapi drinking, for it does not account for the
fact that the Naskapi express almost unanimous
satisfaction with their life in Schefferville, and
does not allow understanding of the disparate forms
of behavior evidenced by persons whose alcohol
consumption patterns are near identical.
Furthermore, among the Naskapi drinking, rather
than involving personal withdrawal is pre-eminently
a social act, guiding the person to certain types
of social interaction defined by both the situation
and the identity of the participants. Accordingly,
the view followed here is that drinking behavior,
rather than being explained by alcohol's "toxic
assault on the seat of moral judgment," is behavior
that is culturally defined and given meaning within
a given social nexus (McAndrew and Edgerton 1969;
see also Mandelbaum 1965:287). Furthermore, to
understand the nature of alcohol use and drinking
behavior of the Naskapi, one must focus on the
social interaction accompanying the drinking act.
With this in mind we will be concerned with three
aspects of Naskapi alcohol usage. First, what are
the different types of behavior individual Naskapi
exhibit when drinking? Second, what are the social
positions in a drinking interaction of the actors
vis-a-vis each other, and in what way does this
position determine drinking behavior? Finally, what
is the nature meaning, and significance of the social
interaction that among the Naskapi accompanies the
drinking act?

Patterns of Alcohol Usage

     By far the most frequent beverage imbibed by
the Naskapi is store-bought beer. Hard liquor can
be ordered at the Provincial-run liquor store, but
the wait before such beverages are delivered - 2 to
7 days - deters most Naskapi from utilizing that
source. Hard liquor and mixed drinks are purchased

172

at the two local bars, although the bulk of drinking
activity takes place in the Indian Village. Most
drinking groups are small, usually from two to three
persons, and on no occasion did I observe a group of
more than six (see Table 5). There are a number of
reasons for the small size of drinking groups, not
the least of which is the fact that beer is only
supplied by one or, at most, two persons in such
gatherings, an amount not sufficient to provide more
than 5 or 6 persons. It would also be difficult as
we shall see for the social interaction that
accompanies the drinking act to be engaged in with
groups of more than 5 or 6 individuals. In addition
to the size composition of drinking groups, a
pattern also emerges in the types of relationships
between individuals drinking together. Almost half
of the drinking groups I observed were composed of
persons who stood as nistaw to each other, while
68% were composed of persons who stood either as
nistaw, or as nistash-nishim to each other. In
other words, drinking is most frequent between
persons who are tied together by a colleague
contract.

As noted, it is difficult to determine the
quantity of beer consumed by each person since local
merchants keep no records of beer purchases, and
even if they did one could not be certain that those
who purchased it consumed it. However, except for a
number of women, there are few abstainers among the
Naskapi. In fact, I knew of only one adult male
(65 years old) who claims never to drink and whose
claim is substantiated by others. Furthermore, he
is a virtual recluse whose most frequent interactions
are with some older Montagnais who, as far as I could
gather, do not drink either (see Szwed 1966).
Otherwise all Naskapi males drink, and most drink
heavily. But in spite of the high frequency of
alcohol consumption (or perhaps because of it),
virtually all Naskapi when asked their opinion will
state simply that "drinking is no good." Often a
person is characterized as a "good man, except when
he drinks," and even persons who are frequent
consumers will look askance at someone who is
drinking and say, "People are no good when drinking."
These negative attitudes toward alcohol consumption

173

are reinforced from both within and without the
Naskapi community. The Anglican Missionary often
uses church services to speak on the harmful effects
of alcohol, as does the Roman Catholic Missionary
with his Montagnais congregation. The Iron Ore
Company sends home persons who come to work
inebriated, firing those for whom it becomes a
repeated offense. The police reinforce these
attitudes through arrests, and townspeople will
usually ignore the attempt of a drinking Indian to
engage in conversation. Within the community
drinkers are often the subject of deprecating
gossip, and it is believed by most Naskapi that
drinking causes stomach trouble. Yet to focus only
on these stated attitudes is misleading for while
drinking and alcoholic beverages are condemned,
what is usually intended is an objection to that
type of drinking that leads to socially disruptive
behavior. Virtually all Euro-Canadian agencies,
including the missionary and the police, express no
objection to drinking in moderation, and the Naskapi
themselves state that it is all right to drink to,
as they put it, "get happy."

As with a number of other societies (see Berreman
1956; Simmons 1959; Whittaker 1963; Hamer 1965; Curley
1967), the Naskapi does not hold anyone responsible
for his behavior when drinking. If a person becomes
aggressive when imbibing his actions will be overtly
forgotten by others the next day in the belief that
he was "not himself," or was "crazy," and only when
such behavior results in injuries to others will
negative sanctions be applied. One person, for
example, severely cut one woman with a pipe,
threatened his wife with a loaded rifle, and struck
another man over the head with a shovel. Only
after the third incident were negative sanctions
applied to him, the person's father-in-law, in whose
house he was residing, asking him to leave.
Nevertheless, actual injuries and the application of
negative sanctions are relatively rare, surprisingly
so to someone who has witnessed the frequent,
apparently aggressive behavior that accompanies the
consumption of alcoholic beverages.

174

Time and Alcohol

Any casual observer in the Naskapi community is
certain to note the familiar weekend drinking spree.
It is a rare Saturday night when less than 50 Naskapi
adults are drinking, and rarer still when the R.C.M.P.
or town police do not make several trips to the village.
That alcohol consumption, at least in its more
socially disruptive form, is most frequent on weekends
is evidenced by the fact that half of all arrests
made for drinking occur on Saturday. However, there
are other temporal criteria for the staging of
drinking activities. At the end of the workday,
Naskapi mine workers will stop off at the bar for a
drink or two. Paydays, and the night preceding and
following a trip into the bush signal drinking
activity, as do such holidays as Christmas and New
Years. What is most apparent in this temporal
distribution of alcohol consumption is that
drinking is heaviest when it least disrupts the
flow of everyday life.

Drinking Behavior

Naskapi males do not all react the same way to
the consumption of alcoholic beverages. Nor from
my observations do their reactions necessarily
coincide with the amount of alcohol consumed (see
Berreman 1956). Persons who on some occasions would
show no signs of inebriation after 6 to 10 cans of
beer, would, on other occasions show signs of
inebriation after as little as one half can of beer.
In other instances, persons reacting aggressively to
alcohol would sober up as soon as someone new
entered the interaction.

The form that drinking behavior takes varies
from a friendly, amicable type, to an assertive,
sometimes violent type. The friendly reaction
usually takes the form of the drinker loudly
declaring his friendship to a drinking partner, or
may take the form of a give-away. There were
frequent cases of a drinker writing checks to others

175

for amounts ranging from $5 to $50,[7] or giving away such personal valuables as radios, clocks, or wrist watches. The person exhibiting the friendly reaction will also usually insist that others share his beer with him. The assertive reaction to alcohol usually entails overt boasting by the actor. The most typical verbal statements that accompany this reaction are "me big man," or "I'm boss in my house," or simply "everybody likes me." Often such assertions will become more insistent and include the verbal downgrading of others, sometimes in their presence. On these occasions such a downgrading will lead to a like response from the accused, such interactions often culminating in physical violence.

My thesis in this paper is that Naskapi drinking interactions serve as identity-resolving forums; that when drinking a person is permitted to defend an identity that has been challenged, claim an identity he believes he is entitled to, or rectify an identity that has been spoiled by failure, and, that such interactions aim toward allowing the person to receive from others information which confirms the identity he is seeking. Furthermore, drinking interactions demarcate identity struggles within the Naskapi community. To give the reader the flavor of these drinking interactions, I have selected four incidents involving alcohol consumption, incidents which will reveal both the regularities and variations in Naskapi drinking behavior.

Interaction 1. It was 5:30 p.m. and the bus back to the Indian village was filled with returning workers and shoppers. Bill had been drinking in town, and when he boarded the bus he shouted as he took his seat, "I been in Schefferville 9 years now.

[7] Such checks are often written when the writer has no money in the bank. However, since any paychecks from the Company go directly into a person's account, the holder of the checks can wait until there is money in the bank, and then present it.

Nobody push Bill around, everybody my friend." Bill
is 50 years old and at one time was one of the most
influential men in the Naskapi community. He was
known to have been one of the best hunters in the
village, but while he still spends considerable
time in the bush, he realizes little income from his
exploits. When he came to Schefferville from Fort
Chimo he was unable to find work at the mines because
a back condition prevented him from passing the
Company's physical examination, although he quickly
informs people that he doesn't work in the mines
because, as he puts it, "I'm my own boss." His
major source of income is from relief and he is
reputed to be one of the heaviest drinkers in the
community. Bill continued his tirade on the bus
enroute to the village, and soon began directing
his comments to John (Bill's nistaw) who was
returning home from work bedecked in the yellow work
hat employed Naskapi wear virtually all the time.
Bill shouted at him, "You no good," and continued
in much the same vein all the way back to the village.
John, who had stopped off briefly at the local bar,
apparently tried to ignore the outburst, his only
reaction being embarrassed laughter.

Interaction 2. Joseph and Tommy had just returned
from town carrying with them two cases of beer which
Joseph had purchased. They were joined by Moses,
Thomas, and myself, and promptly opened the first
case with Joseph doing the honors of distributing
a can of beer to each participant. As the drinking
progressed, the conviviality of the group increased.
Joseph was the first to finish his can and rose and
handed those present another can, although no one
had yet finished their first. However, everyone
readily accepted, offering their thanks to Joseph
and praising his generosity. As the party continued
into the fourth round of drinks, Tommy began
repeating what a "good man" Joseph was, looking to
the others for their nod of approval, and by the
fifth round Thomas had taken out his checkbook and
was writing a check for $25 to give to Moses. By
the sixth round and into the second case of beer,
Thomas had given Joseph his watch and cigarette
lighter.

177

Interaction 3. Tom had already been drinking when he came into my room and asked me to go visiting with him. He put four cans of beer into his pocket and said: "Come, we go visit George, I give him beer." George is a permanent employee at the mines, and his English surpasses any other adult Naskapi. In Fort Chimo he lived with the manager of the local Hudson's Bay Company outpost, and was once elected to the band council. However, at present, he has very little status in the community, has extremely few household possessions, and has been in frequent trouble with Euro-Canadian authorities. In Fort Chimo he threatened an R.C.M.P. officer with a loaded rifle when the officer tried to take his wife into custody to send her south for treatment of tuberculosis. When his daughter Sally was to be married George wanted to Sponsor a big feast - he approached the Roman Catholic Missionary for a $1000 loan for the party - but the then Anglican Missionary would not let the feast take place because Sally was pregnant. Nor would the Missionary allow Sally to wear a white dress for the wedding ceremony. Whether this incident was the direct cause or not, neither George nor his wife has been to church since. In addition, the wife of the lay preacher (who is George's brother) has publically announced that she wouldn't allow George in church. When Tom and I arrived at George's house Tom pulled the beer out of his pocket and told me to give it to George.[8] George accepted, told Tom to "shut up,"

8   It should be noted that the author is by no stretch of the imagination a heavy imbiber of alcoholic beverages. When I arrived in Schefferville, complete with fairly negative ideas about alcohol, I tended to view Naskapi drinking as nothing short of self destructive, and hence had no intention of adding to what I first perceived as chaos by buying and distributing beer. However, as my time in Schefferville increased, the Naskapi, mostly through subtle teachings, tried to convey to me that my status required that I make frequent distributions of beer. This incident with Tom was, I think, one such lesson in my education.

explaining that he spoke better English than Tom.
He then proceeded to tell me that he had worked at
the Hudson's Bay Company store in Fort Chimo, and
that he had been on the village council for two years:
"We had a good chief then, better than now, but I
didn't like to be councilman. The people didn't
like me." Tom then interrupted: "No, George good
man. Doesn't drink too much." Two days earlier Tom
had told me that George drinks more than anyone
else in the village.

Interaction 4. Sam and I were visiting with Willie
when Sam's wife Martha came into Willie's house,
grabbed Sam by the arm, and proceeded to drag him
home. Sam had been drinking, and as he walked home
he kept complaining that he had given Martha two
checks (relief payments), one for $200 and the other
for $97. "My money," he kept repeating. When they
got home Martha sat Sam at the kitchen table and
began making him supper. Sam said he hadn't eaten
in two days. Martha tried to give him some water
(a native cure for hangovers), but he refused saying
he wanted meat. Then he began arguing with Martha,
Sam repeating in English, "I'm boss in my house,"
and Martha repeating in Cree that Sam was crazy.
Martha then cooked some Spam and gave it to him
along with a cup of coffee, but Sam pushed the food
aside, spilled the coffee into the plate with the
meat, and proceeded to pour himself another cup.
After two hours of bickering they went to sleep.

Analysis: The Drinking Interaction

    In analyzing the nature of the interaction
process that accompanies the consumption of alcoholic
beverages it is important to note the reaction of
others when a drinker adopts either a friendly,
assertive or aggressive pose. In the case of the
friendly actor, the most marked response of others is
one of deference. When a Naskapi offers another a
drink, the recipient will usually shake his head
and proclaim what a "good man" the donor is. There
is also a sharp difference in the demeanor of the
giver vis-a-vis the receiver. The donor tends to

179

be more assertive in his actions, distributing beer
or other goods with an obvious flourish while the
receiver tends to be more subdued and deferential.
In Interaction 2, for example, Joseph, who is a
permanent employee at the mines, was the recipient
of considerable praise for his generosity. Thomas,
who works only part-time, also began to make
presentations, but the check he gave to Moses was no
good, and the goods he distributed to Joseph he
asked for back the following day through an
intermediary. One may view Thomas' presentations
to Joseph (who is nistaw to Thomas) as his attempt
to balance the exchange initiated by the
distribution of beer. However, it is largely a
fruitless effort on Thomas' part because he has
got just so many watches and cigarette lighters
to give away during such interactions, and he does
not have a steady income with which to replenish
his supply of such goods or purchase sufficient
quantities of beer to present to others.

As is the case with friendly drinking behavior,
the reaction of others to the assertive drinker is
also marked by deference. When a drinker begins
proclaiming what a "big man" he is, or how he is
"boss" in his house, others usually react with
profuse agreement, nodding their heads or
specifically stating that the drinker is indeed a
"good man" (see Hamer 1969). In some cases
drinking partners will review the accomplishments
of the assertive person: "He used to be councilor,"
or "Tom's a good mechanic." Or they may support
some future ambition of the actor: "Sam is going
to be the next chief." But while deference and
support are characteristic of others' reaction to
both friendly and assertive behavior, deference and
support are, I believe, given for different reasons.
In the case of the friendly drinker, the reaction
of others is dictated by the real situation of the
actors - the giver and receiver of gifts. In the
case of the response to the assertive drinker
nothing is actually given although others react
as though something had been received. Given the
value that the Naskapi place on the personal
attribute of reticence, the reaction of others to

the assertive drinker may be viewed as their way
of minimizing possible conflict, since any
disagreement to the boasts of the drinker or any
appearance of remaining indifferent to them may,
and often does, lead to physical violence. In
Interaction 3, for example, Tom reacted quickly to
squash George's suggestion that people didn't like
him, as well as agreeing with his boasts that he
spoke good English.

When drinking behavior shifts from being
assertive to being aggressive, the interaction
often resembles a contest between two protagonists,
each trying to convince others of their higher
social standing, as I believe Bill was trying to
do in his verbal attack on John in Interaction 1
(see Ridington 1968). It is also significant that
Bill's behavior on the bus is in marked contrast to
his drinking behavior when interacting with his
45-year-old step-son, Pete (Bill's second wife is
15 years older than he). Pete has rarely been
employed, living on relief and income he earns
collecting bottles to exchange for deposits at
the local grocery stores. His wife left him 10
years ago to be treated for tuberculosis, has since
refused to come home to live with him, and has had
two illegitimate children since she left home.
When Pete does drink, he often launches into a
tirade against Bill, and on one occasion had to be
forcibly restrained from attacking him. On this
occasion, Bill didn't even look at Pete, but
appeared to remain completely indifferent to the
attack. One can see that in this incident and in
Interaction 1, the person being assertive or
aggressive in the interaction is someone who is
less successful than the person to whom the
assertions are directed, or is someone who is not
able to fulfill his obligations to the other, as
Sam is unable to do in regard to Martha (see
Interaction 4).

I am proposing that in all of these interactions
persons are attempting to resolve identity struggles
in those interpersonal relations in which the
identity claimed by the person is different from the
identity attributed to him by others; that those

persons who have ready access to those goods which
serve to maintain a desired identity will, when
drinking, attempt to elicit confirmation of their
status and power through the presentation of gifts.
On the other hand, those persons who do not have
such access will, when drinking, attempt to defend
their identity threatened by their lack of access
to identity validating goods through the use of
assertive or aggressive behavior. In order to
substantiate this proposition a comparison was made
of the prevalent drinking behavior of those persons
with a steady income and a ready supply of identity
maintaining goods with the drinking behavior of
those without a steady income, or without a
substantial number of such goods. Town police and
R.C.M.P. records were used for the purpose of
determining the types of behavior characteristic
of Naskapi male drinkers, since both law
enforcement agencies do not arrest Naskapi unless
their behavior becomes assertive or aggressive.
Since virtually all Naskapi males drink but only
those who are assertive or aggressive are likely
to be arrested, we can assume that those persons
with a high frequency of arrests tend to be more
assertive drinkers, while those with a low
frequency of arrests are likely to react to
alcohol in a friendly manner. Table 6 shows the
number of arrests of those persons that are
employed full-time by the Company and those who
are, at best, part-time employees. It indicates
that the average part-time employee was arrested
three times while the average full-time employee
was arrested 1.6 times. Since there are other
sources of money income, a tabulation was also made
of the number of arrests of persons according to
gross income, but again the results are similar
(Table 7). Finally, since money itself does not
confer a desirable identity, a comparison was made
of the number of possessions owned by each household head with his number of arrests (Table 8).
Those persons who own 8 or more such items were
arrested on the average of 0.6 per person, while
those individuals with less than 8 items showed an
average of almost 4 arrests per person. In short,
the above data suggests that the form of drinking

182

behavior takes for individual Naskapi is due, not
to the amount of alcohol consumed, but to the social
position of the actor (see Bruun 1959: Honigmann
and Honigmann 1968).

To summarize, I suggest that drinking
interactions serve as a vehicle for the reordering
of interpersonal relations unsettled by economic
change; that alcohol sets the stage for persons to
make status claims, claims which can only be made
when drinking, since status claims in any other
setting would violate the desired personal attribute
of reticence. Thus, in addition to allowing persons
to present claims to a desired identity, (something
I maintain is inevitable given the changes in the
Naskapi community), alcohol also permits the
maintenance of the reticence ethic. Furthermore,
status claims made while drinking demarcate
identity struggles resulting from economic change
with the drinking interaction providing an
opportunity to resolve such struggles. Those
persons whose recent success has encouraged them
to view themselves as being entitled to a higher
status than others recognize will claim that status
while drinking by initiating presentations to others
in the form of beer or other goods. Those persons
who have seen their prestige decline relative to
specific others, that is, who do not have ready
access to identity-maintaining or confirming goods,
will attempt to resolve the discrepancy between
their self and public identity through the use of
assertive or aggressive behavior.[9] In this sense,
assertive or aggressive behavior much resembles

[9] The analysis followed here is similar in some
respects to that used by Graves (1967) in his
paper on drinking in a tri-ethnic community.
The major difference is that whereas Graves
views alcohol itself as a means of escaping the
frustration generated by lack of access to
desired goals, I am treating _drinking_ behavior
as the means by which persons attempt to cope
with the inconsistencies in interpersonal
relations generated by economic change.

Haitian spirit possession as analyzed by
Bourguignon (1965). In Haiti trance occurs when
a person is "mounted" by a spirit of loa which
itself is ranked in a status heirarchy. Others
react to the person in trance, not according to
his social standing, but according to the status
of the possessing spirit. One case cited by
Bourguignon is illuminating: "A.C.'s father is a
mild-mannered man, generally ignored and pushed
around by his kin. Yet, he has one of the most
powerful deities of the family, and when
possessed, he is given great deference by his wife,
who has left him, by his children, by his
successful half-brother, and by others.
Significantly, his possession on ceremonial
occasions appears to linger on longer than most
others" (Bourguignon 1965:53).

Economic Change and the Identity Struggle

     The Naskapi usage of alcohol is not an
isolated or unique adaptation to the consequences
of economic change. This is not to imply that all,
or even most, societies use alcohol in the way
described above - although research suggests at
least some do (see Hamer 1969) - but rather that
in all societies in which economic change follows
the lines typified by the Naskapi there will be,
in some form, an increase in the frequency of
identity struggles, and an increase in activities
or interactions which serve in that society as
identity-resolving forums. Earlier, I mentioned
that following the introduction of a money economy,
status conflict apparently increased among the
Kwakiutl, Siane, and Lugbara. I propose here to
further examine these three societies to determine
if economic change can account for this conflict.
More specifically, I will be concerned with 5
questions. First, what are the major attributes
by which a person's identity is defined in these
societies? Second, what are the behaviors or
activities in these societies by which identities
are maintained? Third, what are the avenues of

184

access to identity-maintaining goods or activities?
Fourth, how has economic change affected the
availability and distribution of those behaviors
or things which serve to define a desired identity?
And finally, has there been any change in frequency
of those activities, behaviors, or interactions
which serve as identity-resolving forums?

The potlatch is the prototype of that aspect
of economic activities that involves the
maintenance or confirmation of a social position.
Codere (1950:63) makes this clear in her
definition of the potlatch: "The Kwakiutl potlatch
is the ostentatious display and dramatic
distribution of property by the holders of a fixed,
ranked, and named social position to other
position holders. The purpose is to validate the
hereditary claim to the position and to live up to
it by maintaining its relative glory and rank
against the rivalrous claims of others." In short,
the potlatch is essentially competition for power,
a form of activity that both manifests struggles
for status and serves as an identity-resolving
forum (see Wallace and Fogelson 1965).

According to Codere, Kwakiutl property was
divided into two categories: those things used for
potlatching and "trifles" or "bad things" (Codere
1950:63-64). The former category included such
items as blankets - fur and cedar before contact,
Hudson's Bay Company blankets after contact - canoes,
and "coppers." Trifles, on the other hand, consisted
of items such as deer skins, mats, and baskets before
contact, and flour, silk scarfs, and sewing machines
after contact. Potlatch goods were given away or
destroyed at ceremonies to demonstrate the high
social position of the giver, and to humiliate a
rival. One feature of these ceremonies was a hymn
or chant sung by the giver relating his own self-
glorification and ridiculing his opponent, statements
which bring to mind the self-aggrandizing of the
assertive Naskapi drinker: "I am the great chief
who vanquishes .... I am the great chief who makes
people ashamed .... You are my subordinates .... Oh,
I laugh at them, I sneer at them who empty boxes (of

185

treasure)in their houses, their potlatch houses,
their inviting houses that are full only of hunger
.... I am the only great tree, I the chief ...."
(Benedict 1959:272).

Before contact access to those goods which
were potlatched, and hence access to a desired
identity, was determined by inherited social rank,
wealthy persons apparently being heads of extended
families who held custodianship over the goods of
the group (Drucker 1966:142). However, with the
introduction of a wage-money economy two changes
occurred; first, goods used for potlatching changed
from locally produced items (cedar, blankets, canoes)
to Hudson's Bay Company products, most notably
blankets. Second, the means of access to potlatch
goods changed from inherited social rank to
activities such as hunting, fishing and wage labor,
that is, activities through which money could be
obtained (Codere 1950:33). With these changes
persons who because of a low inherited social rank
were aboriginally unable to potlatch, and hence
claim a favored identity, could now improve their
positions by obtaining money, purchasing blankets
at the Hudson's Bay Company store, and potlatching.
On the other hand, those persons who before contact
had exclusive access to potlatch goods would now
have their social rank threatened by those, who by
the new criteria for obtaining potlatch goods, could
now make status claims. The result would be an
increase in identity struggles wrought by the
increase in social mobility. As Codere then points
out, these changes were accompanied by an increase
in potlatch activity (1950:96).

Among the Siane, a group of tribes in the New
Guinea Highlands who until the 1930's and '40's were
virtually untouched by Western society, the most
desired identity is that of "big man." While
technically anyone could attain this status - the
attributes being skill in oratory, a mature age,
procreation of children and wealth - such persons
are usually yarafo, senior members of the various
generations within a lineage. The village headman,
or bosboi, is usually a senior member of the senior
generation within a lineage.

186

To maintain or acquire a desirable identity
among the Siane, a person must have access to
subsistence goods such as sweet potatoes and taros.
However, for a person to raise in status and power,
to become a "big man," he must have access to goods,
such as pigs, which are involved in exchanges
between clans on such occasions as marriage, birth,
or death. When such goods are received from other
clans on such occasions they are first distributed
to the bosboi of each lineage, who then
redistributes them to others, thus maintaining his
high status (Salisbury 1962:101). Technically
anyone who has a number of valuables may increase
his prestige by making presentations, but the power
of the "big man" is solidified by the fact that
it is they who lend pigs to young men to be used
as brideprice, and the debtor cannot enter into
clan councils until the loan is repaid. So while
a person could claim a desired identity, this
identity could be confirmed only when he was free
from his obligations to the "big men."

There were two stages in the change of the Siane
economy. The first occurred in the form of sporadic
contacts with Europeans, most often government
officials, most of these contacts being made by "big
men" serving as guides. For their labor these
persons received goods classified by the Siane as
valuables, with the result that the power of the
"big men" increased further. An additional
consequence of this initial contact was an inflation
of brideprices. Those groups living nearest
European settlements, who hence had greatest access
to European goods, would obtain these valuables and
offer more in payment for women to groups living
at a greater distance from the settlements.
However, the outlying groups from which the women
were obtained soon experienced a shortage of
marriageable females, although they quickly became
rich in valuables which they then used to pay
greater prices for women from even more outlying
settlements. As a consequence of this increase in
the number of valuables (which were distributed
in the same manner as before the increase), the
"big man" had greater access to valuables while
young men were forced to borrow even more pigs in

order to pay the now inflated prices for women. In other words, the wealth and power of the "big men" grew, while the power and status of the young men remained static (Salisbury 1962:117).

However, this increased status differential between persons lasted only until the second stage of economic change, the introduction of indentured labor. Young men could then go to work on the coast and return with money which was classified as a valuable. This development potentially enabled young men to free themselves more quickly from their obligations to "big men" since they could now use their wages to pay off their debts incurred in obtaining a wife. Put another way, the criteria by which a Siane could rise in status and join the clan councils changed from the production of pigs - a lengthy process - to obtaining of money through indentured labor - a far speedier process.[10] One would then expect that the young men would use their newly found riches to make status claims through ceremonial exchanges, claims which they were unable to make under the old system, and that the "big men," that is, those operating under the old power distribution system, would see their status threatened by these new developments, and in turn, initiate ceremonial exchanges. This proposition is, I believe, substantiated by the fact that, as with the Kwakiutl, these changes in the economy effected an increase in ceremonial activities (Salisbury 1962:107).

The Lugbara are a Sudanic-speaking people in Uganda and what was the Belgian Congo. Their elementary social, political and economic unit is

[10] My analysis of the effects of economic change differs somewhat at this point from Salisbury's analysis, for he states that indentured labor did not reduce the status differential between "big men" and others (1962:131-132). I am assuming that since young men could free themselves from their obligations sooner, that the status differential was, in effect, reduced (Salisbury 1962:156).

a group consisting of a cluster of elementary or
joint families, which Middleton refers to as a
"family cluster" (1966:142). This unit is a
patrilineage varying in composition from a dozen
to as many as 150 persons. The leader, or elder,
of these groups is selected for his position on the
basis of his senior genealogical status in the
lineage, and, ideally, has complete control over
members of his family cluster (Middleton 1966:142).
Each of these social units is further divided into
status grades, a person's position of these grades
being determined by his age and position of
authority in the joint family. However, these
status grades are extremely flexible, and there is
periodic tension between persons who wish to
increase their authority and prestige and those
who wish to maintain their authority. These
identity struggles may be resolved in one of two
ways. The first involves what Middleton terms
ghost invocation, and the second involves
accusations of witchcraft.[11] When a Lugbara makes
a status claim, and any member of the family
cluster may attempt to exert authority, the claim
must be legitimized by the senior members of the
lineage, who, in turn, must seek statements from
the dead ancestors to determine whether the person
making the status claim is entitled to a higher
ranking in the group. This they do by communicating
with the dead through specters, omens, dreams, or,
most commonly, through oracles (Middleton 1966:145).
When someone's claim to a more desirable identity
is confirmed by the dead, it follows that those of
once equal status to the claimant lose prestige.
Their means of rectifying this loss of status
relative to the claimant is to level a witchcraft
accusation against their rival, accusing him of
obtaining confirmation of his new identity through
witchcraft. If he is able to convince others of
his charge his rival is, as Middleton puts it,
"cast out from the everyday system of authority"
(1966:148).

[11] While Middleton distinguishes between these
two processes, they appear to be complimentary
aspects of the same phenomenon, with the native
term - ole rozv - applying to both.

The aboriginal economy of the Lugbara was
organized around the family cluster with the elder
being invested with the authority to distribute the
goods of the group - grain, iron objects and
livestock (Middleton 1962:575). The changes in this
economy, as they did with the Siane, occurred in
two stages. The first was marked by the Belgian
practice of setting up chiefs who were paid tribute
in the form of cattle and grain. These chiefs then
used their earnings to acquire wives and large
families, signs of high status, which increased the
status differential between them and those not
having the same favored access to these goods, a
circumstance parallel to that existing among the
Siane when "big men" acquired virtually exclusive
access to European goods. The second phase of
economic change occurred with the introduction of
migrant labor and money. Before this change a
young man could move up the status grades only by
first marrying, which changed his status from
"youth" to "big youth," and then producing
children, increasing his status to "man behind"
(behind more senior men). This he could do only
by acquiring bridewealth from his elders. But with
the acquisition of money he could hasten his
increase in status by using the money to buy wives,
or to buy beer for his seniors, becoming less
dependent upon his elders in the process. In other
words, as with the Kwakiutl and Siane, economic
change effected a situation where the power of
traditional authorities would be threatened by the
newly acquired status of those having access to
new status-conferring goods, as well as initiating
a scramble for power among those who have access to
such goods. One would then expect an increase in
identity struggles, Middleton noting that
accompanying these changes in the economy there
was an increase in the incidence of witchcraft
accusations (1960:228).

Summary and Conclusions

The arguments presented in this paper may be
summarized as follows: First, Naskapi drinking

190

interactions represent identity-resolving forums
defining identity struggles and permitting persons
to make status claims or defend an identity
threatened by a lack of access to identity-
maintaining goods. Second, the form drinking behavior
takes among the Naskapi is determined by the social
identity of the participants in such interactions;
those persons experiencing success at wage earning
will attempt to gain confirmation of what they see
to be their increased status through the use of the
friendly reaction to alcohol, while those who have
been less successful manifest assertive or
aggressive behavior when drinking to defend an
identity threatened by their lack of access to
identity-maintaining goods. Finally, Naskapi
drinking interactions represent but one form of a
class of phenomena that accompany economic change.
Given a situation where economic change results in
an increase of "free-floating power," and a change
in the means of access to things, persons, or
behaviors which serve to maintain a desired identity,
there will be an increase in identity struggles.
These struggles will stem from either a threat to
the power of established authority, contention for
power among those for whom the status system has
opened up, or from the uneven distribution of
goods among those of once equal status. Further,
the increase in identity struggles will produce an
increase in the frequency of those activities or
behaviors which serve in a given society as identity-
resolving forums. The extent that such forums
permanently resolve identity struggles, however, is
another matter. A person may give a potlatch, make
a witchcraft accusation, or become assertive when
drinking attempting to resolve a contradiction
between his view of himself and the way others view
him, but may in the process threaten others who, in
turn, may feel it necessary to give a potlatch, or
make a witchcraft accusation. So while a person
may resolve, at least temporarily, discrepancies in
some of his social relationships, the whole process
may lead to a steady spiral of identity struggles
for the community at large, and hence lead to a
steady increase in the frequency of those activities
that serve as identity-resolving forums.

I began by drawing a parallel between those conditions that promote millenarian movements, and those that promote increases in identity-resolving forums. It appears, however, that there are at least two differences in the antecedents of the two types of phenomena. First, in millenarian activities all participants are denied access to identity-confirming information (see Wallace 1970), whereas when there is an increase in the frequency of identity-resolving forums only some members of the group are denied such access. Second, in millenarian activities the reference point from which participants measure their identity tends to be external to the group partaking of such activities. Put another way, the reference point tends to be the dominant group (see Burridge 1969:41). On the other hand, when one finds an increase in the frequency of occurrence of identity-resolving forums, one finds that the reference point for measuring identities lies within the group. If a New Guinea native includes within his field of competition the Whites he has recently come into contact with, then his perceived failure at such competition will likely lead him to millenarian activities and beliefs. If, on the other hand, his field of competition includes only those of his own society or group then he will likely take recourse in competition manifested in those activities that serve in his society as identity-resolving forums. The Naskapi, for example, appear to be competing only with other Naskapi, and not, as yet, with Euro-Canadians or, for that matter, the more acculturated Montagnais, a proposition that is substantiated by the fact that only rarely do they engage in assertive or aggressive behavior with non-members of their community.

Finally, the hypothesis presented in this paper suggests we further examine economic aid programs, for, rather than introducing economic or social stability, they may, in fact, promote social instability and conflict by the mass introduction of new goods and resources, or by changing the means of access of persons to goods and activities vital in identity maintenance. If this is indeed the case we need to be able to determine the form this

192

interpersonal conflict will take, and what cultural
mechanisms will be used to resolve it.

Table 1

Sources of Naskapi Income for the
Period Jan. 1965 through June 1966

Wage Labor

Source	Amount
Iron Ore Company	$115,596
Town	2,351
Guide	2,250
Trapping (est.)	1,150
Other	2,126
Total	$123,473

Government Relief

Source	Amount
Relief	$33,052
Old Age Insurance	7,740
Needy Mother Allowance	1,350
Clothing Allowance	11,200
Total	$53,342

TOTAL INCOME $176,815

Table 2

Days Worked and Number of Naskapi Part-
Time Workers from Jan. 1962 through June 1966

	1962	1963	1964
Number of Days Worked	1442	701	227
Number of Men Employed Part-time	20	14	6

	1965	1966 (through June)
Number of Days Worked	1606	377
Number of Men Employed Part-time	21	12

Table 3

Range of Household Incomes From
January 1965 through June 1966

Income	Number of Households
Over $10,000	2
$8,000 to $9,999	4
$6,000 to $7,999	8
$4,000 to $5,999	5
$2,000 to $3,999	13
Under $1,999	5

Table 4

Allocation of Naskapi Income Among
Categories 2, 3, and 4

Category 2	Number of Households
Washing Machine	24
Sewing Machine	9
Freezer	18
Refrigerator	1
Electric Iron	13

Category 3	Number of Households
Canoe	9
Outboard Motor	4
Rod and Reel	7
Gun	34

Category 4	Number of Households
Television	19
Radio	18
Record Player	15
Camera	11

Table 5

Size of Drinking Groups

Number in Groups*	Number of Times Observed
2	26
3	17
4	6
5	6
6	2
Total Number Of Observations	57

*The size of drinking groups did vary with ti▮ with the above number referring to when the g▮ was first observed.

198

Table 6

Percentage of Arrests of Naskapi
Able-Bodied Men According to
Employment Status

Number of Arrests	Part-Time Employees	Full-Time Employees
zero	11%	33%
1	11	42
2	21	8
3	23	0
4	9	0
5	9	0
6	9	8
7	6	8
Total Number	(34)	(12)
Total Number of Arrests	102	20
Mean	3.0	1.6

199

Table 7

Percentage of Arrests of Naskapi
Able-Bodied Men According to
Gross Income

Number of Arrests	Income Category	
	$0-1,999	$2,000-3,999
zero	0%	0%
1	28	18
2	17	9
3	28	9
4	11	28
5	6	28
6	0	9
7	11	0
Total Number	(18)	(11)
Total Number of Arrests	53	40
Mean	2.9	3.6

Number of Arrests	Income Category	
	$4,000-5,999	Over $6,000
zero	75%	25%
1	0	42
2	0	17
3	25	0
4	0	0
5	0	0
6	0	17
7	0	0
Total Number	(4)	(12)
Total Number of Arrests	3	21
Mean	0.8	1.7

200

Table 8

Percentage of Arrests of Able-Bodied Household Heads According to Number of Possessions*

Number of Arrests	Number of Possessions		
	0-4	5-8	Over 8
zero	10%	0%	44%
1	10	12	56
2	10	25	0
3	10	0	0
4	10	25	0
5	20	12	0
6	20	0	0
7	10	25	0
Total Number	(10)	(8)	(9)
Total Number of Arrests	39	32	5
Mean	3.9	4.0	0.6

*Possessions used to formulate Table 8 include: washing machine, clothes dryer, refrigerator, freezer, sewing machine, electric iron, electric stove, electric razor, radio, television, camera, store-purchased sofa, store-purchased armchair, and phonograph.

REFERENCES

Barth, Fredrik
    1969 "Pathan Identity and Its Maintenance",
    In Fredrik Barth, (ed), Ethnic Groups and
    Boundaries. 117-134. Boston: Little, Brown,
    and Company.

Benedict, Ruth
    1959 "Anthropology and the Abnormal." In
    Margaret Mead, (ed), An Anthropologist at
    Work. 262-283. Boston: Houghton Mifflin Co.

Berreman, Gerald D.
    1956 "Drinking Patterns of the Aleuts."
    Quarterly Journal of Studies on Alcohol
    17:503-515.

Bourguignon, Erika
    1965 "The Theory of Spirit Possession."
    Melford E. Spiro, (ed), Context and Meaning
    in Cultural Anthropology. 39-60. New York:
    The Free Press.

Bruun, Kettil
    1959 "Significance of Role and Norms in the
    Small Drinking Group for Individual
    Behavioral Changes While Drinking."
    Quarterly Journal of Studies on Alcohol 20:
    53-64.

Burridge, Kenelm
    1969 New Heaven, New Earth: A Study of
    Millenarian Activities. New York: Schocken Books

Burton, Roger V. and John W. M. Whiting
    1965 "The Absent Father and Cross-Sex
    Identity." In William A. Lessa and Evon Z.
    Vogt, (ed), A Reader in Comparative Religion.
    610-614. New York: Harper and Row.

Codere, Helen
    1950 Fighting With Property. Monographs of
    the American Ethnological Society, No. 18.
    Seattle: University of Washington Press.

Cohen, Yedhudi A.
    1964 "The Establishment of Identity in a
        Social Nexus: The Special Case of Initiation
        Ceremonies and Their Relation to Value and
        Legal Systems." American Anthropologist 66:
        529-552.

Curley, Richard T.
    1967 "Drinking Patterns of the Mescalero
        Apache." Quarterly Journal of Studies on
        Alcohol 28:116-131.

Drucker, Phillip
    1966 "Rank, Wealth, and Kinship in Northwest
        Coast Society." In Tom McFeat, (ed), Indians
        of the North Pacific Coast. 134-146. Seattle:
        University of Washington Press.

Evans-Pritchard, E. E.
    1940 The Nuer. London: Oxford University
        Press.

Foster, George M.
    1967 "The Dyadic Contract: A Model for the
        Social Structure of a Mexican Peasant
        Village." In Jack M. Potter, May Diaz, and
        George M. Foster, (ed), Peasant Society: A
        Reader. 213-230. Boston: Little Brown and
        Co.

Goffman, Irving
    1956 "The Nature of Deference and Demeanor."
        American Anthropologist 58:473-502.

Goodenough, Ward H.
    1963 Cooperation in Change. New York: Russell
        Sage Foundation.

Graves, Theodore D.
    1967 "Acculturation Access, and Alcohol in a
        Tri-Ethnic Community." American Anthropologist
        69:306-321.

Hallowell, A. Irving
    1955 Culture and Experience. Philadelphia:
        University of Pennsylvania Press.

Hamer, John
   1965   "Acculturation, Stress, and the Functions
   of Alcohol Among the Forest Potawatomi."
   Quarterly Journal of Studies on Alcohol 26:
   285-301.
   1969   "Guardian Spirits, Alcohol, and Cultural
   Defense Mechanisms." Anthropologica 11:215-
   241.

Honigmann, John J.
   1964   "Indians of Nouveau Quebec." In Jean
   Malaurie and Jacques Rousseau, (ed), Le
   Nouveau Quebec: Contribution a L'Etude
   de L'Occupation Humaine. Bibliotheque
   Arctique et Antarctique 2. 315-373. Paris.
   Mouton and Co.
Honigmann, John J. and Irma Honigmann
   1968   "Alcohol in a Canadian Northern Town."
   Paper presented at the 1968 Meeting of the
   Canadian Sociology and Anthropology
   Association.

Horton, Donald
   1967   "The Functions of Alcohol in Primitive
   Societies." In Clyde Kluckhohn, Henry
   Murry and David Schneider, (ed), Personality
   in Nature, Society, and Culture. 680-690.
   New York: Alfred A. Knopf.

Laing, R. D.
   1962   The Self and Others. Chicago: Quadrangle
   Books.

Leach, Edmund R.
   1965   "Two Essays Concerning the Symbolic
   Representation of Time." In William A. Lessa
   and Evon Z. Vogt, (ed), Reader in Comparative
   Religion. 241-249. New York: Harper and Row.

Leacock, Eleanor
   1958   "Status Among the Montagnais-Naskapi of
   Labrador." Ethnohistory 5:200-209.

MacAndrew, Craig and Robert B. Edgerton
   1969   Drunken Comportment. Chicago: Aldine
   Publishing Co.

Mauss, Marcel
1967 The Gift. New York: W. W. Norton and Co.

Mandelbaum, David G.
1965 "Alcohol and Culture." Current
Anthropology 6:281-294.

Mead, George H.
1934 Mind, Self and Society. Chicago:
University of Chicago Press.

Middleton, John
1960 Lugbara Religion. London: Oxford
University Press.
1962 "Trade and Markets Among the Lugbara of
Uganda." In Paul Bohannan and George Dalton,
(ed), Markets in Africa. 561-578. Evanston:
Northwestern University Press.
1966 "The Resolution of Conflict Among the
Lugbara of Uganda." In Mark Swartz, Victor
W. Turner, and Arthur Tuden (eds), Political
Anthropology. 141-154. Aldine Publishing Co.

Miller, Daniel R.
1963 "The Study of Social Relationships:
Situation, Identity, and Social Interaction."
In Sigmund Koch, (ed), Psychology: A Study
of Science. Vol. 5:639-737. New York:
McGraw Hill Book Co.

Peacock, James L.
1968 Rites of Modernization. Chicago: University
of Chicago Press.

Preston, Richard J.
Ms "Reticence and Self-Expression in a Cree
Community." Unpublished Manuscript.

Ridington, Robin
1968 "The Medicine Fight: An Instrument of
Political Process Among the Beaver Indians."
American Anthropologist 70:1152-1160.

Robbins, Richard H.
1972 "Identity, Culture and Behavior." In
John J. Honigmann, (ed), Handbook of Social
and Cultural Anthropology. Rand McNally.

Rogers, Edward
    1965 "Leadership Among the Indians of Eastern
    Subarctic Canada." Anthropologica 13:263-284.

Shalins, Marshall D.
    1965 "On the Sociology of Primitive Exchange."
    In M. Banton, (ed), The Relevance of Models
    for Social Anthropology. A.S.A. Monographs,
    No. 1. 139-236. London: Tavistock
    Publications.

Schwartz, Gary and Don Merten
    1968 "Social Identity and Expressive Symbols:
    The Meaning of an Initiation Ritual."
    American Anthropologist 70:1117-1131.

Simmel, Georg
    1950 The Sociology of Georg Simmel.
    Translated and edited by Kurt H. Wolff.
    Glencoe: The Free Press.

Simmons, Ozzie G.
    1959 "Drinking Patterns and Interpersonal
    Performance in a Peruvian Mestizo Community."
    Quarterly Journal of Studies on Alcohol. 20:
    103-111.

Speck, Frank
    1931 "Montagnais-Naskapi Bands and Early Eskimo
    Distribution in the Labrador Peninsula."
    American Anthropologist 33:557-600.

Szwed, John F.
    1966 "Gossip, Drinking and Social Control:
    Consensus and Communication in a Newfoundland
    Parish." Ethnology 5:434-441.

Thomas, Elizabeth
    1959 The Harmless People. New York: Alfred A.
    Knopf.

Turner, Lucien M.
    1889-90 Ethnology of the Ungava District, Hudson
    Bay Territory. Eleventh Annual Report of the
    Bureau of American Ethnology.

Turner, Victor W.
    1957   Schism and Continuity in an African
           Society. Manchester: Manchester University
           Press.

Veblen, Thorsten Bunde
    1931   The Theory of the Leisure Class. New
           York: Random House.

Wallace, Anthony F. C.
    1966   Religion: An Anthropological View. New
           York: Random House
    1967   "Identity Processes in Personality and
           in Culture." In Richard Jessor and Seymour
           Feshback, (eds) Cognition, Personality, and
           Clinical Psychology. 62-89. San Francisco:
           Jossey-Bass, Inc.
    1970   "Review, New Heaven, New Earth."
           American Anthropologist 72:1103-1104.

Wallace, Anthony F. C. and Raymond D. Fogelson
    1965   "The Identity Struggle." Ivan
           Boxzormenyi-Nagy and James L. Framo (eds)
           in Intensive Family Therapy. 365-407.
           New York: Harper and Row.

Whittaker, James O.
    1963   "Alcohol and the Standing Rock Sioux
           Tribe: Psycho-dynamic and Cultural Factors
           in Drinking." Quarterly Journal of Studies
           on Alcohol 24:80-90.

CHAPTER VIII

Indians on Skid Row - Alcohol in the Life of

Urban Migrants

by

Hugh Brody

The principal objective of this study was originally conceived as an account and exploration of drinking and drunkenness among urban migrant Indians. It was evident from the outset that field work for such a project would have to be centered on bars and street corners of a skid row. While the emphasis was committedly sociological, it was anticipated that the background to Indian drinking lay in the directions of stress and adjustment contingent upon migration. Thus to anticipate the form of the explanation, if only as an emphasis to the work, was to follow the general directions of former studies of heavy drinking; that is, to incline towards a perspective which places drinking in proximity with stress.[1]

In dealing with the skid row context, this view emphasises the loneliness and rootlessness of the milieu. Moreover, it enjoins a view of the drinker which identifies him more with the psychopathic or chronic alcoholic, isolated by the nature of his personality if not by the consequences of his addiction. Skid rows are associated by outsiders with stress and individual isolation. Theories of Indian drinking might be expected to concentrate on the isolation of the Indian within Canadian society, and the difficulties of making an adjustment to urban life. Heavy drinking

Reprinted from Indians on Skid Row, 1971 by permission of the author and Canada Department of Indian Affairs and Northern Development

[1] Examples of studies which emphasise the stress in relation to drinking: Washburne 1961, Clairmont 1963, Heath 1962, Berreman 1964.

placates stress, and skid row offers an environment within which such placation is conventionalised.

But to drink on skid row, like drinking almost everywhere else, is to drink within a community, and it is to drink with members of the community who offer a welcome and a way of life. This way of life provides more than recurrent inebriation, simple forgetfulness, or the palliating effects of alcoholic stupor. Drinking is basic to the community, but it is essential that emphasis be given to the community itself. The gratification of skid row life are inevitably going to turn on that community form -- it is the factor which both attracts and retains the migrant. One key question thus becomes: What has the community to offer? In answering this question it is important to isolate the discussion of gratification from the issues of stress at least at a theoretical level. We must begin this report by turning away from any commitment to view the Indian's drinking as a direct function of misfortune or demoralisation, and towards the possibility that skid row is able to offer the Indian a more gratifying life than either the relative sobrieties and exclusiveness of middle-class White Canada, or the isolation, accompanied by the sense of weakness, of the native reserves.

Composition of the Community

To drink on skid row is to enter a heterogeneous society. It is a society composed of Whites as well as Indians, more permanent residents as well as migrants. The permanent White residents are predominantly alcoholics, with a few exceptions among the younger men, who thrive on some aspect of petty crime or prostitution. Migrant Whites are almost entirely young men who work for a few months in the North, spending time between jobs, and money they have earned, on skid row. The Whites are predominantly male, and the few exceptions are to be found among the young prostitutes. The Indian residents are all ages, most types, and both sexes:

210

many of the older men and women are alcohol-
dependent, and the younger people also drink very
heavily. But as well as these Indian residents,
there are also groups of migrants, for the most part
young, who have come into town for a visit or to
find a job.

It is the Indian groups which concern us here,
but they are divisible into those who do and those
who do not drink in the bar. This division is largely
a consequence of age -- bars do not allow entry to
minors -- but many young people have acquired
adequate if not legal identification, and once they
have become known to barmen and bouncers no doubts
as to their age are raised. In the bars and coffee-
houses the minors are conspicuous and important.
Details of their life will be given later, but at
this point they serve to illustrate the fact that
skid row is more than bars and drinking: the bar
frequentors and the minors are quite evidently part
of the same community. For all the elements -- with
the possible exception of the few isolate White
alcoholics -- to drink on skid row is to come into
contact with more than a bar stool; is to imbibe
and enjoy more than alcoholic beverages.

The Bars

The social quality of skid row bars reflects
their community context. In general, bars in other
parts of the city are quiet: a group may collect
around a table, but such groups are usually small
(rarely more than four people) and do not interact
with other groups. Customers in these bars do not
move around freely; much playing of bar games is
unusual; the isolation of each group of drinkers,
the relative quiet and calm, the lack of movement,
all tend to emphasise the separation which exists
between the bar and the community or area in which
the bar is located. Entering such a bar one enters
a milieu which neither connects with the street
nor encourages any contact between the drinkers
themselves. Bars outside the skid row, that is
to say, tend to be subdued and individuating.

211

In each respect the skid row bars have qualities precisely opposite to that norm.

Groups around tables tend to be large - very often eight or nine drinkers crowded together, and always ready to make room for others. More important, it is frequently impossible to determine where a group ends: three or four groups merge into one another, joining conversation and exchanging drinks. Also, people are continually moving from one table to another. On a crowded night, each of the skid row bars tends to become a single, if amorphous, group of highly mobile participants. It is still the case that the waiters bring drinks to the tables, but there are always many people moving about freely, both between tables and in and out of the bar itself. The atmosphere of such bars is animated, not at all restrained or subdued. Shuffleboards are often the centre of enthusiastic competition, display and social mixing.

Similarly, the vitality and communality of such a bar includes close incorporation of both the street into the bar and the bar into the street. People gather outside the bar; passers-by are drawn into conversation and banter; 'regulars' are on the look out for friends to drink with. A large majority of the drinkers live or stay in the neighbourhood, and are in no hurry to make their ways home. Also, cafes and restaurants adjacent to the bars are included in something of a circuit: an evening's drinking would involve visits to most of the skid row cafes and bars.

Two levels of integration - of drinkers in the bars, and of bars in the neighbourhood - are thus strikingly contrary to the individuating and isolating qualities of bars outside skid row. It is not possible to spend any time in skid row bars without becoming implicated in this solidarity, and any person who drinks there with regularity can quickly establish himself in a network of friends and companions.

Of course, this applies most particularly to the Indian drinkers, and there tends to be a divisiveness within the bars which keeps the Indians and non-Indians in somewhat discrete groupings. So flexible are these groupings, however, that the forceful integrative quality is more apparent than racial isolationism. The relationship between Indian and non-Indian drinkers will be discussed later, but it is necessary to note at this stage in the discussion how the bar life affects the new migrant.

All migrants are aware that skid row is where they will find the greatest density of Indians. In any case, the skid row of each city has a substantial reputation -- for licence, excitement, and the chance of money. This reputation makes skid row a natural starting point for the impecunious new arrival; if he is Indian the reputation is almost certainly reinforced by the contacts he expects to have among the skid row Indians. Most of the migrants on arriving at the city already intend making their way to skid row, and expect to find a specific relative or friend there. In fact, when the newcomer does arrive downtown, he probably discovers that his contact is not to be found with quite the ease he had anticipated. In such a situation, the migrant naturally goes into the bars, and there seeks out his friends and relatives.

Once in the bar, however, he does not really need his friend and relative, for he will find quick acceptance, and within an hour of drinking will have become integrated into a group of drinkers. This group will be of Indians, and all will be curious about where he comes from, what language he speaks, and where he has been. In most cases, there is sufficient shared experience for them to strike up conversation. These friends keep the newcomer with them, will take him from one bar to another, and he will quickly come to meet a large number of others like himself.

This experience confirms the migrant's expectations of city life, and holds him in the bar for maintenance of the friendships he established at first. The solidarity which the bar offers protects the migrant from the isolation which

213

cities otherwise tend to involve, but also renders
non-bar life of the city relatively inaccessible
and certainly frightening. At the integrated
community bar the Indian can avoid the worst features
of migration, and at the same time find ready
acceptance in a vivacious community.

The Cafe and Street Corner

Bars stay open twelve continuous hours each day,
but some open earlier than others in the morning.
By taking a first drink at the first bar to open,
and a last drink at the last to close, an
enthusiastic drinker could spend at least thirteen
hours of every day, six days in the week, in the
bars. In fact, even the heaviest drinkers spread
their time between bars and other places. There
are a number of reasons for this. First, bars only
sell beer; second, those who seek interaction with
minors must do so outside the bar; third, both
sleep and unconsciousness are causes for ejection
from bars, and many heavy drinkers like to lie down
and sleep where they drink; fourth, the street is an
important place for contacts, and when a drinker
is running short of money, there are always
encounters on street corners which can lead to the
purchase of a bottle of wine.

It is around wine drinking that such extra bar
contact tends to be built. Many drinkers converge
on the liquor store, making their way from the bars
to the store hoping to meet others who will either
subsidise a bottle of wine or will choose to join
them in a larger purchase. In this way small groups
form, and these groups must find a place where they
can drink in secrecy -- it is illegal to consume
liquor on the street or in any unlicenced public
place, and the bars themselves do not allow the
consumption of any beverage on their premises which
has not been bought there. In empty ruined houses,
along quiet alleyways, or in the back garden of a
friend's house, these groups gather. They are very
tight circles, their intimacy enjoined by the covert

214

nature of the activity as well as by the need to be
within reach of the circulating bottle. Moreover,
they are quite silent groups, amicable and
unaggressive in a feeling of solidarity but without
much talk or activity. The sense of unity which
such drinking fosters must be stressed: it was
evident in _every_ such group I encountered. Also, it
is in these groups that the Indians can sometimes
be heard singing their native songs; the formation
of real friendships is much more a quality of the
secret wine circle than the bar. This means that
the circle provides an excellent location for the
planning of crimes, for it secures both the bonds
between the participants which a combined crime
requires, as well as privacy in which to make plans.

Often a member of such a circle passes out,
and others will continue drinking while he recovers
consciousness. In these concealed places there is
no anxiety about passing out, and no fear of either
legal intervention or reproach by friends. Indeed,
it is in this form that city drinking approximates
most closely to the sprees documented in much of
the literature dealing with drinking on the
reserves.

The cafes are usually frequented by drinkers
who are completely impecunious or suffering from
dire after-effects; the two conditions tend to
accompany one another. As in the case of the bars,
these drinkers are continually moving from one cafe
to another, lingering on the street corners between.
Many of the cafes have a Juke-Box and it is not at
all unusual for a few people to gather around it,
discussing each tune with keen animation, and
occasionally dancing if the proprietor allows.

In these cafes and also on the street corners,
the same conditions and atmosphere pertain as were
noted in the bars: talkativeness, mobility,
integration between people and between atmospheres
of street and cafe. Indeed, given the degree of
drunkenness attained by almost all during the
previous hours and days, this vitality is as
impressive as it is apparent.

Even when the bars are open, therefore, drinking and communality both take place outside them. But it is when the bars are closed that the cafe, street-corner, and other locations become especially important, if somewhat less conspicuous. At closing time in the bars many drinkers make their way to the liquor store to buy a supply for the night, or to a coffee bar to talk -- in the hope of finding access to another drink. In both places -- liquor store and cafe -- new groups are formed. It is these new groups which tend to include the minors and the girls. Many of the groups turn into parties, in hotel rooms, rented rooms, or local homes. In any event the activity of skid row is not terminated by the closing of the liquor outlets. At night the people from the bars can join with the minors as well as with others who are relatively peripheral to the skid row world itself: wives at home; acquaintances with convenient rooms (if different life-styles); whites who have come to the more notorious coffee bars out of curiosity or with hopes of finding a prostitute.

These parties take place every night, though it is at the week-ends when they are most numerous and frenetic. They are complementary to the bar drinking, less public but just as integral to the community life. They are also characterised by much excited and extroverted behaviour: at the parties sexual liaisons have a more explicit part; there are few, if any, restrictions of the kind imposed by bartenders preoccupied by the maintenance of customary proprietaries and a minimum of order.

On Sundays, when the bars are closed, stock-piling ensures some continuation of parties and drinking, but for the most part the more regular skid row people are obliged to use the bootlegger. The bootlegging involves much visiting around the neighbourhood, and in many homes a group of drinkers sit around a kitchen table with a bottle of wine. It must be noted that these Sunday walks and visits are enjoyed for their own sake, and are

not merely hysterically alcohol-dependent guests
despairing for a drink. Seeking out a drink is the
form social contacts assume, and these are enjoyed
even when the guest is unsuccessful.

This is further evidenced by the role of the
cafes on Sundays. Several of them stay open, and
are frequented by many people who wish to sit and
talk and sober up. The community does not expire
with the closure of the bars. Equally it must be
emphasized that there are activities in the skid
row district which have no direct relation to the
consumption of alcohol. There are numerous billiard
saloons, cinemas, a dance-hall and shops, all of
which are much patronized. It is therefore quite
false to suppose that activity on skid row is
confined to the chronically isolated and depressed.

Alcohol and Community

To drink on skid row is to do more than drink.
This kind of drinking, stretching as it does over
a long period, entails residence in the neighbourhood,
with the attendant need for a place to stay, for
food, and for ready cash. The needs of these
drinkers are not the minimal needs of the clinical
alcoholic: conversation and the pursuit of sexual
conquest are elements in this as in other forms of
life. The gratifications of the life here extend
beyond the pleasure or palliations of drunkennes. To
understand the Indian skid row drinker, it is
essential to understand both the fullness and
limitations of the community. There are accordingly
two contextual aspects: the drinker in skid row,
and skid row in terms of the norms and institutions
of middle class white Canadian life. These contexts
must be related in any attempt to discover what is
happening; neither the individual drinker nor the
skid row community as a whole exist in vacuo, aspire
as they may to do so.

It has frequently been pointed out that the
hardened alcoholic is unable to function without his

daily consumption of alcoholic beverage. This leads
the alcoholic into whatever drinking mode he can
secure, be it in the thick of a vibrant community or
in the solitude of his own room. It is not the
purpose of this report to deny that there are among
skid row Indians such chronic cases of alcoholism.
But the insistence upon community in this chapter
is intended to reflect a vitality which could not
exist if isolated drinking were widespread. It is
fair to say that the absence of community would
precipitate an end to the drinking. Indeed, such a
hypothesis is barely conceivable, since the
community and the drinking are indissolubly linked.
For a majority of the drinkers, to drink is to be
part of the community, and to be part of the
community is to drink. Chronic alcoholism has a
minimal place.

The literature dealing with the use of alcohol
among the North American Indians has so
preponderantly concerned the situation of the
reserve as to render a discussion of that literature
in danger of irrelevance. It is central to this
report that the predicament of the skid row Indian
is distinctive; its relationship to the reserve is
obviously important, but the urban milieu presents
a new context, and the skid row involves a
distinctive form of life as well as a unique
relationship to Canadian society as a whole. It
can be noted, however, that the social dimension
to drinking, and the correlative absence of the
individual alcoholic has been remarked upon in a
number of studies of reserve drinking. Lemert, for
example, writes: "The most careful inquiries failed
to uncover a single instance of an Indian who drank
in solitide".[2]

But Lemert also remarks that "In our culture,
persons who get drunk usually can be presumed to
have conflicts or tensions which they are seeking
to escape or narcotise; but this cannot be presumed

[2] Lemert 1954 p. 310.

218

for peoples who customarily get drunk".[3]   Thus the
reserve drinking is both community oriented and
frequent. But in the reserve this observation
naturally leads the sociologist into a comparison
between the past or aboriginal social structures and
those of today, in the belief that such comparison
will bring to light the crucial change for which the
persistent use of alcohol is functional. Thus, for
example, one sociologist writes: "As for function it
is evident that in Mescalero, drinking serves as a
substitute for the various forms of institutionalised
activity and group relationships that have been lost
to the Apache during a hundred years of deculturation".[4]
Similar considerations lead Edward Dozier to say: "I
believe that group or gang-type drinking among
Indians represents a greater problem in terms of crime
rate and community disorganization than addicted
drinking".[5]

     Thus, the view of Indian drinking which has
dominated the literature suggests that drinking is
intelligible by use of a model which sets present
disarray, the disruption of established social
institutions and practices, against former social
coherence. In this interpretation, the commentators
have the large body of general and theoretical
literature on the whole study of alcohol to support
them. But the disintegration of the tribal society
is long-standing, and the contrast of alcohol use
among contemporary Indians with the highly integrated
aboriginal life tends to be a comparison that
disregards two generations of social change, within
both the native bands and Canadian society.

     To point to the distance between the two
elements in the prevalent comparison is not to deny
the disintegration of the Indian societies. But it
has been suggested already in this chapter that the
primary relationship for the skid row Indian, and

[3]   ibid p. 317

[4]   Curley 1967 p. 121-2

[5]   Dozier 1966 p. 72-3

219

probably for the Indian of the contemporary reserve
as well, is with the urban milieu. Hence the contrast
ceases to be between tribal past and present, and
instead revolves upon a contrast between the
integration of the white middle-class and the non-
integration of the Indian into the urban milieu.
In this case the emphasis remains upon the communal
role of drinking, but interpretations do not
concentrate upon the replacement of the solidarity
associated with tribal institutions.

Indeed, the solidarity of the skid row way of
life has been described so as to indicate its highly
communal qualities. And the skid row does have its
institutions as well as its norms. What this report
must be directed towards is the perception of the
relationship between the structures of skid row life
and those of the large centre within which it is a
small and distinctive sub-culture. That is to say,
the function of alcohol cannot be asserted by
reference simply to the Indian tribal past, or its
demise. Further, the function of alcohol is not a
single thing, and probably is not amenable to the
kind of theoretical isolation that conventional
functionalist approaches pre-suppose. Instead, we
must deal with the community which it has been the
purpose of this chapter to introduce. In such a
situation, alcoholic drinks do more than vitalise a
quiescent society: it is transparent that they do
not mark moments of indulgence or solidarity within
an overall life of isolated withdrawal; they do not
simply serve to ease problematic social
relationships, either among Indians or between
Indians and Whites; they do not provide an outlet
for an otherwise restrictive sexuality; they neither
temper nor permit aggression in a community where
inter-personal relations are fraught with constraint
and inhibition. All those features of alcohol may
be well-known qualities of its use in the rural or
native community. Since this report is specifically
concerned with a community which is neither rural nor,
within the ordinary use of the term, native, it is
prima facie unlikely that such features will contain
the heart of the issue.

Drunk and Fighting

Now, drunkenness itself will be considered more closely, and the relationship between skid row drinking and fighting will be pursued. It must be noted at the outset that the majority of the violence which erupts in and around the bars does not involve theft, while the participants in fights are invariably very drunk. Sober or calculating attacks on others are extremely rare.

Attitudes to Drunkenness

Among skid row Indians the state of drunkenness is valued. I never heard an Indian discuss alcoholism at any length, and reference to alcoholism was made without guilt, fear, or anxiety. This contrasted remarkably with non-Indian drinkers, who often insisted that they were or were not alcoholics. Where they insisted that they were not, the insistence was strikingly aggressive; where they noted that they were, it was said in terrible despondency and self-recrimination. For the White, being alcoholic involved loss of status and missed opportunities. One White from Montreal repeated to me over and over: "I was a chemist, I had a good life; now I am alcoholic. Are you alcoholic?" Another man from Calgary took me aside many times and told me: "I come here because it's interesting. I don't need to come here. I own a truck. Would you like to come hunting for a few weeks? I have good guns. I'm going to the north to work tomorrow."

Obviously a number of the Indians decide that they do not want to be alcoholics, and the half-way houses as well as the Alcoholics Anonymous programmes have a number of Indians who are bent on self reformation. But all such people I talked with explained their presence in the programmes by reference to a chain of events which terminated in a desire to avoid alcoholism, and which began with prison and dealings with social workers; the sense of guilt, an awareness of alcoholism as such, had

221

usually been implanted by contact with non-Indian agencies. And the small measure of success which meets the endeavours of such agencies in their work among Indian drinkers may testify to the absence of guilt and anxiety.

Lemert has noted much the same thing: "In none of the interviews I conducted with Indians in prison for liquor offences did I discover any sign of guilt or remorse on their part."[6] He also notes the distinction which can be made between drunkenness itself and the consequences of drunkenness, and remarks on the security with which it is made by the Indians themselves: "To the Indian drunkenness appeared as a desirable thing which outweighs its unpleasant consequences."[7] This apparent lack of guilt among drinkers also seems reflected in the way in which they recount their drunken experience. There is never any emphasis on the possible folly. The characteristic phrase: "I got good and drunk" is extremely revealing, and is not one we would usually expect to hear from a non-Indian. The non-Indian equivalent is something like: "I got so damned drunk" -- in which the so, the curse, and the tone all reflect at least a token concession to the error of having got drunk at all. Equally, it is usual to find among non-Indians a valuation upon resistance to alcohol, as illustrated by the careful quantifying of what was drunk, and patronising reference to others who got sick or just couldn't go on drinking. Among Indians such quantifying is rare, while the narration of a spree includes quite proud reference to having passed out oneself.

Moreover, the Indians do not seem to fear the loss of self-control or awareness in the way that non-Indians do. Berreman quotes the lament of a young Aleut: "I can't get good and drunk. It always seems like I know what I'm doing, even when I can't walk straight."[8] On skid row this distinction is much the

[6] Lemert 1954 p. 356.

[7] ibid p. 354.

[8] Berreman 1956 p. 507.

222

same. It is unusual to see non-Indians delighting
in their loss of self-control. This difference also
reflects the apparently quite different levels of
anxiety which surround drinking as between the
Indians and Whites, even on skid row.

It is of course possible to over-estimate the
degree of this difference. In Canadian society as
a whole, as in most industrial societies, there is
a degree of pride attached to having been drunk.
The entry into a bar is a sign of maturity, and
the drunken adventure is something like the sowing
of wild oats -- testament to on-going manhood. What
is important, however, is the measure in which being
drunk is conceived as a deviation from adherence to
the social values. Among the non-Indians the way
in which drunkenness is described of itself suggests
that the narrator really subscribes to the values
constraining drunkenness. Indeed, the very
affirmation of his maturity surrounds his ability
to deviate from strongly felt values -- it is such
deviance which our society often regards as 'growing
up'. Among skid row Indians, however, there seems
to be no such qualification to the drinking. It is,
in their case, the drunkenness which is valued more
certainly than any moral proscription around it.

The Form of Drunkenness

The form which drunkenness takes yields more
important insights into its nature than the form in
which it is described by the drinkers. Too many
studies of the role of alcohol neglect to note that
drunkenness has highly various expressions, not only
between cultures but within cultures. That the
peasant farmers of central America have traditions
of quiescent drinking is regarded, rightly enough,
as an example of a cultural form to drunkenness.
Equally, the variety of drunken expression in our
society is seen to reflect the heterogeneity of
value systems, and to highlight the individuation
of behaviour. But recourse to explanations of such
behaviour in terms of cultural norms can too easily
obscure the significance of the behaviour itself;

223

the argument comes treacherously close to saying
that coherent or homogeneous behaviour, as typically
found in simple society, is _beyond_ explanation.
The importance of drunken behaviour, however, can
be seen in the small villages of rural Ireland,
where drunkenness varies between extremes of
vivacity and despondency, according to the time of
year.[9] An examination of that variation yields
considerable insight into the societies. It is
important to reduce norms as well as exceptions in
behaviour to sociologically important factors.

The popular view of the Indian drunk is well
known. He is liable to excesses of any and every
kind; he fights savagely for no clear reason; he
destroys property -- even his own -- with no
thought to his actions; he is sexually aggressive
and liable to outlandish indulgences; he becomes
crazy; he can't hold his liquor; he passes out. In
every part of Canada I visited most, if not all, of
this stereotype pervaded the attitudes of non-
Indians.[10]

Before embarking on the description of the
drunken behaviour that I witnessed on skid row,
it is worth making a few general remarks about this
stereotype. First, there is no evidence within the
literature on alcohol to date to confirm the view
that Indians, as a race, are less able to tolerate
the effects of alcohol. Lemert has pointed out that
Indians of the Northwest Coast quite remarkably seem
to sober up when the necessity arises -- which
suggests that drunkenness was perhaps not so great
as the behaviour might have lead an observer to
suppose.[11] I found no basis for the view that
Indians have as a matter of chemistry, constitutionall
less resistance to alcohol. It may seem laborious
to continue emphasising this lack of evidence, but

9 See Aalen and Brody 1969.

10 For discussion of this in relation to the Indian
   view of himself see chapter 5.

11 Lemert op. cit. p. 322.

the insistence with which non-Indians hold the
belief is disturbing since it provides in all social
contexts -- perhaps most relevantly in the employment
situation -- a rationale for discriminatory
practices.[12] Second, the evidence that Indians tend
to fight, or be sexually aggressive, or generally
become 'crazy', is not quite as substantial as the
upholders would have us believe. Berreman says of
the Aleut, for example, that aggression and violence
are unusual, but sexual freedom is normal; Honigmann
points to the release of sexual inhibitions, a
genital awareness, and a reduction of inhibition on
aggression, all of which are strikingly in contrast
with normal and sober behaviour, but the aggression
is limited and there is no suggestion that the
drinkers are excessive. Indeed, it is mostly from
the writings of earlier travellers that one can
gleen data about the "drunken excesses" of the
native people.

Yet it is the case that Indians, when they are
compared with other Canadian groups, do behave
distinctively when drunk. Since they tend to be
more actively in pursuit of the effects of alcohol,
they are much more ready to behave like drunks. And
behaving like a drunk is determined by how the drunk's
behaviour is conceived. In our society there is a
tendency to expect drinking to make social relations
more fluent, and to allow conversation to flow. Among
many Indians drink is expected to remove far more
restraints than that. That many Indians are able
to accept this removal of constraints, that they
acquiesce in the more extravagant consequences of
drinking, reflects their comparative lack of fear
about loss of self-control. And that in turn may
reflect their dislocation from any proscriptive
moral framework.

That a group of people should be less afraid
of drunkenness, should in fact enthusiastically
look for the extremes of drunkenness, is not in
itself surprising. Probably most pre-industrial
societies have been far more at ease with what we
are inclined to term abnormal states of mind --

[12] e.g. see King 1967.

225

from the trance to the regular use of narcotics.[13]
The fear and anxiety which surrounds such mental
states in our society, however, do succeed in impeding
responsiveness to stimulants used to precipitate the
abnormal conditions. It is well known that the effects
of marijuana are slower in coming to those who are not
accustomed to it, and this unresponsiveness to the
drug reflects anxiety and fear about the drug's effects
With habituation these fears become minimal, and
the effects of the drug accordingly increase.
Among skid row Indians, as we have already pointed
out, guilt associated with drinking and drunkenness
appears to be minimal. It follows that more
conspicuous drunken behaviour will set in more
quickly. The evidence which is usually adduced in
support of the argument that Indians can't take their
liquor may, instead, be used to support two quite
different arguments: one about the Indian's lack
of anxiety over the stimulant itself, the other about
how Indians conceive drunken behaviour. Indians
do get drunk more quickly -- from a behavioural
point of view -- but this has social and psychological
rather than bio-chemical dimensions. The reasons
for this responsiveness thus return upon the two
orders of explanation -- one may look at the
traditional culture's attitudes to the dream and
hallucinogenic experiences and abnormal states of
mind, or at the moral frameworks operative on a
group in that particular socio-economic position.
That there are differences between forms of
drunken behaviour in Indians and whites is important,
but these differences reflect the difference between
the Indian's cultural heritage and the non-Indian's
inevitable co-operation within the more puritan
value-system outside skid row. But this will be
considered more fully later.

Within skid row bars, drunken behaviour is
strikingly ambivalent. The drunk is full of
camaraderie (with the qualifications that were
mentioned in the last chapter), and gathers around
himself a group of friends with whom he engages in
excited conversation and banter. As he becomes

[13] See Devereux 1951 and Erickson 1950.

226

drunker, so this conversation becomes less and less
coherent, until eventually the drinker subsides
into a stupefied silence, and eventually passes out
altogether. At any point along this continuum,
short of unconsciousness, the drinker can become
extremely angry and violent. There is a readiness
to begin fighting, and the drinker seems to be
keeping a careful look out for possible provocation.

The things which count as provocation includes:
malicious reference to family; suggestion of lack
of generosity; attempt to take anything for nothing;
comment on some former dispute. Of course,
occasions for violent animosity are not confined to
these, and there is often a willingness to find
offence in anything that is said at all, but these
particular provocations do seem to precipitate a
conflagration whatever the apparent mood of the
drinkers.

The ambivalence of the drinkers' moods is
reflected in the sudden speed with which a bar that
is full of animated and seemingly happy conversation
at one moment can become in the next moment the
scene of four or five large-scale fights. Indeed,
the fighting actually seems to be infectious. One
table gets involved in a noisy and conspicuous
dispute, a glass is broken, the table is pushed
over, two people are swinging blows at one another,
and within moments there are other fights in the
bar. Such incidents are quite a normal feature of
life in these bars. It would not be possible to
find a skid row bar which did not, in the course of
a busy night, see at least one such fight. More
often there are three or four -- most particularly
at weekends.

In the vast majority of these fights, however,
there is a certain lack of seriousness on the part
of the combatants -- they do not really try to hurt
one another, and are quite quick to sit down again
at the same table, or if they are thrown out of the
bar, may go together to another bar. Once such
fight has happened, it tends to erupt through the
evening, and often over a few days -- but with the
participants remaining on quite cordial terms

227

between eruptions. Examples give some impression
of the fights themselves, and some of the factors
which are involved:

1.   Dave (who is half Cree and half French) was
with his old friend Harry (who is Cree) when a
younger man who knew them slightly came to sit at
the table with them. As soon as he sat down he
asked if they would buy him a drink, and also
picked up a packet of cigarettes that was lying on
the table, took one, and began to smoke. Dave and
Harry had been having a very friendly and relaxed
conversation, but as soon as the newcomer took the
cigarette they both tensed up and began to insult
him. Very soon Dave and the newcomer were fighting,
and soon after that Dave and Harry took the
newcomer outside and quite severely beat him up.
There was no reconciliation with him.

2.   A large group of drinkers were at one table,
and had been there for a long time. All were very
drunk. One of them was much larger than the others,
and was teasing a very small young Indian about
his family. The small man replied at first very
defensively, then fell silent. The large man began
to nudge him, in a jocular way but also by way of
escalating the tease. Suddenly the young man hit
out at the large man. The match was pathetically
hopeless for the young man, but he attacked very
viciously. As soon as the fight had begun the
brother of the smaller man came to his rescue, and
tried to take over the fight himself. Also, the
friends of the larger man tried to prevent him from
fighting at all. These two secondary encounters
both turned into fights themselves: the two
brothers began to fight, and the large man began to
hit out wildly at the friends who were seeking to
restrain him. As the numbers involved in the one
fight increased, so fights which did not appear to
have any direct relation to the central one also
broke out. Quite soon the bar was taken over by
fighting groups. Eventually the two brothers agreed
to a pause, and they returned to the attack on the
big man. But meanwhile he had been persuaded to
calm down, and they all sat at the table again. As

228

soon as they did so all the other fights stopped as
well. In the course of the next hour that central
fight broke out again twice, each time precipitating
others.

3.   Two brothers who had just come from the Great
Slave Lake area asked me to drink with them.   For
half an hour we got along well, talking for the
most part about England.   Suddenly one of the
brothers asked: "Who owns the Northwest
Territories?"   "The U. S. A." was my tentative
answer.   "Bullshit", he said, "England does."   At
this point the other brother joined in: "I'll tell
you who owns the Territories, it's England that owns
the Territories."   Immediately the first brother
turned on the second: "What the fuck do you know
about it?   You know fuck all about anything.   It's
England that owns the Territories."   The second
brother defended himself, saying that he knew
pretty well who owned what, and the one thing he
did know was who owned the Northwest Territories.
At this the first brother became extremely enraged,
and warned that anyone who said he didn't know what
he was talking about had better watch out.   The two
then began to shout menaces, and I am certain that
if I had not been there actively interceding on
behalf of peace a violent if brief fight would have
broken out; I am also certain that it would have
died down as quickly as it happened.

4.   Bernard is half Indian, and comes from British
Columbia.   He had just arrived on skid row when I
had been there about a month.   He is extremely
tough, but when he first arrived was unknown to many
of the regulars.   He tended to be very quiet at first,
but was always on his guard against possible slight
or criticism.   One night a young local Indian asked
him for money to buy a drink.   Bernard said he
wouldn't give him any.   The young man persisted in
a friendly way asking for enough to buy one beer.
Bernard suddenly shouted at him to go away, but the
young man didn't want to lose face in front of
everyone else, and made a joke.   Bernard
immediately stood up and pushed him out of his
chair; both the man and the chair went sprawling
across the floor.   A very confusing fight then
broke out, involving most of the people around --

229

especially those whose drinks had been knocked over by the falling chair, and others who seemed to want to join in. In the end the bouncer came over to Bernard and tried to push him out of the bar. Bernard then turned on the bouncer and with a sudden heave threw him onto the floor. When the bouncer picked himself up he pushed the young man out of the bar. Later that night the bouncer made a point of becoming very friendly with Bernard.

5.   I was walking into a bar with some Indian friends and because I was talking very intently to one of them, almost walked into a young Indian who was coming out. The Indian as he was about to bump into me caught me by the collar and held a knife close to my neck. I asked him what was bothering him, and he replied: "some White guy's fucking my old lady and I'm going to stick this knife right into his heart." As I talked to him he relaxed his hold on my collar, and put the knife away. Quite quickly he came to suggest that we have a drink together, and that perhaps between us we could "get the guy who was fucking his old lady."

These are all examples of bar fights. There are also many fights which take place in the street. It is much harder to judge what is involved in street fights, simply because it is unusual for an outsider to have the chance of overhearing the preludes. On a few occasions, however, people I was with got involved in street fights, and on those occasions they seemed to constitute either something of a prolongation of a bar fight or were attached to an outstanding dispute of much the same order as the bar fights. Many of the street fights take place around the liquor store, and these seem to involve almost exclusively the claims people were making on one another for money as they tried to get up the cash for a bottle of wine. The other special features of street fights lies in the involvement of the older women; several times I witnessed a fight involving an older woman, and it was also noticeable that these fights rapidly drew other participants in defence of one or other of the principal combatants. On the whole, however, there

230

is reluctance to become involved in fights in public places for the police are quick to intervene.

Two forms of fighting need special mention: aggression directed against outsiders, and violence directed against the police and other social authorities.

The stranger is drawn into violent situations because skid row people are nervous of him -- he is considered a threat to the established regulars while his intentions and strength must be assessed. In this respect my own experience is representative. On first appearing on skid row I was quite often stopped and asked a particularly provocative question, like: "What kind of fucking jacket is that?" or "We don't like people like you around here; do you want a poke?" or "What are you, some kind of fucking hippy?" In these situations the questioner anticipates a counter-attack, and also expects that the exchange will eventually become violent. In none of these cases did the encounter become violent, and in a number they provided the basis for good and lasting friendships. So long as a stranger can avoid inducing nervousness, and can establish that he has no intention of challenging the influential regulars, he is welcomed. Moreover, once he is welcomed no more questions about his doings are raised. Challenging questions of the kind just cited excepted, I was never, at any time, asked how I earned my money, why I was on skid row, or when I was intending to move along. In a sense everyone there is a stranger to everyone else. It is all the more important to the regular populace, therefore, that confrontations be effected between the newcomer and themselves.

In the case of the police, the aggression is quite different. There appears to be a tendency among them to 'go easy' on skid row Indians. The police seem to have realised that over-enthusiastic intervention in the skid row world does nothing but aggravate relations between police and Indians, and certainly does nothing towards improving the social conditions of the area. Also, the police are frankly nervous of too much intervention -- there are many people who are quick to be provoked, and who, when provoked, are willing to resort quickly and effectively to violence. It is extremely rare to see a policeman in a bar, and few walk on the streets. However, the patrol car is a familiar part of skid row traffic. But when a drunk does encounter a policeman he is glad to find some way of challenging or annoying him. Two examples can illustrate the various form such challenges take:

Jim, a Cree, had broken his leg, and walked on crutches. As he was making his way down the street, very drunk, a police car drew up almost alongside him. The policeman in the car looked out at Jim and his group of friends. Jim promptly waved one of his crutches at the car and shouted: "Come on out, come on out and I'll fight you both without the crutches; come on, you ....." The Police did not come out of their car, and Jim walked away triumphant, shouting further abuse and obscenities back at them as he departed. Though I heard reliable accounts of many in the recent past; skid row old-timers assured me that it was still 'tough' in other places, but that in this city a sudden and considerable change for the better had recently taken place.

It should be said that I never witnessed a case of police brutality. The second example here is more representative of the kinds of challenge which the police must be familiar to:

An old and very fat woman was asleep on a patch of grass by a waste lot. A young policeman came up to her and told her to move along. She was not easily able to do this as it was only an hour since she had passed out after a bout of heavy drinking. Moreover, it was quite obvious that the policeman had picked on her because he was nervous of interfering with the extremely tough men who were also lying around on the waste lot. After some time, the woman understood that the policeman was trying to make her get up and move away. And quite suddenly she did get up, just as the policeman was walking away from her after delivering his final warning. But instead of going the opposite way,

232

she rushed towards the policeman shouting as loud
as she could: "Come back, come back. I want to
fuck you. I want to fuck you." The policeman, no
doubt unwilling to be seen to run away, could not
avoid being caught up with, and the woman tried to
catch him into her arms, still shouting out her
desire. Needless to say a substantial crowd was
beginning to gather, and all of them were enjoying
the spectacle. Eventually the woman sat down --
almost at the policeman's feet -- and he was allowed
to walk away. Everyone was laughing and shouting
in their pleasure at the sight, and the old woman
returned to her corner to sleep, screaming with
laughter. The policeman did not return.

The forms and objects of drunken aggression
are thus various. But perhpas the most important,
both from a theoretical and practical point of view,
is the internecine violence of the bars. It is that
violence which seems to reflect a situation of
stress and which most demands a better understanding.
Before returning to that problem, however, the
discussion must move on to drunken sexual behavior.

Sexual encounters play only a small part in the
activities of the bar. Many drinkers have their
established companion, as has already been noted,
and couples drink together. Some women do move from
table to table, flirting with many different
drinkers, but it is usually the case that these
women have definite partners, and everyone knows who
the partners are. In general the sexual lives of
the skid row people are rather limited. The younger
Indian men cannot establish sexual contacts among
young white girls, while the young Indian girls
systematically select young whites as partners. The
older men and women appear to have relegated sexual
conquests to a very peripheral element in their lives.
But such sexual encounters as do take place tend to
be full of aggression and tension. Much of this
will be discussed in the next chapter, but it must
be noted here that this aggression is drunken.

The Indians, when sober, are extremely shy and
reserved, both within their close groups and in more

233

public places like bar and street corner. As in
the case of criminality and fighting, drunken
behaviour in sexual encounters is the opposite of
the sober norm. The drunk makes direct and almost
hostile advances to the woman, and if she is not
instantly compliant he often becomes aggressive.
This aggression does not take the form of blows
where the couple are not established, partly
because anyone who hits a woman other than his wife
or regular partner is quickly attacked himself, and
partly because hitting would end all possibility of
a successful outcome -- the aggression is designated
in the form of persuasion. Between regular couples,
however, there is a great deal of fighting, both
verbal and physical. Women are often to be seen
with their faces swollen and their arms bruised
from these fights, and the fights are almost always
associated with drunkenness. It has been noted
that the wife is frequently the target of drunken
aggression on the reserves[14] and the same is true
of skid row.

Women when drunk often fight among themselves.
The rationales for these fights seem to reduce in
almost every case to sexual jealousy, and involve
angry recriminations about past deceptions. In
many ways the ferocity of these fights is greater
than any among the men. Also, when the women fight
there is much greater reluctance to become friendly
again, and feuds seem to last for quite long periods.

The Consequences of Violence

If we are to arrive at a satisfactory account
of the aggressive behaviour which seems to attach
to drunkenness among skid row Indians, we must
assume that the behaviour is in some sense purposive.
Things are not done without an end at least
subliminally in view. People may fight at times
because they are very frustrated, but where the
fighting has some fairly precise objectives.

[14] e.g. see Whittaker 1963.

In fact I have already suggested that the challenges which are issued to the stranger have a very definite purpose, namely to ensure that the stranger does not disrupt the situation to anyone's disadvantage. If this suggestion is followed more closely, it can also be noted that within the community the people have some fairly clear idea of where their advantage lies. It is ex hypothesi not economic, nor can it be any orthodox institutional status which is at stake. The social hierarchy which is in danger of disruption is not easily pointed. I have argued that the most important features of this group is their lumpenproletarian position that they have no clearly defined or orthodox social scale. Being without the customary social ethics and ideologies, it follows that they are also without a corresponding status system, whereas in more ordinary social groups assertiveness is aimed at guarding or building a particular position, in the skid row world of the lumpenproletariat it is more likely that assertiveness will constitute of itself the status system. Where objectives are not amenable to rationalisation, the means tend to become ends.

In a recent unpublished paper, Richard H. Robbins suggests that "a Naskapi who is exhibiting assertive behaviour during a drinking episode is an individual who is not receiving information, needed to reinforce a role that he sees himself as playing." Robbins notes three types of drunken behaviour: moving from friendliness to stupor directly, with assertiveness, and with both assertiveness and aggression. He tested his hypothesis by correlating the presence of assertiveness with the absence of alternative role reinforcement by income level. In that paper it is a reserve group which is being discussed -- people whose community status system is at least vestigially present.[15]

On skid row no such vestigial status system exists. The Indians there do not come from any one

[15]   Robbins 1968.

band, or even any one culture. Instead, there
exists no role of importance other than being or
not being an assertive person. Given that one's
reputation for assertiveness is the one form of
reputation that can be maintained, it is·tautological
to say that assertiveness is vital to status.

   But tautologies are true, and within the socio-
economic group which makes up the skid row
population, that assimilation of assertiveness to
status is to be expected. By being aggressive a
skid row drinker establishes a reputation: he is
not a man who can be toyed with; he is someone to
whom everyone else does well to show friendliness
and generosity; he is a man of importance. What
the violent behaviour achieves, therefore, is status
within a community where no other criteria for
status exist.

   The question to which this much over-simplified
account gives rise is: Why, within such a community,
should there be any need for status at all? Why,
in a situation where there is no extrinsic objective
to assertiveness, should people actually be
assertive? The answer to this question is complex,
but it can be begun by remarking quite simply that
skid row is not a total world. The people there
have been socialized within a quite different kind
of milieu, where status and hierarchy always are
relevant and often a crucial part of the social
structure.[16] Just because there is no material

[16] The individualism and atomism which once
      characterised many Indian groups might be
      cited as evidence for a contrary argument. Two
      replies can be given to this: first, two or
      three generations of cultural decline have
      eroded the force of such an observation in the
      present; second, the culture contact has, from
      the first, implicated the Indians in trade and
      then education within a system dominated by
      European conceptions. In that contact
      institutionalised status is likely to be imported
      where traditional systems of status are not
      re-inforced.

basis for inequality, it does not follow that inequalities themselves will promptly disappear from people's minds. If the significance of being an Indian is also considered, at least insofar as it intensifies the lack of possibility for attaining other forms of status, then the aggression of skid row drinkers becomes still more intelligible.

The explanation of aggression must be held there for the moment, for it cannot be adequately extended before the relationship between Indians and non-Indians of skid row is taken into account. But this far it is evident that the multifarious nature of the violence, its widely various precipitants, objects, and consequences, combine to indicate that we are dealing here with an extreme social predicament. Where status turns on assertiveness, then assertiveness becomes omnipresent.

It remains to consider a feature of Indian drinking which most writers comment upon at some length -- the measure in which the drunk is exempted from responsibility for what he does.[17]

Curley gives an example from the Mescalero Apache of a policeman who blinded an Indian, but who was not blamed because he was drunk when he did it.[18] The whole idea that a man is 'not himself' when he is drunk accompanies that kind of indulgence. And in a society where drinking is occasioned or at least intermittent, such indulgence is obviously of great social importance. But it has its importance if and only if there are times when people are responsible for what they do. Indeed, implicit within the argument lies the view that the deeds carried out while drunk are the very deeds which are most definitely censured in sobriety. It is this kind of Freudian account which has placed so centrally within most essays on the role of alcohol the concept of released

17 Honigmann 1945, Berreman 1956, Curley 1967.

18 Curley 1967 p. 121-2.

inhibitions. The drunk, on that view, is a man
without his super-ego, in a milieu where everyone
has also abandoned claims on the drunk's super-ego.

On skid row, however, drinking is too persistent,
and drunken behaviour too large a proportion of
total social behaviour for arguments which revolve
around moral indulgence to carry much weight. It
is not the case that everything is indulged or
explained away on account of temporary loss of
responsibility; it cannot be the case that ascription
of blame is confined to sobriety. In this
situation the people involved must make distinctions
as well as judgements which are independent of being
or not being drunk. And of course they do; a man
who becomes only violent when drunk is disliked,
and the consequences of his violence are blamed
just because he is blamed for being too violent.
The man who balances self-respect (i.e. a correct
degree of assertiveness) with generosity in
deserving quarters, is praised. The man who never
pays his own way is blamed.

It is worth noting that the operations of
blame and praise are also necessary because a man
is accepted as a drinking partner in virtue of
considerations other than community membership.[19]
If a man is to be blamed for being too persistently
a bum, and if that man is also a persistent drunk,
then he has to be judged for his parasitism despite
his drunkenness. The suspension of responsibility
therefore requires two preconditions: first, a
pattern of intermittent drinking, second, a social
context where community membership secures entry
into the drinking circle. On skid row neither of
these conditions can be met.

It follows that the problems of skid row
drunken fighting urge the sociologist to move away
from the kind of considerations which dominate
discussion of the reserve, and towards an awareness
of the conditions which pertain in the urban milieu.
This leads to social factors which involve more than

[19] See chapter 1.

238

either   details of a particular band or generalities
about 'Indianness' as such.

The Middle Class Idea of the Indian

Canadian attitudes to the Indians seem to vary
considerably according to both region and income
level.[20]   Generalisations are not easy but it seems
that the middle class is effectively discriminatory
if theoretically 'understanding'. Those who have
any knowledge of the way in which Indians have
suffered from the intrusion of Europeans refer
sympathetically to the past. But many of these same
people, having paid homage to past error, express
their irritation with the Indian's failure to
overcome misfortune. All too frequently,
unfavourable comparisons are made between the
Indian's demoralisation and resilience of many
immigrant groups in Canada. More significantly,
those who deprecate Indians find the most
compelling expression of Indian failure in their
non-middle class habits and attitudes: relative
uncleanliness, lack of reliability in work,
drunkenness, and violence. Discrimination is a
consequence of this view, for it entails a
disinclination, if not downright refusla, to employ,
house, or even interact with such unreliable
dangerous people.

This discrimination is tempered by pious hopes
and positive ideas about government policy. Some
examples: 'Indians should be given British Columbia,
so they could have their own state'; and 'they get
too much money for nothing; that should be stopped,
then they'd get down to work.' Even the more benign
and liberal, noticeably the younger people, admit
to nervousness and unease when they are with Indians
-- though many of them remark that their unease is
a racist hang-over.

[20] For an account of the variation by regions see
      Indians and the Law, 1967, p. 55.

Such views are all too familiar to those who have had experience of White-Indian relations, but their frequency does reflect an extremely strong attitude adopted by the middle class, and that attitude bears keenly, if often indirectly, on the predicament of the urban migrant -- most importantly in employment and housing. The confusion of myth, stereotype, self-fulfilling prophecy and truth which makes up this prevalent attitude cannot be fully unpacked here. It suffices for the present purpose to say that the attitude amounts to a racial prejudice and creates widespread discrimination.

An incident from my own experience may once again serve to illustrate the seriousness of the problem.

When I went on a trip to the Northwest Coast I gave the use of my apartment to an Indian friend. When I returned from the trip the door of the apartment was padlocked from the outside, and I was obliged to get the key from the caretaker. It transpired that the occupiers of the next door apartment had complained about the presence in their building of Indians, and the complaint had reached the landlords. It also transpired that the landlords did not permit the letting of any of their property to Indians, and the caretaker was instructed to refuse access to them. In protesting with the caretaker about this measure, he confided to me all the unwritten and confidential instructions that landlords in the city usually give to caretakers and whoever else may be responsible for letting rooms. I was given a great many examples from the block I lived in of extremely ugly cases of outright discrimination. One of these is worth repeating: a professional couple had taken an apartment in the block and were beginning to move in their possessions; when the other tenants saw that the couple were Indian-looking (they were in fact immigrants from Asia) they demanded that the apartment be withdrawn from the market. The caretaker said that this was impossible, and the other tenants then canvassed the landlords, saying that they themselves would all leave if the new tenant was not sent elsewhere. The landlord duly

240

told the caretaker to tell the new tenants that there
had been an administrative error, and that the
apartment was in fact already let.

Examples of refusal to employ Indians came to
me from many social workers and others concerned
with finding employment for Indians. Some of these
cases were more flagrant than others, but the overall
picture was extremely unpleasant. It is most
striking in the cases of Indian girls who go to
interviews and are immediately told that the job is
taken. One hotel makes their policy quite explicit
on the phone, and justifies it by saying that they
would lose business if they employed Indian
receptionists. A senior Administrator of a
provincial jail told me that there would be no
point in developing training programmes in jail
since the Indian girls who are most in need of them
in any case cannot find employment outside the jail.

Finally, it must be said that on many occasions
I was taken aside by middle class Canadian
acquaintances who had noticed me talking to Indians,
and warned against too much association with them.
These warnings centred on the imminent dangers from
sudden and unpredictable fits of violence and
alarmingly virulent forms of venereal disease they
attached to all Indians. It is difficult to take
these kinds of beliefs at all seriously, blatantly
irrational as they are. But their seriousness,
from the Indian's point of view, is considerable
indeed.

Skid Row Whites' Attitudes Towards the Indian

Among Whites of lower income and social status
there is less sophistication and articulateness.
Because the principal qualifications to middle class
racism lies in the verbal concealment of it, it is to
be expected that lower class Whites will at least
sound more racist. Both the non-Indians of skid row
come more directly and frequently into contact with
Indians than any other Canadian group. In

understanding the Indian response to Whites -- a
response which inevitably plays a significant role
in his social predicament and adaptation -- the
relationships between skid row groups are likely to
be important. Since these are people who have daily
contact with, and even some dependence upon Indians,
it is also to be expected that they should display
ambivalence. It is the high degree of this
ambivalence, with all the attendant confusions and
tensions, which is surprising. These can be
illustrated:

1. I was talking in a bar with a middle-aged
Indian woman and an Indian friend of hers. The
woman was very drunk and very muddled. She was
telling how she had lost a child, and how badly
she needed to find it, and how important it
probably was to the child that she succeed. Her
confusion consisted in a failure to express any way
of achieving this end, which was either consistent
or remotely plausible. At an adjacent table a
White had been over-hearing this conversation, and
eventually came and joined us. From time to time
he asked me what the woman meant, and it eventually
became clear that he did not speak very good
English, and that he was in fact from Montreal.
He was unemployed and drinking heavily. It
transpired subsequently that he had been employed,
but was not alcoholic. Eventually, this Montreal
man began to solicit the favours of the Indian
woman: propositioning her in husky whispers he
laid his hand on her knee. As he sought responses
from the woman he talked to me in French. As he
talked the general question of the Indians came
to the fore, and he began to confide to me his
views. These views were quite forthright: he
insisted that all Indians were good for nothing,
never to be trusted, lazy, dirty, and altogether
inferior -- 'presque animaux'. As it happened, the
Indian woman rejected his advances, and he continued
to talk to me, occasionally trying to recapture the
woman's attention. The talk with me simply confirmed
the anomalous situation; his hand periodically
reaching towards her, he meanwhile condemned and
despised the object of his interest.

2. During the first few weeks of the fieldwork I
became particularly well acquainted with four young
Whites, all migrant workers and petty criminals,
all very well known and respected regulars in the
community of drinkers. Moreover, these four young
men often drank together with the Indians in whose
company they appeared at ease and content. One day,
however, they took me aside and delivered a
'friendly piece of advice'. They insisted that I
was too trusting, that the Indians I was spending
so much time with were concerned only with getting
money out of me and everyone else like me, that they
would be nice in the afternoon and 'roll' me at
night, and what's worse, when they fought with me
they would 'put the boot in' (i.e. kick in my eyes
and genitals as I lay on the ground defeated).
Such warnings were given to me by these four and
many others on numerous occasions, and always the
warning involved a general view of the Indian as
dangerously devious and peculiarly treacherous in
both intention and action. Sometimes the
explanation for this predicted behavior (none of
it actually ever came to pass) was said to lie in
the Indian's failure to hold alcohol, but that was
less common a view on skid row than among the
middle class community. More often the explanation
was purely racist -- an Indian, the argument runs,
is dangerous and nasty because he is an Indian.

3. As I became familiar with the bars, and came
to know numbers of both Indian and White drinkers,
so a very special difficulty arose. When sitting
at a table alone, people would come and join me.
Often it happened that one or two Whites would
come and sit at my table, and then an Indian I knew
particularly well might come and join me too. On
one such occasion, after which I sought to minimize
the possibility of recurrence, an elderly Indian
came and joined me at a table with two young Whites.
Both the Whites lived by crime and bumming; neither
had brought any substantial amount of money into
the community for several months. They did not know
the Indian well, and he did not appear to be
particularly poor and made no requests for drink
or cigarettes. But a few minutes after the Indian

243

sat down, one of the young Whites said: "Well, are you going to get us a fucking drink?" The man promptly said yes he would, and drew out a dollar bill. The White continued, shouting at the man: 'go ahead then, get the drinks, you fucking bum'·. Quite soon the Indian left the table, and I was once again treated to warnings about Indians.[21]

These incidents all show the White's involvement with his superiority, his specific charges against Indians of material inferiority, and his concern with communicating these beliefs both to strangers and to Indians themselves. But there is another face to the whole relationship, which is brought out best by the first example above. The Whites do stay with the Indians, and they are not forced to do so. They participate in the way of life, a way of life which is as open to Whites as it is to Indians. They are always trying to form sexual relations with Indian women. They often commit small crimes with Indians. There are very rarely fights between Indians and Whites. Some Whites, including the two young men in the third example above, also insist that Indians are really good people, if and only if they are pure Indians; it is the people of mixed blood they say they despise and can't trust. And of course the vast majority of the Indians on skid row are partially non-Indian.

We find in the attitude of the skid row White, therefore, three principal ingredients: first, the Indian is regarded as a bum; second, he is regarded as unreliable; third, he is regarded as unduly violent. But we also find that in practice the Whites do many 'jobs' with Indians: many Whites have Indian girl-friends, with whom they co-operate for the purposes of hustling and petty theft; much drinking is done by Whites and Indians jointly. It is evident that there is considerable divergence between protestation and practice.

21 It should be remembered that these aggressions towards Indians were very much for the benefit of the stranger; had I not been there it is possible that they would not have occurred.

244

Indian Attitudes Towards Themselves

On skid row the Indians from different regions tend to keep together, at least during the day-time when groups gather in houses and on corners, talking in their own languages. Equally there is some tendency for the Indians as such to keep apart from the Whites -- but this is subject to all the qualifications which arise from the various forms of co-operation just noted.

To these qualifications another must be added: the Indian girls definitely prefer to be with White men. The reasons they give for this are surprisingly similar to the reasons which the middle class White gives for avoiding Indians. They say that Indian men drink too much, that they cannot hold their drink, and that they become violent when drunk, and so the girls are forever getting beaten up by them. One Chipewayan girl told me that she had had an Indian boyfriend when she was fourteen and would never have one again, because he treated her so badly. He was fifteen at the time. Since then this girl married a White, was beaten very badly by him three times, found him in bed with another woman, left him, and went to live with another White. That White also beat her very badly, and she decided to go back to her husband, who said he wanted her back. She went back, and was then beaten up again several times, and she again left him. This same girl refused to talk to me in the bars when I was with the Indians I knew, and when I asked her why she was being so unfriendly she mysteriously replied that there was something she would tell me about one day. Finally the day came, and she told me: "I don't like Indian people, and I won't spend any time with them'. When I asked her why this was, she referred back to that first boyfriend and to the drunken violence of the Indian.

The Indian girls of this kind represent the extreme in negative feeling towards their own race. But it is also to be seen among older people, many of whom are extremely preoccupied with maintaining friendly relations with all whites they meet. On one occasion I was in a bar with an elderly Indian

who had begun to teach me Cree. We had become good
friends, or at least so it seemed, and most of the
initial tensions had begun to fade. After an hour
in the bar, during which we talked about the language
and his past times and exchanged notes about England
(he had been in the navy during the second world war),
he suddenly declared: "You must be tired of talking
to an old Indian; I'll go and find a white person
you can talk to.' I tried to dissuade him from doing
this, and insisted that I was very much enjoying
talking to him. But since it was possible that he
was using this as an excuse for extricating himself
from my company without casting any unpleasant light
on myself, I let him go and find this White.
Eventually he returned with a middle-aged White
woman -- whom he had never met before -- and sat
her next to me. He then sat down again himself,
and told the woman that I wanted to talk to her.
The woman looked confused, and began to talk to
the Indian. But every time she addressed anything
to him, he replied: 'no, no, you talk to him; he's
going to want to talk with a White woman'. After
a few awkward exchanges between us, the woman went
away. And as soon as she had gone the Indian returned
to the Cree lesson.

This kind of over-acceptance of Whites was a
recurrent feature of many of my contacts with
Indians on skid row. It had a less troubling, but
probably no less significant, counterpart in the
large number of jokes that Indians made against each
other which turned on the backwardness and violence
of Indian people. Some of these jokes referred to
the Indian of the cowboy and Indian paradigm, but
their relevance was carried into the skid row context.
One Indian would quite often go up to another and
say: 'O.K. cowboy, I'm going to scalp you'. Also,
it was common practice for an Indian man to say to
an Indian girl something about her being a squaw.
A Cree I knew tended to argue with his Blackfoot
common law wife, and in these arguments he always
infuriated her by stating that the Blackfoot women
were only Indians, and would ask her to take him to
her Tepee. Between the Indians, however, these
jokes were usually taken in good part, but if a
White called an Indian girl a squaw it was

considered a sign of gross disrespect, and often led to very violent exchanges which culminated in blows.

The attitudes of the girls to Indian men, the older men's anticipation of the White's lack of interest in the Indian, and the jokes, all indicate a fairly high level of introverted aggression. Franz Fanon has suggested that there is an intimate connection between this incorporation of non-native attitudes into the native's attitude towards himself and the persistence of violence.[22] He writes of the Algerian native: 'The first thing which the native learns is to stay in his place, and not to go beyond certain limits. That is why the dreams of the native are always of muscular prowess; his dreams are of action and aggression.' Also; 'The native's muscles are always tensed. You can't say that he is terrorised, or even apprehensive. He is in fact ready at a moment's notice to exchange the role of the quarry for that of the hunter. The native is an oppressed person whose permanent dream is to become the persecutor.[23] Of course the situation of natives in Algeria was radically different from that of the present day Canadian urban migrant, but there is no doubt that internalization of the non-Indian's hostility towards the Indian is a significant factor in skid row, and one should not be hasty in dismissing the possible connection between that factor and the prevalence of violence. In many respects the Indians are hostile towards their Indianness, and the stress which that hostility imposes is all too easily underestimated.

Indian-White Relationships on Skid Row

It transpires that the racism of skid row is no

22   See Fanon 1967 & 1968.

23   Fanon 1967, p. 41.

less substantial than elsewhere in Canadian society,
although it receives a somewhat different expression.
The puzzle which must now be faced is the acceptance
both Indians and Whites accord each other on skid
row.   There exists a unity between the two groups,
as well as divisiveness. The Whites on skid row
insist upon the inferiority of the Indians, but
live in a context where their relationship to the
Indians is in practice greater than their relationship to the non-skid row world. On skid row, racist
theory is qualified in practice. In the bars and
on the street corners the interaction between Indians
and Whites suggests a firm mutual acceptance which
is quite different from the strikingly inconsistent
with the disrespect which the Whites confer upon
the Indians in word.

There are two aspects to this unity which can
be discussed here: first, the unity which derives
from a common socio-economic position; second, the
desire for collaboration which stems from the
special circumstances of that socio-economic
situation. The first is a socio-economic, the
second a psychological account.

The Unity of Socio-economic Condition

The skid row Whites are either migrant workers
between jobs or regular quasi-alcoholics. The
migrants have spent or are in the process of
spending their 'roll'. Both in spending and having
spent their 'roll' they are very much part of the
skid row world -- they are either in the position
of spree drinker or bum. One qualification to the
assertion that skid row Whites and Indians are in
the same socio-economic position derives from the
concentration of the young Whites in migrant labour.
But since skid row Whites, whether migrant labourers
or not, have identified with the skid row world,
this qualification is not as important as might
otherwise have been the case.

The lumpenproletarian is someone who has no
regularized relationship to the means of

248

production -- he is neither owner nor qualified
worker, there are no continuities to his economic
life. On this definition the skid row population,
Indian and White, are all in the same or very
similar relationship to the means of production.
They may be there for somewhat different reasons,
and they may have arrived by different paths, but
they have arrived -- be it by choice of necessity --
at very much the same position. The same
relationship to the means or production, in the
case of skid row, also involves very similar forms
of social life: it is no coincidence that people
in this socio-economic predicament gather in
communities which are committed to and dependent
upon modes of earning and living which lie
substantially outside the law, modes best defined
as in systematic opposition to those of the
mainstream or middle class.

Indians and Whites can, objectively, be said
to have a real unity on skid row -- objectively
because whatever they themselves might think about
their positions relative to one another they are,
in fact, in a very similar economic position.

Mutual Dependence

As well as this objective unity between Indians
and Whites on skid row, there also exists a striking
argument for subjective unity. It has already been
noted that Indians and Whites seem very willing
indeed to share way of life, while at the same time
regarding one another as different. Moreover, it
has been noted that the Whites regard the Indians
as inferior, and the Indians seem to acquiesce in
this judgement.

It is the most dispossessed of society who
gather together on skid row. Although this idea
of dispossession is most emphatically a conception
from mainstream life, it is all the same a conception
of which skid row people are fully aware. It can
be repeated that almost no-one on skid row has been
socialized there, and the majority of mainstream

249

conceptions are brought in by the migrants themselves. Even in the terms of the migrant, therefore, skid row is associated with failure within the society as a whole.

But within the skid row the relative failure of the two groups is different. That is to say, while the skid row White feels he is at the base of the social system, he can qualify that position to his advantage by being a racist, consoling himself in the belief that the Indians form a substantial group below him.

On the other hand, the Indian can qualify his sense of failure by sharing his life with non-Indians. If it is accepted that non-Indians are inevitably superior to Indians, then in making an identification with non-Indians the Indian is not as socially relegated as he is in separation from the White. And if we remember that it is the urban migrant we are discussing, the argument is more persuasive. The migrant comes to the city to avoid isolation. He associates the city with a fuller -- and more equal -- life. In living on skid row his life is fuller, in purely status terms, in virtue of the skid row mixture of Whites and Indians. That is not the case in any other part of the city. Outside skid row the Indian is in danger of being systematically excluded from a life shared with Whites, at least on a day-to-day social basis. Thus it can be seen once again that skid row offers the Indian a milieu in which his self-respect is enhanced. But it is a corollary of this enhancement that he must accept the White's racism; status accrues just because being with Whites is better than not being with Whites. Where Indians find that satisfaction, it follows that they are also subscribing to doctrines of White superiority.

Thus, in the bar, on the street corner, and in every part of the skid row world the White can console himself that he is not at the base of society, for there are Indians beneath him. And the Indian can feel that he is socially advanced just by being with Whites. Each sector of the

250

community gains by sharing its life with the other. For the White this involves the merging of racism in theory with assimilation in practice: for the Indian it involves the internalization of White views of Indians. From what has been described so far in this report, it should be evident that these conditions are definitely met.

This mutual dependence in practice, combined with a shared theory about the relative status of the Indian and the White, can be seen as a social symbiosis; both social groups depend on the other for social and personal reassurance. Combined with the objective unity which derives from shared socio-economic status, and is supplemented by the joint belief in myths of racial superiority, the solidarity of the community as well as its racial divisiveness becomes intelligible. That the expression of the divisiveness should surround beliefs about economic parasitism and violence should not be surprising in the light of the argument of Chapter 4. It is now possible to add an additional insight into the violence.

It is obviously central to the present argument that skid row Indians and Whites are both, as groups, troubled about their social positions. Given that there is this malaise, assertiveness as a means of forming status per se becomes more intelligible. As well as using assertiveness as the one means of making an impression on others, thereby securing a position of some importance within the skid row community, assertive individuals are also compensating for their more general, but probably no less profound, sense of failure. If we add to this the remarks by Fanon about the introversion of violence per identification with the value systems of the socially ascendant group, class, or race, the violence of the Indians should cease to be surprising at all.

Social Work and Social Workers

In the course of field-work I had occasion to
talk to many social workers, and spent some time
in different institutions which aim at meeting the
needs of the groups I have been describing. In this
chapter some brief outline of the people and the
institutions will be given. This outline is
important if only to reveal the enormous gulf that
exists between the helpers and the helped: not
only do they come from opposite social classes,
different life-styles, and different races in a
race-conscious society, the helpers do not seem
to be able to grasp that there exists in skid row
a way of life which is gratifying, and which has
evolved around the very difficulties which the
social workers regard as the heart of the problems.
Skid row life, that is to say, accommodates the
marginal people far more completely than any of
the institutions. The operators of the institutions
for the most part cannot understand how such a
situation could exist. This difficulty in
understanding the gratifications of skid row life
reflects, of course, the vast moral and ideological
gulf between social workers and the socially
problematic group.

I shall divide social work into two broad
categories: that which is aimed at providing
shelter and the more directly material benefits,
and that which is directed at moralizing or
rehabilitating. The two cannot easily be separated
since the second kind of work almost invariably
offers many of the benefits of the first category,
while many who claim to be offering no more than
material benefits are, in fact, hoping, if not
expecting, that the recipients will automatically
be rehabilitated without any further intervention.
In practice, however, the distinction is quite real,
and those institutions which explicitly direct a
substantial proportion of their energies towards
rehabilitation can be classed in the second
category -- whatever their material benefits --
while the institutions which offer only material
benefits do not effect rehabilitation on any

252

significant scale. And if the categories be
considered from the point of view of the recipients
the distinction is plainly very real. Many refuse
to have any dealings with the work which is directed
towards rehabilitation, and all are very conscious
of the two aspects of whatever kind of social work
they come into contact with.

Housing and Homes

There are on skid row many people who have
nowhere to live, so that housing poses a grave
problem. It is extremely hard to quantify the size
of the problem, but one table of figures compiled
in 1969 by a group from the Y.W.C.A. seeks to give
an accurate account of the housing needs for girls
in one city. The figures are estimates for a one
year period, 1968-9.

ESTIMATED NUMBERS FOR GIRLS ARRIVING IN THE CITY, 1968-9

category	reported in need	cared for	not cared for
A. Girls coming to city with resources, but needing accommodation and orientation to city life.....	455	195	260
B. Destitute girls who may require residence and orientation to city life.....................	594	49	545
C. Girls who may require supervised residence away from own homes...........	55	40	15
D. Girls released from institutions who may need supervised accommodation..	157	45	112

category	reported in need	cared for	not cared for
E. Girls without resources who are in the city for special purposes (e.g. education)..	134	34	100
F. Transient girls coming to the city......	78	28	50
G. Girls with pathological problems (e.g. alcoholism and prostitution).................	872	62	810
H. Expectant and unwed mother not in above categories.............	215	197	18
I. Girls in need of accommodation not categorised...............	2,220	1,721	499
	4,780	2,371	2,409

(Figures compiled by the Y.W.C.A., 1969)

This table does not distinguish between Indians and non-Indians, but the evidence suggests that a substantial proportion of categories B, F, G, and H are in fact Indians or Métis. Further, the compilers of the figures told me that they regarded the estimates as extremely conservative, largely because Indians who move between reserve and city are not easily quantified. Many make their way into the skid row district because they have no recourse to a route which would bring them into contact with agencies which might assist them.[24]

The Indian migrants would benefit enormously from a scheme aimed to provide accommodation at a

[24] Y.W.C.A. employees keep a close watch on the bus depot for arriving girls who are conspicuously in need of help, but so do pimps, bums, and lonely people on the look out for friends.

reasonable rate, and which also provided an information centre about employment so those who did think that employment would help them through their adjustment to city life would be able to determine what work was available in a fairly casual manner.

There is, in fact, one such institution in the city, though it does not provide for residence. This is the Native People's Centre. The Centre is run entirely by native people, and every afternoon it is possible for anyone to go there and get coffee and bannock free. There is a small library at the Centre, and a few musical instruments for visitors to play. The instruments are quite popular, and most days one or two people strum on guitars or play music on guitar and fiddle. The Centre also gives news about Indian affairs, and tries to keep classes in Cree well subscribed. The staff are qualified to give a great deal of advice and help on legal and social problems. The principal staff member is a court worker, and seems to be quite influential in the city. Certainly Indians can go to him for legal help and he intercedes on their behalf in the courts. Now that the Centre has become somewhat better known, the court occasionally refers a case to him, and the police sometimes contact him over a particularly difficult problem.

There is certainly a very relaxed atmosphere in the Centre, and though visitors are not permitted to drink or sleep there, most transients in serious need are accommodated whenever possible. The Indians of the city trust the staff of the Centre, and the staff do succeed in avoiding the excesses or moralization and latent criticism which infuse so much non-Indians' dealings with Indian problems. Skid row Indians often leave the bars during the afternoon and go to the Centre for a few hours, and in increasing numbers they look to the staff for advice and help -- particularly when in the courts.

What the Centre needs is a programme of massive expansion, but it seems that funds are just not forthcoming. At the moment, there is the nucleus

255

of an excellent staff, but the building has only
one large room for use of visitors. A residence
which grew out of the Centre would meet a very
pressing need, and could by itself do more to
alleviate the problem of the migrant than any other
single factor. At present there is in Vancouver
such a Centre, and its progress should be watched
closely for the same reasons.

The Y.W.C.A. functions in some measure as a
primarily residential institution, though girls who
have any difficulties are very closely watched
over. In the Y.W.C.A., however, there is very
little special awareness of the problem of Indian
girls, and accommodation is used chiefly by people
who are in the city for special purposes, such as
education.[25] Of course, it is necessary for the
majority of the girls there to pay for their rooms
keep, and some women use it rather like an hotel.
What the Y.W.C.A. does offer, however, is a youth
club for Indians -- both young men and women --
which is organised extremely intelligently and
could have a great deal of success. But it must
be noted that the majority of the people who come
to the youth club are students in the city and they
tend to regard skid row Indians as people from
another world. This attitude probably reflects
in considerable measure a desire to convince the
organizers of the club that they, the club users,
are not just bums and alcoholics -- but the very
fact that they should feel a need to give this kind
of reassurance reflects the nature of the club if
not the Y.W.C.A. itself. While it has that
character it will barely touch the problem of the
skid row population.

Much the same must be said of the Y.M.C.A.,
though in its case the large majority of users are
not Indians. Skid row men who are desperate for a
place to stay do not go to the Y.M.C.A. because they
do not need to. Instead they use the Salvation
Army Hostel.

25 The Y.W.C.A. accommodates 60, of whom 1/3 are
    usually Indian.

256

The Salvation Army Hostel is in the middle of skid row, and it is possible for even the very drunk to find their way from an adjacent bar into the entrance hall. The difficulty with the Salvation Army Hostel lies in its closing at 9:30 every night. This means that it is impossible for the men who want to drink until the bars close at 11 p.m. to stay there. It is not easy for a man to extricate himself from a group of friends who are having a very happy time, and make his solitary way to the Hostel. It may be that the Salvation Army regards this small act of self-discipline as a minimum sacrifice for the use of their facilities, but if the Salvation Army is seriously trying to alleviate the problem of the homeless on skid row it might reconsider its policies in the light of the objectives. It cannot be denied, however, that some do leave the bars and go to the Hostel, but they tend to be the older men who are afraid of having nowhere to stay at all. For the younger men, the Hostel has only very limited use.

For those who do not get into the Hostel, have no friend to stay with, and prefer not to sleep in the open (and in the winter this is impossible) the cheap hotels are the only resort. All the skid row bars are located in hotels where it is possible to rent a room for as little as three dollars a night, and when the bars close many people are obliged to do so. To pay for these rooms many of the drinkers spend the last hour's drinking time borrowing and begging money. It is quite possible that a substantial proportion of the small crimes in the streets after closing time are thus motivated.

Of course the purely commercial hotel is the residence least concerned with the rehabilitation of its residents. In the hotel rooms many drinking parties are continued long into the night, and they offer the most effective protection against the most pervasive vulnerabilities -- the night's place is sure, there is no need to fear the intrusion of unwelcome outsiders, be they forces of law or friends. The hotels are full every night.

257

Rehabilitation

The provincial jail is the institution concerned with rehabilitation which skid row Indians come into contact with the most. During fieldwork I did not meet a single Indian who had been on skid row for more than a few months who had not been in jail. Many of the sentences are very short, and many of the offenders make a very conscious distinction between sentences served in the provincial jail and those served in the penitentiary. The provincial jail takes all offenders sentenced to less than two years. Between fifty and seventy-five per cent of the inmates are usually Indian or Métis.

The actual rehabilitation work done in the jail is small. There are programmes for educational up-grading, but they are not popular. There are some facilities for technical training, but they are very limited, and the prisoners are allowed little time out of their cells. Outside speakers are occasionally invited to talk to Indian inmates, but there is inevitably a great deal of suspicion and wariness of strangers.

It is necessary to emphasise the relaxed attitude which Indians tend to have towards jail. It is not, in the skid row world at least, a source of remorse or guilt to be jailed. Indeed, it is substantially the opposite: the 'rounder' is a person who is likely to build up some prestige, especially if the offences for which he is jailed are impressive for their daring or monetary returns. Many people from different towns meeting in skid row bars remember one another from jail; most conversations between Indians who are uncertain if they have met before or not centre on jails and prisoners they have known. Jail is an important shared experience, and is valued so much by virtually all skid row people. Many Indians and non-Indians told me that they did not mind the shorter sentences at all, for they gave a chance to rest, get some better food than usual, and meet many old friends. There is never any mention of

258

the embarrassment or stigma which attaches to jail
sentences in most communities outside skid row.

It is not surprising, therefore, that
recidivism among the skid row population is extremely
high. It is in fact highest in the twenty to thirty
age group, and next highest in the forty to fifty
group. Altogether the numbers in jail have decreased
in all age-groups, but not due to the deterrent effect
of jail or to the success of skeletal programmes
for rehabilitation: the police have decided to
reduce the number of arrests they make for simple
drunkenness and other minor offences, while the
magistrates have realised that over-zealousness in
jailing for first offences can only reap negative
returns.

In jail the Indians tend to be more friendly
than the non-Indians. The social worker in the
women's section told me that the Indian girls are
very glad to sit and talk and laugh with the
counsellor, and, once initial defensiveness and
shyness is overcome, are very glad to maintain a
relaxed joking relationship with all social workers
who come into contact with them. In contrast, the
White girls are very serious, and seem very
concerned about what is going to be done for them.
They aggressively insist that something must be done.
This difference in response to the social worker
is the one indication of a difference in attitude
to being in jail at all.

Given that the Indians in jail are forced to
be there for a definite period, and that they have
very few negative feelings about being in jail,
the rehabilitation aspect of the institution is not
likely to be effective. The argument that going
to jail at all is reformative, or at worst likely
to frighten offenders out of repeating their
offences quite obviously does not apply. Jail,
therefore, barely qualifies as part of social
rehabilitation, despite the protestations by social
workers to the contrary. Perhaps the one
qualification to this lies in the presence of
social workers in the jails -- it is in jail that

most of the Indians are brought into contact with a social worker or counsellor, and in the course of their lives this contact can prove influential. But even that qualification probably applies only to the younger women.

Apart from the jail, there are a number of half-way houses and similar institutions. The half-way house was conceived as a way of easing the route between the closed institution and normal social life. Ideally, the prisoner being rehabilitated can leave jail for a half-way house where residence is provided and counselling is continued. Here it should be possible for the resident to pursue some training or seek some job without the desperate lack of home, security, and money which customarily greets the prisoner on release.

The half-way house is the one institution in a position to overcome the paradoxical situation of the Indian prisoner who goes to jail for offences which arise out of his marginal social position (petty theft, prostitution, false pretences, drunken fighting) and his ability to integrate into the economic opportunities of the society as a whole, but who comes out of jail even less capable of integration than before. The Indian girls in jail complain that they cannot find the jobs they want, most commonly nursing or social work. But to become a nurse's assistant a girl must have attained grade ten. Very few Indian girls have reached more than grade seven. Once they have been in jail the difficulty of finding any employment is much increased, and those girls who do find some work tend to do so only with deception. I heard several cases where the deception was uncovered, the girls who for several months had proved quite satisfactory employees were summarily dismissed because they had been in jail and had not said so when applying for their jobs. It is this kind of difficulty that the half-way house aims at alleviating.

There are two such houses for women in the city, but none for men. Both the houses for women

260

had the same difficulties: the Indian residents
tended to use the house as a place to come to when
in desperate straights, but would not settle into
its rehabilitative modes. Living in an institution
organised entirely by middle class Whites is not
easy for an Indian girl. Her experience and the
kind of attitudes which her experience has moulded
are at odds with those of all others who have
dealings with her. Hence the Indians tend to remain
feeling marginal, keep to themselves, and in
withdrawal do not take advantage of the
opportunities which the half-way house is trying to
give them. Instead they look to skid row for
company, and to hustling for a source of income.

It must be added that these Indian women have
a good deal of rationale on their side. The social
workers and resident staff say that they should
stop drinking, stop hustling, and find some other
way of living. But in fact drinking is the route to
friends and companions with whom they do not feel
awkward, and the difficulties which face an Indian
woman with low educational grade attainment in a
search for employment are so severe as to
highlight the benefits of the hustler's life.

The half-way houses not only take women out
of jail, but in fact tend to concentrate on women
who are picked up on the streets and seem to be
in need of help. Some women simply come to the
house and ask to be taken in. Many of these are
very ill from prolonged drinking when they arrive,
and often have been seriously beaten. They need,
therefore, a period of recuperation and some medical
attention. But as they recuperate, so the utility
of the recuperation comes to be outweighed by the
disutility of their isolation within the homes. For
the Indian this isolation is very severe. Unable
to relate to the other residents, who are either
non-Indian or of a very different age-group, and
forbidden to go out drinking, they increasingly
feel the strong appeal of skid row.[26]

26 Anyone who returns to the house drunk is in
    danger of being turned away. In one house

Much as the staff of these houses are
understanding and sympathetic to their residents'
problems, they are effectively unable to grasp how
isolating their homes are for the Indians, and they
also seriously underestimate the difficulties which
would face the Indian women in a search for
employment and integration into mainstream Canadian
life.

If the social workers succeed in communicating
to the Indians that they are there to find jobs
and provide facilities which Indians need, and if
they can avoid implying or suggesting that there is
a price in terms of rehabilitation to be paid for
these benefits, they are able to do useful work.
Much effort goes into the social work that is
carried out, but far too much of that effort is
under-informed or too flagrantly middle class in
its tones. The Indians, as this report is
emphasising throughout, constitute a sub-culture
within the industrial society which has moral and
social qualities systematically at odds with those
of the mainstream society. The opposition in these
values, and ways must be dealt with intelligently
by all who wish to offer benefits and services and
counsel to Indian migrants. Many of these migrants
are glad of help. What they are much less glad
of is a presumptuous claim by the helper that the
Indian on skid row is quite obviously in desperate
need of reform. The experience of the skid row
Indian in many cases quite manifestly disconfirms
that view, for he frequently knows very well just
how difficult, hostile, and alien the alternative
forms of life in the city are. Skid row has much
to offer, and social workers can help where there
is need before claiming the right to determine
the correct social paths.

the stricture is so strong that the best
established residents get turned away for coming
to the House drunk.

REFERENCES

Aalen, A. A. and H. R. Brody
1969 Gola, the Life and Last Days of an Island Community. Cork: Mercier Press.

Anderson, R. T. and G. Anderson
1960 "Sexual Behaviour and Urbanisation in a Danish Village". Southwest Journal of Anthropology, Vol. 16;93-109.

Aron, R.
1967 The Industrial Society, New York: F. A. Praeger.

Berreman, Gerald D.
1956 "Drinking Pattern of the Aleuts", Quarterly Journal of Studies on Alcohol. Vol. 17, No. 3-503-14.

Berreman, Gerald D.
1964 "Aleut Reference Group Alienation, Mobility, and Acculturation", American Anthropology. Vol. 66:231-47.

Canadian Corrections Association
1967 Indians and the Law. Ottawa: Crown Publication.

Chance, Norman
1962 "Culture Change and Integration: An Eskimo Example", American Anthropology. Vol. 62:1028-44.
1965 "Acculturation, Self-Identity, and Personality Adjustment", American Anthropology, Vol. 62, No. 2:372-89.

Curley, R. L.
1967 "Drinking Patterns of the Mescalero Apache", Quarterly Journal of Studies on Alcohol, Vol. 28, No. 1:116-131.

Clairmont, D. H. J.
1963 Deviance Among Indians and Eskimos in Aklavik, N.W.T. Ottawa: Northern Co-ordination and Research Center, Department of Northern Affairs and National Resources. NCRC-63-9.

Desgoffe, C.
    1955 "Le Gas des Esquimaux des Iles Belcher", *Anthropologica* No. 1:45-61.

Devereux, George
    1951 *Reality and Dream*. New York: International Universities Press.

Dozier, Edward P.
    1966 "Problem Drinking Among American Indians: The Role of Socio-cultural Deprevation", *Quarterly Journal of Studies on Alcohol*. Vol. 27, No. 1:72-87.

Elkin, A. P.
    1951 "Reaction and Interaction: A Food Gathering People and European Settlement in Australia", *American Anthropology*. Vol. 53: 164-83.

Erickson, Eric H.
    1964 *Childhood and Society*. New York: Norton.

Fanon, Franz
    1965 *The Wretched of the Earth*. New York: Grove Press.
    1968 *Black Skin, White Masks*. New York: Grove Press.

Frank, A. G.
    1967 "Sociology of Development and Underdevelopment of Sociology". *Catalyst* No. 3.

Goldfrank, Ester S.
    1945 "Changing Configurations in the Social Organization of a Blackfoot Tribe During the Reserve Period", *Monographs of the American Ethnographic Society*. VIII.

Hawthorn, H. B., C. S. Belshaw, and S. M. Jamieson
    1958 *The Indians of British Columbia*. Toronto: University of Toronto Press.

Hawthorn, H. B.
    1967 A Survey of Contemporary Indians of
    Canada. 2 Volumes, Ottawa: Indian Affairs
    Branch.

Heath, D. B.
    1962 "Drinking Patterns of the Bolivian Camba",
    Society, Culture and Drinking Patterns, eds.
    Pittman and Snyder, York. New York: Wiley.

Honigmann, John J. and Irma Honigmann
    1945 "Drinking in an Indian-White Community",
    Quarterly Journal of Studies on Alcohol.
    Vol. 5:575-619.

Hughes, C. C.
    1960 An Eskimo Village in a Modern World.
    Ithaca: Cornell University Press.

King, A. R.
    1967 The School of Monpass: A Problem of
    Identity. Montreal: Holt, Rhinehart and
    Winston.

Lemert, Edwin M.
    1954 Alcohol and the Northwest Coast Indians.
    Berkeley: University of California Press.
    1958 "The Use of Alcohol in Three Salish
    Tribes", Quarterly Journal of Studies in
    Alcohol. Vol. 19, No. 1:90-109.

Lewis, Oscar
    1962 The Children of Sanchez. London: Secker
    and Warburg.
    1965 La Vida. Toronto: Random House.

Lurie, Nancy Oestrich
    1969 A Suggested Hypothesis for the Study of
    Indian Drinking. Unpublished paper read at
    CSAS Meeting, May 1-4, Milwaukee.

Mead, Margaret
    1932 Changing Culture of an American Tribe.
    New York: Capricorn Books.

Nagler, Mark
    1970 <u>Indians in the City</u>. Ottawa: Canadian
    Research Center for Anthropology.

Rivers, W. H. R.
    1962 "The Psychologica Factor", <u>Essays on the</u>
    <u>Depopulation of Melanesia</u>.

Robbins, Richard H.
    1968 <u>Role Reinforcement and Ritual Deprivation</u>.
    Unpublished paper. Dartmouth College.

Sutcliffe, Robert B.
    1969 <u>The Third World and Social History</u>. Paper
    read at the Social History Group, Oxford.

Vayda, Andrew
    1967 "Pomo Trade Geasts", <u>Tribal and Peasant</u>
    <u>Economics</u>. G. Walton (ed). New York:
    Natural History Press.

Washburne, Chandler
    1961 <u>Primitive Drinking</u>. London: College and
    University Press.

Whittaker, James O.
    1963 "Alcohol and the Standing Rock Sioux
    Tribes", <u>Quarterly Journal of Studies in</u>
    <u>Alcohol</u>. Vol. 24, No. 1.

Worsley, P.
    1969 <u>The Third World</u>. London: Weidenfeld and
    Nicolson, World University Library.

CHAPTER IX

Perspectives on Alcohol Behavior

by

John J. Honigmann

University of North Carolina at Chapel Hill

I

    Several times since contributing to a
description of alcohol behavior by Indians and non-
Indians in a small western Canadian sub-Arctic
community called "Delio" (Honigmann and Honigmann
1945) thirty years ago, it has occurred to me that
the interpretation given there could also be
presented from other cultural perspectives.[1] For
example, the use of alcohol conceived of as a
normal part of culture, positively sanctioned
except when it led to aggression, could also be
seen as deviant behavior indicative of social
disintegration (Honigmann 1966). I am unconcerned
with which view is more adequate, or truer,
though that is a proper question to ask on the
ethnological level of analysis. Instead I propose,

This article was written especially for this
volume.

[1] Attempts to maintain the anonymity of the
    community were soon abandoned, as the interested
    reader will learn by examining the second
    reference. Anonymity seemed important in 1944
    because serious illegal behavior, illicit
    distilling, was being reported on. Today there
    is no danger in identifying the community as
    Lower Post, B. C., and the Indians as Kaska,
    but I will retain the name Delio for consistency.

along with examining how cultural persepctives
arise in ethnographic research, to explain how
different perspectives can be applied to
practically the same set of data concerning alcohol
behavior, and to discuss the significance of such
freedom in interpretation for understanding
ethnographic reports. These questions belong to
the philosophy of science, a field in which I
claim no special competence but to which my
experience in studying alcohol behavior may make
a contribution.[2]

                        II

     In the article written by Irma Honigmann and
myself in 1945 about Delio, a northern Canadian
trading post frequented by Indians and White
trappers, we recognized that many of the community's
practices related to alcohol were illegal when
appraised by the legal norms of the larger social
system. However, we treated Delio as if it were
an independent, primarily isolated, culturally
highly distinctive social system, on a par with
the primitive societies I had recently been
reading much about while an undergraduate and
graduate student of anthropology. Much the way
an ethnographer imbued with the principle of
cultural relativity might regard traditional
patterns of premarital sexuality, feuding, and
head-hunting in an exotic society as normative
while knowing that other societies regard such
acts as morally or legally wrong, we studied Delio

[2] The term "alcohol behavior" is comprehensive
     enough to include not only the drinking of
     alcohol beverages but also to their manufacture--
     "brewing" in northern parlance; sharing them,
     sometimes illegally with minors and other people
     prohibited from drinking; intoxication, the major
     cause of arrest in the northern communities
     where I have done fieldwork; the forms
     intoxicated behavior assumes; and attitudes
     toward alcohol.

in terms of its own norms, minimizing the applicability of Canadian legal and conventional norms. The Indians and the White trappers exercised an extremely low degree of social control over their alcohol behavior, and the only sanctions on alcohol behavior came from White policemen who periodically visited the place. Since we studied the community in summer when the Indians and White trappers were on holiday, drinking did not interfere with work.

In the published account, the normalcy with which we treat alcohol behavior is revealed in the tolerant attitude adopted toward Indians and toward the people's fear and resentment of the police. We also refer tolerantly to bootleggers selling whiskey to the Indians, our tone condemning only the extortionist prices, not the illegal custom. We describe the manufacture of "brew" with the detachment we might apply to cooking.

Drinking we treat as a form of recreation, which is what the Indians presented it as being.[3] In keeping with the infrequency with which the people criticized drinking, our report emphasizes the unobjectionableness of most intoxicated behavior. Our account recognizes that aggression accompanied drunkenness, but we stress attempts being made to control hostile acts and note their infrequency, especially in the subgroup of Indians whom we primarily observed. (All frequency interpretations were based on qualitative judgments and not on objective measurement.) We report depression occurring only infrequently under intoxication, and tolerantly note the marked increased in sexual behavior and of immodesty with respect to urination occurring when Indians were drunk. We also point

[3] However, in the concluding section of the paper, and moreso in another publication (Honigmann 1949), the attitude of cultural relativism applied to the Indians' use of alcohol is accompanied by a nonrelativistic psychodynamic interpretation of drinking. See Footnote 1.

out the capacity of alcohol to facilitate the introverted Indians' social interaction with one another. The value stance in the published account is not as explicit as I present it here, for it is submerged in a value-neutral style of writing appropriate, as I thought, for a professional publication.

The published paper maintains the same style and perspective when it turns from the Indians to the White trappers and their customs of distilling, brewing, and drinking. We call attention to the men's fantasies, tinged with positive affect, depicting intoxicated distillers rolling into town, confirmed drinkers who prefer lemon extract to scotch, and the total community as a "haywire outfit," a haven of libidinous gratification and reckless spontaneity at another pole from the staid conventions of civilized life (for this aspect see also Honigmann 1970:46).

In a concluding section of the published paper we employ a scale of drinking behavior devised by Donald Horton (1943) to rate the community. We judge it to be engaging in moderate drinking and as manifesting moderate insobriety, "Moderate" in Horton's scale being indicated when "drinking usually ends in intoxication, but does not continue for days. Unconsciousness is not regular or frequent." To the Indians alone we apply the theory (also taken from Horton) of alcohol functioning to reduce anxiety. In keeping with our perspective that alcohol behavior in Delio is essentially normal, we judge the Indians' anxiety as only moderate in intensity; correspondingly, their drinking is not to be regarded as an undesirable way of coping with an unpleasant personality condition. Observe how a variety of data is conceptualized and integrated to make it consistent with the perspective that sees Delio's alcohol behavior to be a normal part of the culture. A good part of the behavior would no doubt be illegal and unconventional in the main-line society, but in Delio--it is acceptable to the groups we studied and must be accepted by an anthropologist who identifies with those groups' norms and values. This is the

attitude I had learned from teachers, including
Ruth Benedict (1934:Ch. 8) and A. H. Maslow (1941:
30-38), who had been her student and greatly
influenced my thinking.

Twenty years later among the Eskimo of
Frobisher Bay, a Baffin Island town comprising 1600
persons of whom 900 were Eskimo who had recently
quit hunting and trapping lives for jobs and modern
homes in the town, we looked upon alcohol behavior
from a different perspective (Honigmann and
Honigmann 1965a:14, 43, 108, 135-136, 196-215; also
1965b). The accounts we wrote about the community
present alcohol as a serious personal and social
problem with which the Eskimo were striving to cope
successfully, and we paid considerable attention
to how Eskimo adults belonging to different age,
leadership, and occupational categories were coping
with alcohol. We did not regard the Eskimo an
independent cultural group, as we had the Delio
Indians and White trappers, but as an integral part
of the town, and the town we saw closely linked to
the larger social system. The liquor laws set by
Canadian authorities were now accepted by us as
fully applying to the Eskimo. The Eskimo took
the same attitude, and the degree to which Eskimo
avoided being convicted for breaking those laws
furnished an important index of their successful
accommodation to town life.

Why the difference between a relativistic,
tolerant perspective toward alcohol use in Delio and
a nonrelativistic perspective that sees alcohol in
Frobisher Bay to be a problem likely to be associated
with illegal behavior?

Cultural factors no doubt had something to do
with the perspective adopted in each case, but the
patterns we drew were by no means simply reflections
of what we saw during fieldwork. Looking at Delio
retrospectively, it appears that the perspective we
took there was greatly influenced by a decision
implicitly taken to view the community, especially
the Indian segment, as an autonomous cultural system.
The decision to do so was conditioned by a

predilection, learned as an undergraduate and
graduate student, to see each culture as unique and
in some respects incomparable to others, the
incomparable features being the most interesting for
study. Anti-authoritarian attitudes directed by
White trappers and Indians against external agencies
of social control supported the view of Delio as an
autonomous cultural system. We came to Frobisher
Bay knowing the town's notoriety as a place where
resettled Eskimo had become socially disorganized.
Immediately upon our arrival a non-Eskimo
administrator briefed us on the widespreadness of
native personal and social disturbance promoted by
alcohol. Although our research conclusively
disproved the stereotype of a socially disintegrated
native community unable to deal successfully with
alcohol, we reached that conclusion only by
adopting, as a working hypothesis, the generally
shared view of alcohol as problematic.

Eskimo who drank acted as if drinking was one
of the many satisfying experiences they enjoyed in
town, but they too revealed severely traumatized
attitudes toward alcohol. Their attitude, learned
partly from Anglican missionaries during the past
sixty years of missionary activity, regarded
drinking to be morally wrong. They also looked on
drinking as dangerous because of the sometimes
fatal aggression it provoked. Their fear was
reasonable; a murder had been committed by a drunken
man shortly before our arrival and other cases of
physical violence were also known. An Eskimo leader,
himself not abstemious, branded drinking as the
native townsmen's most serious problem. We met
Eskimo who determinedly avoided drinking and learned
of a movement, organized by non-Eskimo some years
before, that failed to induce the government to
refrain from opening a local liquor store.
Subsequently, to cope with heavy drinking the
government introduced a regulation whereby beer,
wine, and spirits could only be purchased if they
were ordered a minimum of three weeks in advance.
Following the regulation native patronage of the
store fell off and court convictions dropped, though
alcoholic beverages remained available for immediate

272

consumption at the well-patronized, privately owned tavern.

Given the contrasting attitudes and events associated with alcohol in Delio and Frobisher Bay, it does appear as if cultural reality in each community dictated the perspective we applied, in one case regarding even reckless and illicit alcohol behavior as essentially normal and nonpathological and in the other treating alcohol as a problem that seeing who was capable of coping with it.

Such a conclusion, however, is contradicted for Delio by the fact that following fieldwork in Frobisher Bay I adopted quite a different perspective toward Delio's alcohol behavior, one largely consistent with the interpretation of alcohol among the Eskimo. In a paper applying the social psychiatric concepts of Alexander Leighton (1959) to several northern Canadian communities (Honigmann 1966), I apply to Delio Leighton's view of drinking as a short-term mode of recreation, see it as indicative of social disintegration, and frankly recognize the illegal, or deviant, aspects of alcohol behavior in the community. I cite the lack of strong social control within the Indian community and other factors responsible for promoting deviant alcohol behavior. No new data led to the new interpretation. The explanation for the shift lies in two interrelated factors solely associated with the ethnographer. First, in reanalyzing Delio's alcohol behavior I abandoned the principle of cultural relativity. As a result, I no longer looked at events in the community only from the standpoint of the norms held by Indian and White trappers. I now judged events with the universal, or absolute, concepts of social disintegration and deviant behavior in mind. Delio's alcohol behavior was deviant because it failed to conform to the legal norms of the larger society whose sanctions Delio could not avoid. Second, abandoning the view of Delio as an autonomous cultural system and the principle of cultural relativity and adopting social psychiatric concepts mark changes in me, the ethnographer, as a person. New experiences had

273

changed me from the individual I had been twenty-years previously, including fieldwork in Frobisher Bay and other communities with varying patterns of alcohol behavior (Honigmann 1963). Those experiences include exposure to social psychiatry and deviant-behavior theory, interest in applied anthropology, and greater familiarity with the literature pertaining to alcohol. Such experiences encouraged me to try out the new perspective on the Delio data, and I discovered it could be applied successfully.

Following fieldwork in Frobisher Bay, Irma Honigmann and I studied the native sector of another northern Canadian town, Inuvik, located in the Mackenzie River delta. The native sector accommodated some eleven-hundred people: Indians (mostly Athapaskan but including a number of Cree who had migrated northward along the Mackenzie), western Arctic Eskimo, Métis, as well as a few non-native persons married to or living with persons belonging to the native groups. The native population mostly lived in a part of the town separated by a commercial zone (which includes a liquor store and tavern) from another housing area inhabited mainly by non-native families of government employees hailing from many parts of Canada.

In the published account we wrote of Inuvik (Honigmann and Honigmann 1970), we proceed partly as we did in Frobisher Bay. We recognize that some of the native community's alcohol behavior is deviant when judged by Canadian society norms and report the frequency with which different categories of people in the native sector get into difficulties with police through the use of alcohol. But we no longer emphasize the problematic aspects of alcohol as we did in Frobisher Bay, even though our informants did (informants' attitudes collected on tape are reported in Honigmann, Ms.a). Acknowledging the existence of deviant alcohol behavior, we treat such deviance relativistically, as if it were normal in the context of native sector's frontier culture (Honigmann 1971; also Honigmann and Honigmann 1970:Ch. 2).

274

Frontier culture is not the aboriginal or traditional culture of the native population but a style of life that developed in the course of one-hundred and fifty years of acculturation, in the Delta and lower Mackenzie valley. Culture contact stimulated a considerable degree of cultural borrowing on the part of the three major native groups without, however, promoting complete cultural assimilation. Increasingly during the period of culture contact the lower Mackenzie valley witnessed the influx of new institutions claiming superior rank and power for themselves: traders, missionaries, boarding schools, and police. Toward the end of the period, in the 1950's, a relatively large, modern town was built in the Delta and brought about an influx of still more government officials and regulative procedures. In place of fur trapping, formerly the main occupation, the town opened a large number of steady jobs to natives. Inuvik also brought a large contingent of non-native government workers and their families from southern Canada into the Delta. Despite the large degree of cultural borrowing that had taken place among natives, most of whom spoke English and possessed some elementary school education, the families from the south manifested a life style different in many respects from the one followed by the Delta folk. The non-natives' superiority and cultural distinctiveness was symbolized in the better housing reserved for them in a separate, better maintained section of the town. Natives who moved into the town and took jobs, discovered they were being deprived of a large measure of their former autonomy as they became subordinate to rules governing jobs, housing, welfare, and other activities. They also confronted new values exemplified in the life style of the non-native population, value symbolically denoted as superior to those values of Delta folk.

Frontier culture was no sudden creation. It developed gradually during the century and a half while the Delta people devoted themselves to fur trapping, hunting, and fishing. As the name implies, much of frontier culture is adapted to rugged outdoor activities, but it also has its expressive aspects,

of which alcohol behavior is one. In both its
adaptive and expressive aspects the culture contrasts
with the mainline culture of North American society,
the culture which is represented almost intact in
the section of Inuvik where the government employees
and their families live. The norms and values of the
frontier culture with respect to legal marriage,
respect for police, and use of alcohol conflict
sharply with those of the dominant culture, though
members of the native community know the mainline
norms and recognize their ideal legitimacy. In
cases where the mainline norms are disregarded, the
persons who disregard them know they are acting
unconventionally or illegally but generally show no
evidence of personal concern in doing so. Heavy
drinking on payday weekends and other social
occasions, at the tavern or with beverages bought
at the government-owned liquor store is a
conspicuous feature of Inuvik's frontier culture
and contravenes mainline drinking norms. Formerly
unlicensed brewing was also a deviant aspect of
Delta frontier culture and so, still, is the freedom
with which alcoholic beverages in Inuvik's native
sector are shared with minors and persons legally
interdicted from drinking. Public drunkenness,
illegal under the liquor law, is another conspicuous
part of the town's frontier culture and is
responsible for the majority of arrests. Our account
shows that not everyone in the native sector
participates equally in the frontier culture or in
its deviant aspects. Some heavy drinkers avoid the
reckless pattern of alcohol use that leads to trouble
with the police. Other people have tried to
institute a pattern of moderate drinking at home (a
drink after work, before dinner), and some individuals
abstain completely from alcohol. The latter include
members of the Pentecostal Church, a number of whom
were formerly heavy drinkers, and of Alcoholics
Anonymous.

My experience led me to the theory that a number
of people who follow the frontier culture's pattern
of alcohol use, especially with regard to drinking
heavily and appearing drunk in public, do so as a
kind of acting out. They possess a more or less

276

conscious mental representation of the symbolic
significance of their behavior. But whether or not
they are consciously aware of it, grounds exist for
interpreting their style of alcohol behavior as a
badge of cultural identity. Their actions identify
them with the frontier culture and connote their
disaffection from the more confining obligations
of mainline norms and values. Inuvik's frontier
culture in general, but especially its style of
alcohol behavior, is also a way of resisting any
greater concession of superiority and rank to the
dominant society and a means of protecting a measure
of spontaneity and autonomy. Depending on the
strength with which individuals adhere to it, the
culture further serves as a nativistic brake
controlling further assimilation.[4]

The interpretation of alcohol behavior in
Inuvik as a positively sanctioned contracultural
feature of frontier culture is even less directly
justified by objective cultural facts than the view
of Frobisher Bay's alcohol as problematic. With
the western town also possessing a reputation for
disorderliness as great as that of Frobisher Bay,
and arrests for violations of the liquor laws being
higher than in Frobisher Bay (Honigmann and
Honigmann 1970:101-102; see also Clairmont 1963),
we could easily have treated the town in the same
fashion as Frobisher Bay. Where is the

[4] Spaulding (1966:111) reports a closely similar
historical phenomenon from northern Saskatchewan.
There when Metis found their autonomy suddenly
restricted as a result of newly introduced
administrative pressures and puritanical middle-
class values, they withdrew from involvement in
the dominant society, becoming socially marginal.
Withdrawal did not, however, completely shield
them from white people's claim of superiority.
They responded to their invidious assigned status
by integrating themselves culturally on the basis
of opposition to Whites and displayed their
opposition in behavior expressing disdain for the
middle-class values of industry, sexual chastity,
and sobriety.

justification for emphasizing the normative, or positively sanctioned aspects of alcohol behavior in the Delta town? Primarily in the total contemporary cultural pattern and culture history. Alcohol behavior in Inuvik viewed by an outsider in relation to the total cultural pattern -- that is, relativistically and configurationally -- takes on a different meaning than similar behavior in Frobisher Bay. The western Arctic people are much more sophisticated with respect to modern culture than the Eskimo of Frobisher Bay. Most of the adults have had some formal education and, while many of them are also Anglican in religion, they are far more secular in outlook than people in the eastern Arctic. Their view of alcohol and the liquor store is not as traumatized, probably because they have known and used alcohol for a longer time so that it has become an accepted part of the culture. To deal with Inuvik's alcohol behavior as primarily problematic and indicative of disorganization would have been ethnocentric, or would have required us to identify most immediately with those relatively few native people who were strongly committed to mainline norms and values and therefore marginal to the native sector of the town. After finishing with Frobisher Bay we felt dissatisfied with the nonrelativistic perspective on alcohol behavior taken there. We did not want to describe Inuvik in similar negative terms, which would have happened had we emphasized the problems created by alcohol. Even in Frobisher Bay we used police records to document the comparative infrequency and localized extent of personal difficulties with alcohol. In Inuvik, while also pointing out the comparatively limited incidence arrests alcohol, we found the concepts of frontier culture and contraculture ideally suited for interpreting behavior, manifestly deviant from one point of view, as if it were normative in the context where it occurred.

My experience in Inuvik again led me to reconsider the Delio data, in which a closely similar pattern of alcohol behavior now stood revealed. The norms for alcohol behavior in both the Indian and White sectors of Delio were also

278

contracultural in the sense that the actors knew
the legal norms governing alcohol in their society
but deliberately disregarded them. The White
trappers' conception of the community as a "haywire
outfit" indicates they consciously objectified their
community as being culturally at variance with
communities following stricter or more regular rules
of conduct. Among the Indians, the alcohol behavior
reported in 1945 as normatively sanctioned in a
positive way could be seen as a style of behavior
forged by people who for half a century had been
closely involved in western society but who resisted
assimilating all the norms and values of that
society. With the concepts of frontier culture and
contraculture I can maintain a stance of cultural
relativity toward Delio--as I prefer to do--without
the heuristic fiction of treating the community as
if it were equivalent to an isolated, primitive
society incorporating non-western cultural
tradition. Although I have done nothing further
with these thoughts, I expound them to show that
yet another conception of Delio's alcohol behavior
is possible. The new view is also not indicated by
new data but results solely from a different
perspective for conceptualizing the data that
resulted from new experiences I had encountered.
The latest view does not contradict the earlier
interpretations of alcohol behavior in Delio as
normal or as deviant. It reconciles both those
concepts. But whether any of the three views is
superior to another is not at this point a pertinent
question; I suspect arguments buttressed by data and
theory could be offered for and against any one.

The frontier style of alcohol behavior appears
in accounts of other Mackenzie River communities
(cf. Cohen 1962:99-100 and, for frontier culture in
general, other parts of his report; see also Phillips,
Ms.) Such descriptions distinguish the western sub-
Arctic, occupied by Athapaskan Indians who in some
places live in close association with white trappers,
from the eastern sub-Arctic with its Algonkian
population. But because a description turns out to
be reliable obviously does not mean it is the only

one possible given the facts.

IV

Were I to adopt the usual model of ethnography as a mirror of cultural reality, I would conclude this chapter saying I have described three styles of alcohol behavior, three different meanings of alcohol discovered in northern Canadian communities.

But clearly, when the behavior of one community can be described from different perspectives and none of those is false in the sense of being contradicted by another, more is involved in ethnography than just reporting existing phenomena. Alcohol behavior in Delio or any other community is not a single entity, a piece of reality with only one form or meaning. As an ethnographic pattern a community's alcohol behavior is a conception, a pattern that may be conceived of in several ways, looked at from various perspectives, much as a photographer can take pictures of the same scene from different vantage points (the image is used in Maquet 1964). Nor have I taken advantage of all the anthropological perspectives applicable in Delio and the other communities I have studied; there is, for example, the possibility of conceiving it as time out behavior (MacAndrew and Edgerton 1969).

In my view, ethnography is a process in which the investigator actively converts empirical facts into knowledge, not a reflection what is empirically given. Even simple description always contains an element of interpretation, or a theoretical component (N. R. Hanson cited in Suppe 1974:152), representing the perspective from which the events are conceptualized. No perspective directly reflects the reality of alcohol behavior in the communities where it is applied. The convential model of ethnography as a mirror reflecting social reality fails to encompass the inescapable and highly

280

potent role ethnographer plays in writing a report. Even a mirror creates as it distorts what it reflects, but the fieldworker in producing knowledge takes a more active part in creating (Honigmann Ms. b). The fieldworker's account depends on the kind of person he or she is; the contemporary historical and personal situation; the personal skills, talents, and proclivities brought to bear in research; the theory or interests guiding observation; and, most directly, the conscious or unconscious way an investigator conceives of certain features in the behavior under observation. Features like normalcy, deviance, and symbolic value are conceived in the mind of the anthropologist, processed out of cues he receives. Anthropology, I realize, has become dissatisfied with the clearly known extent to which such personal factors operate in traditional ethnography. As a result some methodologists want to see the role of the ethnographer made more explicit by spelling out as many operations in data-creation as possible, or confining ethnography only to concepts and meanings furnished by informants. However much those devices confine the ethnographer's imagination and intuition, they do not eliminate the anthropologist as a potent factor in the production of ethnographic knowledge.

The patterns of alcohol behavior in Delio, Frobisher Bay, and Inuvik depend to a great extent, like any pattern, on factors independent of what is externally given. Before any facts are observed the pattern starts to be formed in the first methodological decisions made by a fieldworker, for example, whether to be culturally relativistic or not. The pattern is further influenced by many subsequent decisions of a methodological and theoretical sort entering into fieldwork, analysis of data, and writing up the report. These decisions, in turn, reflect factors like the state of anthropology at a given time or the state of the ethnographer's society that lead him to select certain concepts for conceptualization of data rather than others. (The concepts of deviant behavior and contraculture had become popular by the time I worked in Frobisher

281

Bay and Inuvik.) The previous experience of the observer is another important variable entering into patterns of culture; one person's experience enables him to perceive constructs in the facts that would be impossible for another. These and similar factors determine the perspectives from which patterns of alcohol behavior are constructed.

Because an ethnographer finds a particular pattern satisfactory, including finding it true by whatever tests of truth he employs, for a particular community at a given time does not promise it will be equally satisfactory at another time, nor that other persons with different values, interests, backgrounds, and theoretical preconceptions will consider it adequate. Argument may properly ensue, for instance, over the fit of a pattern to the data it organizes, over the quality of the supporting evidence, over the theoretical premises, etc. In the course of such argument alternative constructions may be put forward, perhaps successfully, or the original construction may be reformulated in the interests of viability. I believe Geertz (1973:9) has the same dialectical process in mind when he speaks of cultural interpretations being contestable and describes progress in cultural anthropology being achieved not through a proposition being generally accepted as true but as a result of constant refinement by debate.

My principal object in this chapter has been to demonstrate how different perspectives may be applied to the same alcohol behavior while examining how different viewpoints arise. The freedom I described in ethnographic conceptualization signifies that the culture patterns presented in an ethnographic report are not reflections of reality but to a great extent represent constructs dependent on factors inherent in the ethnographer and independent of what is perceived.

REFERENCES

Benedict, Ruth
    1934   Patterns of Culture.   Boston: Houghton
    Mifflin.

Clairmont, Donald H. J.
    1963   Deviance Among Indians and Eskimos in
    Aklavik, N.W.T.   Northern Co-ordination and
    Research Centre Report 63-9.   Ottawa:
    Department of Northern Affairs and National
    Resources.

Cohen, Ronald
    1962   An Anthropological Survey of Communities
    in the Mackenzie-Slave Lake Region of Canada.
    Northern Co-ordination and Research Centre
    Report 62-3.   Ottawa: Department of Northern
    Affairs and National Resources.

Geertz, Clifford
    1973   The Interpretation of Cultures.   New
    York: Basic Books.

Honigmann, John J.
    1949   Culture and Ethos of Kaska Society.
    Yale University Publications in Anthropology
    No. 40.   New Haven: Yale University Press.
    1963   Dynamics of Drinking in an Austrian
    Village.   Ethnology 2:157-169.
    1966   Social Disintegration in Five Northern
    Canadian Communities.   The Canadian Review
    of Sociology and Anthropology 2:199-214.
    (Reprinted in Aspects of Canadian Society,
    special issue of The Canadian Review of
    Sociology and Anthropology.   Montreal, 1974).
    1970   Field Work in Two Northern Canadian
    Communities.   In Marginal Natives, Morris
    Freilich, (ed).   New York: Harper and Row.
    1971   Formation of Mackenzie Delta Frontier
    Culture.   In Pilot Not Commander: Essays in
    Memory of Diamond Jenness. Pat and Jim Lotz,
    (eds.)   Ottawa: St. Paul University.

Ms.a Patterns of Alcohol Based on Tape-recorded
Interviews. Report prepared for the Northern
Science Research Group, Department of Indian
Affairs and Northern Development, Canada.
Ms.b The Personal Approach in Cultural
Anthropological Research.

Honigmann, John J., and Irma Honigmann
1945 Drinking in an Indian-White Community.
Quarterly Journal for Studies on Alcohol 5:
575-619.
1965a Eskimo Townsmen. Ottawa: University of
Ottawa.
1965b How Baffin Island Eskimo Have Learned to
Use Alcohol. Social Forces 44:73-84.
1970 Arctic Townsmen. Ottawa: St. Paul
University.

Horton, Donald
1943 The Functions of Alcohol in Primitive
Societies: A Cross-Cultural Study. Quarterly
Journal for Studies on Alcohol 4:199-320.

Leighton, Alexander
1959 My Name is Legion. New York: Basic Books.

Maquet, J. J.
1964 Objectivity in Anthropology. Current
Anthropology 5:47-55.

Maslow, Abraham H.
1941 Principles of Abnormal Psychology. New
York: Harper and Brothers.

McAndrew, Craig and Robert B. Edgerton
1969 Drunken Comportment. Chicago: Aldine.

Phillips, Llewelyn
1945 Unpublished manuscript.

Spaulding, Philip
1966 The Social Integration of a Northern
Community: White Mythology and Metis Reality.
In A Northern Dilemma: Reference Papers,
Arthur K. Davis (ed) Two vols.

Bellingham: Western Washington State College.

Suppe, Frederick (Ed.)
    1974 The Structure of Scientific Theories.
    Urbana: University of Illinois.

CHAPTER X

Summary and Conclusions

Transactional Aspect

Though alcohol is no longer used as cash in exchange for furs, it continues to serve as a medium of exchange. There is evidence that in some instances its use is still qualitive rather than scaled on a continuum of more or less. Brody indicates that "Indians" are primarily concerned about either being non-drunks or drinking to the point of passing out rather than measuring how much is drunk, as the whiteman is likely to do. Much the same information is provided by Hamer in his discussion of the goal of having enough in order to be able to "pass out" as well as the awareness of the Potawatomi themselves that this goal distinguishes them from the whiteman, who can be satisfied to limit his drinking to set amounts. But the exchange process is most evident in terms of redistributive, reciprocal, and predictive functions. It is not that exchange is absent from the behavior of the whiteman in the form of tavern and dinner party drinking, but it appears to be much less elaborated than is the case for Native peoples.

As in the case of the Naskapi redistribution occurs when someone buys beer to give to others and in so doing obligates others to show him praise and deference. Robbins indicates that to be able to share with others is an indication of successful maintenance of status while the converse holds when one fails to share or others refuse the offer to share. The difference is that instead of the redistribution of meat from a successful hunt to maintain one's position with kinsmen it is now the exchange of beer which has become the functional equivalent of game.

For the Salish there is still an element of the potlatch style whiskey feast in the holding of parties in which a person gains or maintains the

287

esteem of others by the amount of beverage that he can distribute. The big spender in the urban drinking situation described by Brody builds up a network of obligated people and by repaying debts creates relations for potential credit. As he indicates, redistribution provides a means for boasting "conspicuously" about the claims on others in the course of a drinking spree. In the urban slum where sources of income are minimal, such a network of credit is crucial for maintenance of the drinking life style.

Reciprocity is highly patterned for the Chipewyans in the ritual visiting about the village during a drinking spree. So that one who receives a drink from the bottle of another then becomes obligated to join the other on his door-to-door wanderings. The sharing which the Inuit formerly practiced within the framework of the kin structured hunting group, or on the basis of residential proximity, has been changing as people have moved into permanent settings and engaged in wage employment. But the reciprocal exchange of alcohol has helped to maintain the sense of community that was formerly supplied by membership in traditional social institutions.

Alcohol is also a means of introducing an element of predictability into social transactions. Among the Potawatomi it is used to make employer-employee relations more reliable as the need to earn "a little beer money" indicates to a prospective white employer a reliable committment to short term employment. In a somewhat different vein possession of "hard liquor" by the Salish is a predictor of economic success. For it implies that one has the wherewithal to pay the relatively high price of purchase and/or the ability to manipulate white friends. It is much the same for the Natives on Skid Row, as Brody has shown that generous outlays of cash for beer is a way of obtaining, at least temporarily, a position of high status.

For the groups discussed in this book, however, the major problem has shifted from a conflict of values over the use of alcohol as a medium of exchange to that of accommodation to the problems arising out of extensive and heavy usage. The range is from a positive reinterpretation of drinking practices among the Inuit, Chipewyan, Salish, and Naskapi to a negative reinterpretation among the Ojibwa. For the Potawatomi and the urban Natives described by Brody drinking seems to have become an end in itself, a way of life.

The Inuit at Pond Inlet have given new form to the old meaning of cooperativeness associated with kinship, hunting partnerships, and residential proximity. They use the sharing of alcohol as a tangible means of maintaining these relationships in a new community situation. Transition to a permanent settlement has been too recent for them to have lost the old controls against overt aggression, even in a state of intoxication, which would have been so disruptive to a hunting way of life where cooperation was crucial for survival. Thus even though many of them are engaged in a form of migratory wage labor they have not yet broken the communal ties which the drinking party helps to maintain. If and when these ties are broken it may be that they will adopt individualistic, aggressive, drinking behavior that Honigmann labels "frontier culture", as have the Inuit of Inuvik.

Salish reinterpretation, using the "whiskey feast" as substitute for the traditional potlatch, was initially a way of keeping the meaning if not the form of the latter. The older generation continue to connect heavy social drinking with story telling and singing, and they are still encouraged to participate by the present generation in the less organised week-end and holiday sprees.

There is some historical continuity in the pattern of Chipewyan drinking. Van Stone indicates that, as in the fur trading days, the most frequent and intense drinking is in the summer season not only because this is the most appropriate time for preparing the home brew, which must be done outdoors, but because this is a time when men are free from trapping and hunting. The village drinking spree involving sharing and house-to-house visiting is strictly social and highly stylized. It is a form of imbibing which is probably difficult to maintain outside the community and it would seem likely that as Chipewyan leave the reserve to obtain wage labor in northern industrial towns they will be prime candidates for the"frontier culture" drinking pattern.

The Ojibwa described by Steinbring have interpreted widespread and heavy drinking as a threat to their culture. To combat the problems of alcohol they took the whiteman's organization of Alcoholics Anonymous and gave it a meaning appropriate to their traditional beliefs and values. Thus A.A. fits well with traditional concepts of male authority, the testimonial is in keeping with stylized Ojibwa oratory, the non-hierarchical structure is acceptable to the decentralized nature of Ojibwa groups, and traditional individualism is protected by the rule that the individual must come to A.A. rather than the reverse. It is possible, as Steinbring suggests, that even with the demise of the Black River A.A. chapter individuals will continue to accept the tenants of the association which serves as a control on their drinking behavior. His study indicates that a Native community may alternatively unite in opposition to the use of alcohol rather than use it to promote group cohesiveness.

The Naskapi have only recently, within the past 20 years, shifted from a hunting/welfare to a wage labourer/welfare economy. To some extent they have been able to keep their social network intact by reinterpreting the reciprocities based upon hunting to reciprocities based on the distribution of consumer goods. Nevertheless, this has not occurred without status conflict and confusion for which the drinking form provides a means of accommodation.

By contrast the Potawatomi, though living in a rural setting, have been surrounded by an urban, industrial, society for several generations. They

290

have had little opportunity to become wage earners
except on a part-time basis. For them drinking
has become an end in itself, a means of adapting to
a marginal existence in which they have lost most
of the traditional hunting and gathering way of
life without becoming a part of the industrial
social system.

The members of skid row come from many
different groups, but what initially brings them
together is that they share the two attributes
unemployment and a Native status. As a community
Skid Row provides a way of life in which, as in
the case of the Potawatomi, the pursuit of alcohol
provides the rationale for existence. Indeed the
expenditure and acquisition of money is in one way
or another related to drinking. It is different
from "frontier culture" where heavy drinking is
merely an adjunct to outdoor activities,
informality of organization, individualism, and
resentment of urban life (Honigmann, and Honigmann
1970:14-15). Moreover, it is an activity which is
more discontinuous than on skid row, being confined
to social occasions and weekends. Though both
cultures provide alternatives to the mainstream
industrial life style as forms of contraculture,
it is primarily the pleasure of imbibing that
leads to social interaction on skid row.

Though there are differences in accommodation,
certain similarities exist in regard to the goals
and procedure, amount consumed, and the values
regarding alcohol usage among several of the
groups. This pattern of consumption among Native
peoples is clearly at variance with the drinking
practices of Euro-Canadians and Americans.

For all, except the Inuit and the non-drinking
Ojibwa, the goal of imbibing is intoxication to the
point of passing out. There is agreement among
the various authors for a behavioral sequence of
initial conviviality, partial intoxication, various
aggressive acts, and finally the oblivion of total
intoxication. Hamer, Brody and Lemert indicate that
the early euphoria and gregariousness, the opposite

291

of the taciturn shyness of sobriety, may change
spontaneously to a mood of hostile aggression. A
seemingly innocent remark by one of the participants
may precipitate the change, but for husbands their
wives are the favorite targets, which may relate to
the declining status of males relative to females
discussed by Hamer, Lemert, and Robbins.
Nevertheless there seem to be norms regarding the
limits of assault while intoxicated, as in the case
of the Potawatomi where there is a community
concensus about people who are dangerous drinking
companions and should be avoided. Van Stone
indicates that most the Chipewyan combatants are
too intoxicated to do each other much bodily harm
and Brody notes that brawls in bars are of short
duration, with participants assuming cordial
relations between sporadic outbursts of fighting.
Perhaps, as Brody suggests, because people drink
to become intoxicated it takes a minimal amount
of alcohol to produce drunken behavior. The various
authors agree that the presence of alcohol and
drinking companions is sufficient to induce the
simulation of drunken comportment.

It is evident from the discussion by the
contributors that in all of these heavy drinking
groups there are relatively few Native alcoholics.
This may be due to the fact that alcohol consumption
is a socio-cultural phenomenon in which people indulge
not to resolve individual problems, but to achieve
highly valued goals of pleasurable intoxication,
and conviviality. There is clearly none of the
sense of guilt generally associated with the
alcoholism of the whiteman. Instead of being a
random, normless, affair, drinking involves a
pattern of learned, acceptable, behavior. It is a
pattern which is at least tacitly supported by the
attitude of the whiteman that drunken comportment
is to be expected from Native people. Both Brody
and Lemert make this point in regard to the
patronizing belief of white people that Natives
have no control or cannot hold their liquor.
Hamer and Lemert note that even the police adopt
a dual standard in the enforcement of law,
assuming that Natives lack the competence to

292

conform. Not surprisingly the lesser penalties
encourage Natives to ignore the law and lend
support to drunken behavior.

Explanation of Drinking in the Contemporary Setting

Thus there is agreement among the authors for
an observable pattern of drinking behavior among
Native people along with some evidence for a
continuation of the historic exchange function of
alcohol, albeit the socio-cultural situation has
changed in many ways since the fur trade period.
But it remains to provide some explanation for the
pervasiveness of the pattern of drunken comportment.
There are at least three broad explanations that
may be deduced from the various authors, one
concerning identity, a second relating to
powerlessness, and a third pertaining to dependency
needs.

Identity

For Native peoples experiencing the tensions
of socio-cultural change alcohol provides a means
for establishing both individual and group identity,
be it on the reserve or in the urban setting. From
the individual standpoint it is a way of acting
out desireable roles with a minumum of social
disruption. In the case of the group it has become
a strategy for adapting to a subordinate, if
predictable role, vis-a-vis the dominant white
culture, by assuming a pleasurable, though hostile
and subordinate status.

On the basis of a continuum from the least to
the most acculturated the identity explanation is
least relevant for the Inuit, Chipewyans and
Ojibwa. For the Inuit, Mathhiasson indicates,
identity is involved only in the sense that alcohol
exchange provides a ritual means of maintaining
traditional social relationships. In like manner

the Chipewyans and Ojibwa until recently in minimal contact with Euro-Canadians, do not seem to use alcohol as a status testing or contracultural device. Two of these groups remain relatively isolated from the full impact of industrial society. The Chipewyans have much of the old hunting and trapping way of life intact and the Inuit, though engaged in a form of migratory wage labor, are still committed to the traditional social network. Black River Ojibwa, who are relatively unacculturated, also are not faced with an identity problem, but used Alcoholics Anonymous as a means for competing with other Ojibwa bands.

Lemert shows that the Salish who have experienced more intense contact with Euro-Canadian culture than the Inuit, Chipewyan, and Ojibwa are quite conscious of the drinking party as providing a sense of social solidarity against the intrusion of the white man. Since the old feasts are now too costly, drinking provides at least a partial substitute setting in which some of the old culture may be kept alive through story and song. On the individual level Lemert believes that by acting out the stereotype of the "drunken Indian" individuals may be free to express aggression and make the most of the whiteman's patronizing fatalism to escape punishment.

The Potawatomi, who are virtually engulfed by Euro-American culture, are at least, if not more so, as involved as the Salish in using alcohol as a means of identity. Drinking provides an opportunity for individual males who have lost status to regain it and for resentful females to take revenge within the limits of the drinking situation. Though dominance and revenge roles contrast with and can be threatening to the social networks of sober existence these roles are complimentary and desirable within the framework of the alcoholic spree. On the group level there is a similarity to the Salish with the Potawatomi using the steoretype of drunkenness and irresponsibility as a self-fulfilling prophecy. It is a means for escaping assimilation

294

into the whiteman's culture while at the same time
making the contact situation predictable for both
whites and Natives. At the very least it makes
for cultural separation and provides for a part-time
role in the economy, which helps to maintain the
drinking life style.

In regard to individual identity testing
Robbins reports many similarities in the drinking
"forms" of the Naskapi to the Potawatomi. The ways
in which the party of friends and/or kinsmen behave
when drinking constitutes a means of defending,
claiming, rectifying, or confirming status identity
in the transition from hunting and trapping to the
wage labour of an industrial society. As in the
case of the Potawatomi it is not disruptive of the
sober restraint of ordinary existence, but permits
people to claim a new status by lavishing gifts
upon others, or serves as compensation for lost
status through assertive or aggressive action.
Unlike the Potawatomi or the Salish, however, the
Naskapi do not appear to be using alcohol as a
contracultural device against the whiteman. This
may be due to the fact that they have not
experienced a loss of cultural identity and, as
Robbins suggests, they are relatively satisfied
with life as wage earners in Schefferville.

Brody maintains that the suspension of
responsibility through use of the drinking "time
out" is less obvious on skid row than on the
reserves. If we interpret him correctly, he is
suggesting that alcohol is less of an excuse for
violence in the city than on reserves where
drinking is more intermittent and there is a
condition of cultural homogeneity. As a
consequence those Natives who wish to be accepted
on skid row must balance assertiveness with
generosity. Nevertheless, from the standpoint of
the individual there are similarities to the
Potawatomi and Naskapi usage of alcohol in
identity testing. There is the openness between
drinking groups, the ease of movement from one to
another without fear of rejection, and the

295

willingness to spend money and share purchased
beverages which Hamer finds for the Potawatomi.
Though the sober restraint of the Native which
maintains social control on the reserve may not be
as noticeable on skid row there is an analogous
sense of unity of conditions and purpose which sets
limits on aggression and violence. It would seem
then there is a continuous seeking after acceptance
in the drinking group by maintaining the requisites
of assertiveness and generosity. Brody suggests
that assertiveness "...establishes a reputation"
and is the only status on skid row to which others
must respond by showing friendship and generosity.
This is very similar to what Robbins says about
Naskapi assertiveness, that others respond
positively to boasting and threats of violence in
order to avoid conflict. In such a situation
assertiveness becomes a means obligating the
acceptance of others without the actual exchange
of goods, which is reasonable considering the
limitations of access to material means.

The group identity of the skid row Native is
very similar to that of the Salish and Potawatomi.
They seem to have accepted the negative stereotype
and in doing so "over accept" the whiteman. As
Hamer finds for the Potawatomi it eases
communications and provides for interaction between
Natives and Whites. But by accepting a subordinate
group identity it may serve, as Brody suggests, to
turn frustrations and resulting aggressions inward
and account for much of violence associated with
drinking. At best it can provide a negative identity
with the functioning of a vengeful demeaning of the
whiteman's values.

Because drastic economic change disrupts the
whole rhythm of life, creates radically new
material goals, and very often turns the old status
order up-side-down it becomes a threat to individual
and group identity. Accommodative response to such
change varies from one culture to another according
to the historic traditions of the people. It may
involve, as Robbins indicates, an increase in

accusations of witchcraft, more bizarre possession states, an intensification of ceremonial exchange or an inflation of the potlatch ritual as among the Kwakiutl. These are all traditional means of adjusting to the tensions of change that people understand and have used in the past. Since North American Native peoples have a long history of alcohol use in their exchange relationships with Europeans, it is not surprising that they have reinterpreted its use in attempting to preserve their identity from the encroachment of industrial technology. As Honigmann points out Native people are well aware that their usage of intoxicants is counter to the accepted norms of Euro-Canadian culture. But their particular pattern of usage provides one way of resisting total surrender to the dominant industrial beliefs and values.

Power

A recurring theme in most of the chapters in this book is that of the use of alcohol for purposes of demonstrating assertiveness. In the introduction an historical connection was shown to exist between drinking as a catalyst to the traditional acquisition of power through dreaming. The quest for supernatural power through dreams has traditionally been an important part of the culture of many North American Native peoples. Therefore it is important to examine the relation of power-seeking to the consumption of alcoholic beverages.

Boyatzis (1976:265-286) cites several studies that show an association between heavy drinking and "impulsive" rather than "controlled" use of power. To test this hypothesis cross-culturally he developed what he refers to as the "socio-economic simplicity scale" which categorizes societies, in the different culture areas of the world, according to the degree of dependence on hunting, absence of food production, lack of social class and a hierarchical social system, impermanence of settlement, and smallness of community size. It is his contention that men in this type of system experience pressure to achieve power, but with so few alternative status positions have very limited chances for success. From a world wide sample in different culture areas he finds a significantly high correlation between this society type, heavy drinking, and folktale themes expressing the impulsive use of power. It is his thesis that in such societies drinking helps the individual reduce inhibitions and release aggressive behavior. The latter in turn provides tangible proof of successful assertiveness.

With the possible exception of the Inuit there is a close correspondence between the above variables and the conditions found amongst the various groups of Native peoples discussed in this book. The Chipewyans continue to be primarily hunters and trappers, to live in small relatively isolated communities, and to be part of an individualistic, eǫualitarian, social system. The Naskapi of Schefferville are in a transitional state from hunting to wage labour. The Salish, having lost the elaborate title system validated by potlatching, have not obtained alternative status positions that would provide outlets for obtaining power and prestige. With part-time fishing, woods work and welfare they remain peripheral to the industrial system surrounding them with most of the socio-cultural attributes found on the Boyatzis scale. It is much the same for the Potawatomi and for the Natives of skid row. The latter, though in the heart of the urban industri system have established an encapsulated drinking community which from Brody's description has only tenuous links with the outside world. Indeed, Honigmann's "frontier culture" with its emphasis upon heavy-drinking and the acting out of aggressive fantasies through public drunkenness bears many analogies to skid-row. On the other hand, the Inuit described by Matthiasson have only recently accepted alcohol and apparently use it to maintain the traditional social network rather than act out drunken fantasies of power.

298

The pattern of creating an alcoholic fantasy
of power and validating it with physical violence
is in evidence for the Chipewyans. Van Stone
points out that it is the heaviest drinkers who
are most likely to get into fights, but when sober
show a complete reversal of character by being the
most vehement in deploring the violence of drunken
comportment. The demands and billigerency in
disputes over women suggest an attempt at assertive
control which cannot be validated in the reality of
this equalitarian society.

The Salish have more frequent and intense
contact with the whiteman than the Chipewyans,
which may account for aggressively, assertive
vituperation and criminal acts against the latter.
Since aggressive exploits against the white
community have become a means of acquiring higher
status it would seem that the power resulting from
this drunken activity is more of a reality than a
fantasy. The attempt to be violently assertive
toward women also has, in addition to the motive
to dominate found amongst the Chipewyans, a source
of resentment and desire to control the increasing
economic independence of women.

Hamer recounts how Potawatomi men seek to use
the drinking situation to regain lost positions of
power over wives who have acquired superior
economic status through the receipt of welfare
payments. Women in turn use alcohol as a means
for eliciting sex with men other than their
husbands, as a form of revenge against the latter.
As in the case of the Salish both women and men
deviate when imbibing from their customary deference
and passivity vis-a-vis the whiteman. It is only
then that they will demand their rights of government
officials, storekeepers, bartenders, and others in
authority. Men also use the drinking group as a
forum to argue about the position of the chief,
how they as individuals expect to take over the
position and remove the existing chief from power.
But the boasting, plotting, and recriminations
are all figments of alcoholic fantasy, having little
or no connection with the sober reality of
reservation politics. There is only the one position

299

of authority on the reserve and this is so circumscribed that it hardly provides an outlet for the
achievement of power.

Much of Robbin's explanation of Naskapi
drinking is based on the use of alcohol in status
seeking. Those who have full-time employment tend
to use the drinking forum to maintain their status
by giving away beer and consumer goods in return
for deference and praise from the recipients.
Those without the material wherewithal to command
respect resort to aggressive boasting and bullying
to gain deference from other drinkers. The latter
respond deferentially to avoid the violence which
tends to follow indifference or ridicule. Indeed,
Robbins is able to show that the most aggressively
assertive are the most economically insecure
persons.

The nexus between drinking and power for Natives
on skid row is in several ways similar to the
situation on reserves. For example, petty theft
is more important for the bravado effect than
utilitarian gains, persons are always on the look
out for a fight, there are aggressive, vituperative,
encounters with intruders such as the police, and
the familiar fighting between spouses. All of these
incidents occur within the drinking group and are
marked by sudden and unpredictable changes in mood
from jovial acceptance of others to violent name
calling. Generally, however, such outbursts of
violence do not lead to serious injuries. On the
other hand there are differences in the urban from
the reserve setting, which may be largely
attributable to the lack of alternative status
positions to be achieved or preserved. Since
Native peoples come from many different bands and
cultures the positions they have left in their
communities of origin are not necessarily of
relevance to their compatriots on skid row. Because
of this lack of alternative status positions
assertiveness becomes an end in itself, the only
criterion for becoming a person of importance. Being
a native virtually excludes one from the status
outlets in Euro-Canadian culture. At the same time,

since white persons on skid row hold the same socio-economic status as Natives there is a minimum of violent interaction between the two groups. Just as in the case of the Potawatomi who experience limited sharing of social contacts with white, skid row provides the only place for intensive social interaction between the two groups. Thus the opportunities for assertiveness are so limited that, as Brody reports, urban Natives turn their quest for power inwards and do violence to themselves.

Since the Inuit have only recently begun to use alcohol it is too soon to say whether they will find it a convenient means for creating power fantasies. Perhaps the individualism of the Algonkian and Athapaskan social structures engenders a greater tendency toward assertiveness than the comunalistic social network of the Inuit. But once that network is broken, when individuals join the polygot of ethnic groups in the "frontier culture" or the urban centers, the consequences are the same as for the other groups. Nevertheless, Boyatzis' hypothesis is supported by the evidence from all the other drinking groups where alcohol provides the dramatic background for impulsive power seeking. These are communities in which success is elusive for whatever striving occurs for the few available status positions. Even the Native urban community conforms in many ways to the attributes of the "socio-economic simplicity scale" in being an open access group, non-hierarchical, impermanent, and a relatively small segment of the urban whole. Moreover, it is this impulsive use of power, rationalized by the use of alcohol, which may provide at least a partial explanation for "stereotyped drunkenness" or the seeming ease of becoming intoxicated on a minimum amount of beverage.

Dependency

Though it may seem that dependency and aggression are logically incompatible, Barry (1976:249-263) has recently shown how the two emotions go together

301

with heavy drinking. It is his position that
inconsistency in parental reward and punishment of
dependency, combined with consistent encouragement
of self-reliance, leads to a form of psychic conflict
which results in assertiveness. In the drinking
group alcohol becomes a means for muting the effects
of reality, enabling the individual to simultaneously
overcome anxiety about expressing dependency and
self assertiveness. He contends that there is a
sequence to the intoxication process in which
imbibing a small amount of alcohol leads to the
acceptance and giving of nurturance and affection,
but that a progressive increase in the intake leads
to the aggressive expression of "personalized power".
On the basis of a study by McClelland et. al. (1972)
showing a relationship between inhibitory themes in
folktales in connection with moderate to minimal
drinking practices, Barry suggests that self-control
in the use of alcohol may be associated with
societies in which people have been consistently
rewarded for both dependent and self-reliant
behavior. The essays in this volume provide several
examples of this seeking and giving of nurturance
in conjunction with assertiveness as a part of
social drinking.

Hamer is the only author to examine the
development of the dependency-assertiveness
conflict in terms of traditional and contemporary
child training relative to drinking practices. He
shows how inconsistent socialization of dependency
in regard to the traditional guardian spirit quest
with the goal of creating self reliance could
actually have encouraged dependency. Though much
of traditional Potawatomi culture is gone the style
of living on the reserve and coping with a
dominant white society has produced cultural
confusion, intergenerational jealousies and
anxieties, and a continuous round of heavy
drinking. These are all conditions creating an
increase in confusion and discontinuity in the
socialization process which have served to
encourage dependency. Coincident with the
encouragment of dependency is a lack of community
organization which causes a pervasive

individualism and guardedness in social interaction,
noticeably overcome only in the drinking spree.
As to the latter, minimal alcohol intake is
described as leading to a seeking out of others and
a show of affection to be followed, as consumption
increases, by insults and violent assertiveness,
which is identical with the sequence predicted by
Barry. Thus the Potawatomi drinking party is a
kind of drama of acceptance and rejection.

The descriptions of the drinking behavior of
the Salish, Chipewyans, and Naskapi provide at least
indirect confirmation for the dependence/
independence conflict. The Salish show an
ambivalence about alcohol brought out in the
drinking song of the old chief to the effect that
whiskey is bad, but it helps people to overcome a
sense of isolation. For high status Salish
drinking creates a situation analogous to that
attributed to alcoholism in industrial societies.
On the one hand such a person may like alcohol and
should be invited to all parties because of his
position, but on the other hand he cannot afford
to be seen as a drunkard for fear of loss of status.
The Chipewyan are described as following a continuum
of minimal imbibing which creates an attitude of
warm self-confidence vis-a-vis others through
stages of expansive assertiveness leading to
violence as the intake increases. In like manner
the Naskapi of Schefferville are initially friendly,
outgoing, and eager to dispense gifts, only later
as the alcohol intake increases do they resort to
the boasting and downgrading of others which often
results in physical violence.

For Natives on skid row the drinking community
is a refuge from the reserve and the surrounding
Euro-Canadian community. It is a place where
individuals can escape from rejection and
criticism and be assured of acceptance. It is the
one place in the urban milieu where whites and
Natives interact as equals and mutually provide
both social and personal reassurance.

Thus there is indication from the descriptions of drinking behavior of the correctness of Barry's hypothesized association of small amounts with amiable giving and receiving of assurance to be followed by heavy drinking and aggressive power seeking. In so far as the socialization process of the various groups is similar to that of the Potawatomi, with their inconsistent rewarding of dependency, the drinking sequence may indeed provide simultaneously for the seemingly contradictory gratification of dependency and assertiveness. Absence of this sequence among the Inuit of Pond Inlet lends indirect support to the hypothesis in the sense that it is one indication that the pattern is far from universal. The emphasis on communalistic reciprocity in social interaction and shared, rather than individualistic, properties of child-rearing probably militate against the development of contradictory dependency-self reliant behavior. Indeed, Honigmanns report that even within "frontier culture" Inuit tend to reward dependency more than Indian parents and are less demanding in self-reliance training (1970:131-132).

On the basis of the material presented in these essays we are able to form a paradigm relating accommodation to alcohol use to several basic human needs. The paradigm is presented in Diagram I.

Diagram I

Paradigm of Variables Associated With
Accommodation to Alcohol

Antecedent Variables
1) Historic Value Conflict
2) Reinterpretation of Alcohol Usage to Fit Traditional Dreaming and Power Concepts.

Independent Variables   Dependent Variable
1) Identity Needs ←——————— Accommodation
2) Power Needs
3) Dependency Needs

304

In the introductory chapter we discussed how the "more or less" values of European traders were in direct contradiction with the "either/or" values of Native North Americans and how this led to different concepts of drinking and drunken comportment. It was also shown how the meaning of this innovation could have been reinterpreted to fit customary concepts of the acquisition of power through dreams and visionary experiences. If the historical variables explain the precidence for alcohol usage by Native peoples, the accommodation to alcohol usage relates to varying degrees of success in coping with the socio-psychological problems of identity, power, and dependency. In this connection we wish to advance the following hypothesis:

> The amount of drinking and drunken comportment varies inversely with the extent to which Native people are able to establish satisfying individual and group identity, succeed by their own assertiveness to desirable status positions, and achieve a balance between the expression of self-reliance and dependency within and between ethnic groups.

Such a hypothesis is suggestive of the possibility for arranging the groups discussed in this book on a scale ranging from minimal drinking with maximal accommodation of identity, power, and dependency to heavy, continuous, drinking as compensation for minimal accommodation of these needs. At the minimal/maximal end of the continuum are the Ojibwa, Chipewyans, and Inuit. All three of the latter have retained much of their traditional identity and either avoid alcohol as in the case of the Ojibwa, drink heavily only on holidays and between trapping seasons as do the Chipewyans, or like the Inuit use social drinking for retaining traditional work/friendship bonds.

Since much of the traditional culture is intact for the Ojibwa and Chipewyan there are apparently

305

sufficient opportunities for real rather than the
make believe status assertiveness of the drinking
milieu. Amongst the latter it is the heaviest
drinkers who become violent and the fantasy use of
power seems to arise only in regard to tensions
connected with sexual status differences. As for
the Inuit control of assertiveness applies even
when the members of a drinking party are intoxicated.
Though the data on dependency are limited, only the
Chipewyan are reported as gaining increased self-
confidence and assurance from drunken comportment.

The Naskapi in their use of alcohol as a means
for estimating individual success or failure at
status seeking are logically in the middle of the
continuum. In making a relatively smooth transition
from a trapping to a wage economy they seem not to
have lost pride in their traditional identity.
It is notable that status power seeking is a
function of economic security; the least
successful wage earners tend to be the most
violently assertive. Moreover, the latter are also
the most likely to exhibit in drinking behavior
the symptoms of unmet dependency needs.

The Salish, Potawatomi, and Skid Row Natives
are at the maximal/minimal end of the drinking/
needs satisfaction continuum. Salish drinking is
heavy and frequent, so much so that individuals
have accepted the "drunken Indian" identification
as a means for extracting concessions from the
whiteman. The drinking party, which has a precedent
in the old whiskey feast, is a way of expressing
opposition to Euro-Canadian society through verbal
and behavioral acts. But the drinking spree does
not furnish the opportunities for status
achievement provided by the traditional potlatch,
so that drunken assertiveness becomes a substitute,
especially as a means for men to dominate women
who have greater access to economic resources.
Consequently, there are indications of reassurance
seeking and a striving for attention while
imbibing, suggestive of a lack of balance between
self-reliance and dependency within as well as
between groups.

306

The Potawatomi situation is very similar, if
not more extreme, to that of the Salish. Identity,
power, and dependency outlets are so minimal that
drinking has virtually become a way of life. The
Skid Row Natives are the urban counterpart of the
rural Potawatomi. Individual identity has become
dependent upon acceptance in the drinking group,
which in turn has accepted the Euro-Canadian
stereotype of drunken comportment in adapting to
a marginal urban existence. Assertiveness has
become an end in itself and the drinking group
furnishes the sole means of protection and nurture;
an escape from what is perceived as a hostile
outside world.

Social Costs and the Future

For those groups which have made a near total
accommodation to drinking as a way of life it is
evident that there are certain social costs. Hamer
mentions the frequency of automobile accidents,
widespread respiratory problems, and cultural
stagnation that are related to alcohol. Brody
predicts that as the size of the active population
on skid row increases the sense of belonging to
a small drinking group will probably decline and
there will be many more instances of isolated
drinking. This is likely to lead to an increase
in alcoholism. Among the Salish there is evidence
that persons in high positions and women face the
danger of becoming pathological drinkers. In
addition, there are numerous statistical summaries
demonstrating various forms of tragedy connected
with Native drinking. Price, for example, notes
that 3/4 of all arrests of Native people in the
United States and Canada are for public
intoxication, drunk driving, and liquor law
violations (1975:18). Suicides, accidental deaths,
and grievous injuries indirectly, or directly,
resulting from drunkenness are all of much higher
frequency for Natives than for the rest of the

307

Canadian population. All of this leads to the
question of what may be done to diminish the more
extreme forms of accommodation to alcohol. There
are at least three, not necessarily mutually
exclusive, alternative forms of alleviation which
include new models of comportment, the
restructuring of drinking behavior, and
institutional innovations.

     Drunken comportment can be changed by the
acquisition of new behavioral models and/or
acquisition of a stake in society. From his
clinical research among Ojibwa in Minnesota
Westermeyer indicates that many Native people who
have not learned the whiteman's drinking pattern
in their youth do acquire it in later life (1972:
402). But the shift to a restrained alcohol
accommodation is dependent on such variables as
drinking companions, age, sex, past experiences,
and family role. Levy and Kunitz in their study
of Navajo drinking find that persons who would have
been classified as alcoholics in the whiteman's
society abruptly give up alcohol without the
noticeable anxiety or side effects usually
associated with abrupt withdrawal (1974:148).
These are men who after drinking heavily in their
youth came to the conclusion that alcohol is
disrupting their lives physically and socially.
If this means that alcohol is not the
individualistic obsession that it is for white
alcoholics then it is the group that provides the
motivation for drinking.

     This is one implication of the Honigmann's
Inuvik study which shows a significant relationship
between a low Native arrest rate for alcohol
related offenses and what they refer to as a "stake
in society". Indicators of a stake are home
ownership and steady employment. Ferguson comes
to much the same conclusion for the Navajo, except
that for the latter the existence of a stake without
the presence of a non-drinking reference group is
insufficient to control heavy drinking (1976:65-78).

In her study of Navajo participants in an
alcohol treatment program she found that unlike
those who returned to a non-drinking kinship group
on the reservation and experienced a high degree of
success in controlling their drinking, those who
returned to town jobs, where the only reference
group was that of drinking companions, had an
inordinately high rate of failure. The job
situation provided minimal opportunities for
recognition and social acceptance which left only
the drinking group of peers with whom the
individual could identify and experience a sense
of respect and comradeship.

Thus the provision of non-drinking reference
groups appears to be crucial in changing the heavy
drinking accommodation. In towns and cities across
Canada groups with this potential, in the form of
friendship centers and provincial brotherhood
associations may already exist. But whether these
associations are sufficient in number and provide
accessible, companionable, models of. sober
comportment is another matter. The latter are
especially important for they constitute what Levy
and Kunitz refer to as "moral entrepreneurs" (ibid:
189). These may be Native persons with training
in the human service occupations, businessmen,
skilled laborers, and others who have had some
success in adapting to the Euro-Canadian life style
and have had previous experience with alcohol. It
is these persons, both male and female, who by
defining drinking as an unacceptable and
unnecessary means for the establishment of warmth
and friendship with others, or for the attainment
of desirable status goals, may serve as models of
sober comportment. Their presence constitutes
tangible evidence that it is possible to bridge
the gap between Euro-Canadian and Native life styles
without giving up the traditional values of sharing,
support, and group companionship. This may, however,
call for some modification of the customary stance
of non-interference with the behavior of others.

In conjunction with providing new behavioral models controls may be developed by restructuring the drinking situation on and off the reserve. The Honigmann's have shown that in the town of Inuvik Natives with continuous employment records often consume far more alcohol discreetly, and on a scheduled basis, than Natives with records of sporadic employment (1970:97-112). The latter have a high arrest rate for alcohol related offenses which are often connected with public intoxication. Consequently, it is possible to drink heavily off the reserve by scheduling drinking and avoiding public intoxication, without contravening Euro-Canadian norms. There are other examples such as the Camba of Bolivia who apparently drink at least as intensively as any of the North American Native peoples, but with highly ritualized, scheduled, drinking sprees which are in no way socially or physiologically disruptive (Heath 1962:31).

Scheduling, limiting offensive drunkenness and its consequences might also occur on reserves if band councils could control the distribution of alcohol. If the councils controlled the only sanctioned liquor outlets they might be able to regulate the excessive expenditures for bootleg alcohol and the strife ensuing from such activities. Moreover, pubs run by band councils that limit the hours of drinking, have rules against serving intoxicated customers, and prohibit the removal of beer from the premises would provide another means for encouraging the development of new drinking norms. Such establishments could also increase employment opportunities, give communities an option for controlling extreme drinking practices, and make available an alternative source of capital for economic development.

An increase in institutional alternatives of both vocational and religious nature may also be important sources of control. Price, for example, found the arrest rate for public drunkenness to be much lower for Natives living close to prosperous Canadian cities than for those living close to economically depressed cities (1975:22). In many

310

parts of Canada there are already significant efforts being made to train people for skilled trades and professions as well as to increase employment opportunities on and off reserves. That there is encouragement for Natives to enter skilled occupations and acquire training in the universities for positions in teaching, business, medicine, engineering, and law has become almost a platitude in recent years. Nevertheless, this is likely to be the most effective means by which Native peoples will attain a stake in Canadian society.

While it is true that movements such as Alcoholics Anonymous will not fit all Native situations, these associations can be reinterpreted, as Steinbring's essay shows, to function effectively in the control of alcohol abuse. Church groups such as the Pentecostal and the Native American Church have provided institutionalized alternatives to the drinking group. There is even the possibility for reactivation of old curative rituals such as has occurred in recent years among the Salish (Jilck S. Todd 1974:351-355). This revival of winter ceremonial in which a neophyte must be ritually reborn to obtain "spirit power" for a return to health, has been used quite successfully with persons suffering from behavioral and alcohol problems. Such persons are defined as suffering from "spirit illness", but through participation in the year long sequence of rites experience a renewed sense of identity, pride, and responsibility. The experience turns them away from the pursuit of self indulgence.

Where these groups have been successful it has been largely because they are run by Native people and combine traditional concepts and practices with the new. Often these institutions provide Native people an opportunity to innovate for themselves in bridging the gap between their heritage and the surrounding culture of the whiteman. If appropriate respect is forthcoming from Euro-Canadians it is possible that these movements, can eventually become reference groups providing new bases for Native

311

identity, assertiveness, and dependency outlets.

Despite the possibilities for controlling and redirecting drinking patterns among Native peoples one cannot be sanguine about the prognosis. There is a certain self-defeating circularity regarding the present functions of alcohol and efforts to change drunken comportment. Since, as Honigmann suggests, the heavy drinking of the "frontier culture" is a way of resisting the encroachment of Euro-Canadian culture it is likely that drinking control measures will be seen by Natives, as direct, or indirect, attempts to assert the authority of the whitemen. Such an interpretation could conceiveably lead to an increase rather than decrease in drinking. This also creates what Westermeyer (1972:403) has referred to as a "double bind" situation. The individual is trying to adapt to the whitemen's drinking norms, to fit into the mainstream economy, risks breaking with the traditional social network. In effect, to drink like a whiteman in the presence of Natives is considered a sign of disparagement.

Ever since the introduction of alcohol with the fur trade it would seem that the traditional balance between self-indulgence and social responsibility has been skewed toward the former. Indeed Lubart in discussing alcohol usage among the Mackenzie Delta Inuit proposes that it provides a sense of "...infantile euphoria and omnipotence" for both men and women (1969:456). Brody would seem to concur that the pleasure principle is foremost as a motive for drinking on skid row. If this be so, the rather fragile structure of the social drinking groups may not be sufficient in time to prevent a total individualization of alcohol usage, along with a concommitant sense of self-negation and isolation. Thus present social drinking practices could easily lapse into the pathological, and with the exclusive pursuit of self-gratification the possibilities for adaptive change would be minimal.

REFERENCES

Barry, H., III
    1976 "Cross-cultural Evidence that Dependency
    Conflict Motivates Drunkenness" in Cross-
    Cultural Approaches to the Study of Alcohol,
    Everett, M. W., J. O. Waddell, and D. B.
    Heath (eds.). 249-263. Chicago: Aldine.

Boyatzis, R. E.
    1976 "Drinking as a Manifestation of Power
    Concerns" in Cross-Cultural Approaches to
    the Study of Alcohol, Everett, M. W., J. O.
    Waddell, and D. B. Heath (eds.). 265-286
    Chicago: Aldine.

Ferguson, F. N.
    1976 "Stake Theory as an Explanatory Device
    in Navajo Alcoholism Treatment Response",
    Human Organization 35, 1:65-70.

Heath, D. B.
    1962 "Drinking Patterns of the Bolivian Camba"
    in Society, Culture, and Drinking Patterns,
    Pittman, D. W. and C. R. Snyder (eds.)
    22-36 New York: Wiley and Sons Inc.

Honigmann, J. and I. Honigmann
    1970 Arctic Townsmen: Ethnic Backgrounds and
    Modernization, Canadian Research Centre for
    Anthropology. Ottawa: St. Paul University.

Jilck, W.G. and N. Todd
    1974 "Witchdoctors Succeed where Doctors Fail:
    Psychotherapy among Coast Salish Indians".
    Canadian Psychiatric Association Journal,
    Vol. 19:351-355.

Levy, J. and S. Kunitz
    1974 Indian Drinking: Navajo Practices and
    Anglo-American Theories. New York: Wiley and
    Sons.

Lubart, J. M.
    1969 "Field Study of the Problems of

Adaptations of Mackenzie Delta Eskimos to Social and Economic Change", <u>Psychiatry</u>, 32:447-458.

McClelland, D. Davis, R. Kalin, T. Wanner
    1972 <u>The Drinking Man</u>. New York: Free Press.

Price, J. A.
    1975 "An Applied Analysis of North American Indian Drinking Patterns" <u>Human Organization</u>, Vol. 34:17-26.

Westermeyer, J.
    1972 "Options Regarding Alcohol Use Among the Chippewa", <u>American Journal of Orthopsychiatry</u>, 42, 3:398-403.

Dr. John Hamer is Professor of Anthropology and Chairperson of the Anthropology Department at the University of Alabama in Birmingham, Alabama. Dr. Hamer is a psychological anthropologist, with specializations in both African and Sub-Arctic North American cultures. He received his Ph.D. at Northwestern University and was a student of the late Melville Herskovitz. Dr. Hamer has published many professional papers, both in the areas of alcohol behavior, social organization, and ethnography.

Dr. Jack Steinbring is Associate Professor of Anthropology in the Department of Anthropology at the University of Winnipeg, in Manitoba, Canada. He was founder of his department and was chairman of it for many years. Dr. Steinbring is a General Anthropologist with specialties in both Algonkian studies and Sub-Arctic pre-history. He received his Ph.D. from the University of Minnesota, and has published many professional articles on Sub-Arctic ethnography and culture change. He has also published extensively in the field of archaeology.

315